Karel (

Four i ...,_

R.U.R., The Insect Play, The Makropulos Case, The White Plague

'There was no writer like him – no one who so blithely assumed that the common realities were not as fixed and irrevocable as one imagined. Without adopting any special tone he projected whole new creatures and environments onto an oddly familiar, non-existent landscape. He made it possible to actually invent worlds, and with laughter into the bargain. This prophetic assurance was mixed with . . . a brand-new surrealistic humour, and it was honed to hard-edged social satire, still a unique combination . . . He is a joy to read – a wonderfully surprising teller of some fairly astonishing and unforgettable tales.' Arthur Miller

Čapek was one of the most original Czech writers of the 1920s and 30s whose works were the inspiration for much of the science fiction of Europe and America. Endlessly inventive and extraordinary prescient, full of humour and wit, his plays explore and defend man's humanity. This volume brings together fresh new translations of four of his most popular plays, relevant today more than ever. In *R.U.R.*, the Robot – an idea Čapek was the first to invent – gradually takes over all aspects of human existence except procreation; *The Insect Play* is a satirical fable in which beetles, butterflies and ants give dramatic form to different philosophies of life; *The Makropulos Case* (upon which Janáček based his opera) is a fantasy about human mortality, finally celebrating the average lifespan; *The White Plague* is a savage and anguished satire against fascist dictatorship and the virus of inhumanity.

Karel Čapek was born in 1890 in the village of Malé Svatoňovice, north-east Bohemia. He studied philosophy at Charles University, Prague, and went on to become a newspaper journalist and editor and a prolific writer of novels, stories, essays, travelogues, children's books and plays. His novels include *Mass-Producing the Absolute* (1922), *Krakatit* (1924), the *Hordubal* trilogy (1933), and *The War With the Newts* (1936). But it is for his plays that Čapek is best known. His first work for the stage was *The Outlaw* (1920), followed by *R.U.R.* (1921), *The Makropulos Case* (1922), *The Insect Play* and *Adam the Creator* (1922 and 1927, both written with his brother Josef), *The White Plague* (1937), and *The Mother* (1938). He died in 1938, shortly after the Munich treaty had sounded the death-knell of Czech democracy.

KAREL ČAPEK

Four Plays

R.U.R.
The Insect Play
The Makropulos Case
The White Plague

Translated and introduced by Peter Majer and Cathy Porter

Methuen Drama

Published by Methuen Drama

3 5 7 9 10 8 6 4 2

This collection first published in the United Kingdom in 1999 by
Methuen Drama

A CIP catalogue record for this book
is available from the British Library

ISBN 978-0-413-77190-2

Typeset by Deltatype Ltd, Birkenhead, Merseyside
Printed and bound in Great Britain by
Cox & Wyman Ltd, Reading, Berks

Caution

Contents

Chronology

1928   Publication of part one of *Conversations with T.G. Masaryk*

1929   Publishes his mystery stories *Tales From Two Pockets*, and a humorous gardening book, *The Gardener's Year*

1930   Travels to Spain; publishes *Letters From Spain*

1931   Publishes part two of *Conversations with T.G. Masaryk*

1932   Publishes *Nine Fairy-Tales*, *Letters From Holland*, *Zoon politikon* and *Apocryphal Stories*

1933   Publishes *Dashenka*, a children's book about a puppy, and *Hordubal*, the first part of his trilogy of novels of that name

1934   Publishes the second and third volumes of the trilogy, *Meteor* and *An Ordinary Life*

1935   Publication of part three of *Conversations with T.G. Masaryk*. Marries Olga Scheinpflugová

1936   Publishes his novel *War With the Newts*. Travels to Scandinavia

1937   Publication and first performance of his play *The White Plague*. Publishes his novel *The First Rescue Party*. Travels to Austria, Switzerland and France

1938   Publication and first performance of his play *The Mother*. Publishes his essays *How They Do It*. Karel Čapek dies on Christmas Day

1945   Josef Čapek dies in Belsen concentration camp shortly before it is liberated

Introduction

Karel Čapek is one of only a handful of Czech writers, including Jaroslav Hašek and Franz Kafka, whose works have achieved popular international acclaim. In Europe and America in the 1920s, his writings were the inspiration for much of the new science fiction literature then appearing, and contemporary translations of his plays were widely performed.

In his own country, Čapek was a quintessential representative of the generation of intellectuals who entered the cultural scene shortly before the First World War, when Czechoslovakia became an independent republic. Playwright, journalist and newspaper-editor, Čapek was also a prolific writer of novels, stories, essays, travelogues and children's books. Absurd, witty, joyful and endlessly inventive, these writings imagined fantastic new landscapes filled with ordinary people and their ordinary hopes and values. As a poet and playwright, he celebrated this inconspicuous ordinariness of people's lives. As a journalist, he searched passionately for an ideal civil society. As spokesman for his country's artists and intellectuals, his views were sought by the Republic's founder and first president, Tomáš Masaryk, and by Masaryk's successor, Edvard Beneš.

Čapek's working life spanned the two decades between the two world wars, during which the fundamental ideas of Czech humanism and democracy were formed. He was born on 9 January 1890 in the small village of Malé Svatoňovice, in the mountainous Krkonoše region of north-east Bohemia, the third child of a busy country doctor. His mother was a sensitive, cultured woman, who encouraged her children's talents. His grandmother inspired in him his love of the idiom and folk-tales of the Krkonoše region. His brother Josef, two years older, went on to become an outstanding artist, writer and critic, and the two remained close for the rest of Karel's life, writing numerous newspaper columns, prose works and stage-plays together.

Expelled from the local *gymnazium* for joining an underground patriotic society, he moved to another school in the Moravian capital of Brno, and finished his schooling in Prague, where he enrolled at Charles University to study philosophy. He went on to work for his doctorate there on aesthetics, and completed this in 1915 after attending courses at the University of Berlin and the Sorbonne with Josef.

During the renaissance of Czech culture in the mid-nineteenth century, Czech journalism had developed into a highly sophisticated medium of social comment and criticism. Exempted from military service in the First World War by a crippling spinal ailment, Čapek quickly established himself as a journalist with a number of newspaper articles written with Josef. He landed his first newspaper job, on the staff of the newspaper *Národní listy*, in 1917. He made a living from journalism for the rest of his life, and all his subsequent stories and plays have the directness and simplicity of a popular column.

Čapek had a lifelong interest in the Pragmatist philosophy of the American William James, and in 1918 he published a monograph in which he defended basic human certainties and universal values against the institutionalised violence he saw as resulting from the opposing dogmas of collectivism and selfish individualism.

Many of Čapek's later writings criticised the tyranny of reason and the heartlessness of modern technical civilisation, by focusing on some new scientific or technical discovery which he imagined as dehumanising and interfering with the world and driving it to its destruction. Although the world as he knew it remained for him, as it did for Leibniz, the best of possible ones, all his works contained this powerful strand of existential nihilism, in the spirit of Kierkegaard and later existential philosophers and writers such as Camus.

His idiosyncratic nihilism found its earliest expression in his first large-scale stage drama, *R.U.R.*, or *Reason's Universal Robots* (1921). The Robot was the invention of Karel Čapek and his brother Josef, and the play is a gloriously dystopic science-fiction fantasy about them and the brave new world of the men who mass-produce them.

A mechanical humanoid in the tradition of the Golem of Prague, the Robot speaks, calculates, works, fights wars and possesses all human features and abilities except the ability to feel emotion. Robots multiply, are bought and sold and gradually take over every aspect of human existence. As people grow idle and stop procreating, the Robots rebel and destroy almost the entire human race. But they themselves have no future, for in destroying humans they have indirectly destroyed the blueprint for their own design. The guiding idea of the play is that nothing works without love, as is made clear at the end when a couple of Robots are transformed by love into something very much more human than the humans who have made them.

It was at the time Čapek was writing *R.U.R.* that he met the young actress and future novelist Olga Scheinpflugová. His spinal condition made it impossible for them to marry until fifteen years later, but in these years they conducted a passionate platonic affair, and the relationship endured until his death in 1938.

R.U.R. was frequently performed in Europe and America throughout the 1920s, and the outrageous comedy of its central premise, its surrealistic visual effects and experimental use of space immediately caught the popular theatrical imagination. Čapek went on to develop many of the play's ideas in his science-fiction novel *Mass-Producing the Absolute* (1922), a satire on the arrogance of science which sacrifices people in the name of some abstract idea. In this case the idea is infinite production, and the means for it is a machine that scatters electrons, thus catastrophically disrupting the coherence of matter and releasing what was previously bound to it, in other words the Absolute.

Here again Čapek makes common cause with pragmatic notions of simple creativity, the small, the human and the ordinary. All his characters are ordinary, even his Robots. It is this ordinariness which makes them interesting, for from it he unravels the complexity and mystery which underlies the meaning of their lives. In the tradition of the Czech Renaissance philosopher Jan Comenius, and his 'Labyrinth of the World', he leads the lost out of the maze, empathising with and befriending his characters, helping them to discover their unique essence in their own unique but ordinary stories.

Čapek's next major work, written with Josef, was *The Insect Play* (1922), a satirical meditation on different philosophies of life and a powerful anti-war satire. The play's visceral theatricality, playful language and wealth of strong acting parts make it a director's dream, and it is one of the most performed of all Čapek's stage creations in the English-speaking world.

The action is set in a forest and contains a vast cast of insects. Beetles roll along the sacred sphere of their dung-ball investments. Irresponsible butterflies flutter for sex with swelling probosces and trembling wings. Dictator ants march in rhythm and lust for power. Ichneumon-flies drip blood and rip skin. Narcissistic mayflies live and die for themselves. Observing them all, like Comenius' pilgrim in the Labyrinth, is the Traveller, displaced by war, an outsider in his own country. With their tiny eyes, their powerful jaws, their capacity to kill or suck dry, to be blown away or crushed, Čapek's insects are repulsive yet human, and as they scurry effortlessly between the human and insect worlds they show human passions, instincts and vices, and the blood-lusts which make human intelligence hideous.

His next play was *The Makropulos Case* (1922), a tragi-comic fantasy about ageing and human mortality. There are many inspirations for this marvellous play: the Russian zoologist Professor Mechnikov's theories about the ageing process as a self-intoxication of the organism; Shaw's *Back to Methuselah*; the immortal monsters of Frankenstein and Dracula; the French philosopher Henri Bergson, and his explorations of free will and temporality.

The play's plot is now well-known from Leoš Janáček's opera, and involves an opera-singer named Emilia Marty, daughter of the personal physician to Emperor Rudolf II who invented an elixir for eternal life which he tried first on her, causing her to live for three hundred years. The action centres on the legal dispute over an inheritance involving the secret formula for this elixir, and comes to a head through the gradual unravelling of Emilia's numerous identities over the last three centuries, until she is finally and dramatically forced to confront her own mortality.

In 1924, President Masaryk was one of those to attend the regular Friday meetings which Čapek held at his villa outside Prague, and which became a forum for the literary, scientific and philosophical élite of Czech society.

By the mid-1920s Čapek was the acknowledged voice of Czech literature. He travelled to Italy and also to England, where he met G.K. Chesterton, Bernard Shaw and H.G. Wells, and Anglo-Saxon literature, particularly Wells' futuristic fantasies, became a major influence on his storylines. His novel *Krakatit* (1924) was inspired by the volcano Krakatoa, whose devastating eruption in 1883 was still vividly remembered in his lifetime. It describes the annihilation threatening the human race after a scientist's discovery of nuclear fission falls into the hands of a military junta led by a ruthless dictator seeking world domination. The scientist manages to destroy his invention in time to save mankind, then appeals to scientists to re-establish responsibility for the destiny of the world.

As Dr Gall says to Helen in *R.U.R.*, 'Never trust a
man with ideas.' Čapek's characters face God as an
unknown and unknowable entity. In their search for
meaning, they grapple with questions of infinity and find
God's traces in everything, but unable to grasp the
meaning of the eternal secrets, they attempt to
rediscover their faith by turning inward. It was in this
spirit that Karel and Josef Čapek wrote their play *Adam
the Creator* (1927), which deals, like *R.U.R.*, with the
rebellion of the created against the creators. Adam is an
intellectual, an anarchist, who has come to hate the
world and finally destroys it. The only human being left
alive on it, he must create the world anew. However all
his illusions are shattered when he sets out to create a
'superior' woman, and ends up with the foolish Lilith.
Tiring of her, he tries to make a man in his own image.
But his *alter ego* argues constantly with him, and both
realise too late that through negotiation they might have
created a new world of ordinary people.

Čapek returned to this theme of ordinariness with his
great Hordubal trilogy (1933–4) – *Hordubal, The Meteor*
and *An Ordinary Life* – set in rural Ruthenia, then the
poorest, easternmost region of Czechoslovakia. In these
years he also wrote newspaper articles and his mystery
stories *Tales From Two Pockets* (1929), and embarked on
an intellectual history of his mentor Masaryk, based on
his conversations with him.

In 1930 he visited Spain. Shattered by the ominous
trends in Europe in the years that followed – the mass
slaughter of the Spanish Civil War and the growing
military aggression of dictators – he became a passionate
campaigner for peace. His novel *The War With the Newts*
(1936) was a satirical fantasy about the mass psychosis of
war, this time coming from the sea. An old sailor of
Czech descent discovers somewhere in the Pacific a
breed of newts capable of learning human skills,
including speech, and he uses them as pearl-hunters.
The newts gradually become independent and build a

vast underwater urban civilisation. Breeding faster than humans, they soon need more territory and declare war on mankind. The novel's science fiction theme was probably inspired by Wells, and many in Europe who had not seen his plays discovered him in the 1930s with this frightening, comic vision of alien invasion.

In 1935, at the age of forty-five, Čapek finally married Olga Scheinpflugová. By then his outspoken anti-fascist, anti-war stance had made him one of the most respected figures in European culture, and in 1936 he was nominated for the Nobel Peace Prize for literature. But his works had already offended the *petit-bourgeois* and fascist elements appearing in Czech society, and when the Swedish Academy invited him to submit a more uncontroversial work, he refused.

Instead, as Hitler's troops advanced across Europe, he wrote his play *The White Plague* (1937), a savage and anguished satire against fascist dictatorship. The action is set in an unnamed country and under its dictator, the Marshal, the population is poised for the final war which will conquer the world. Science, medicine and production are ruled by *fiat*, and dissent is ruthlessly suppressed. But people are dying by the thousand from a mysterious epidemic for which nobody knows the cure. The disease slays soldiers, rulers and workers alike, depleting the labour force and jeopardising production in Baron Krug's arms factories which supply the country's huge and invincible army. An unknown and humble doctor discovers a cure, and agrees to treat the country's ailing leaders if they sign an undertaking to abandon war. They finally agree, but the doctor is trampled to death by a fanatical mob before the bargain can be honoured.

A humanist by nature, Čapek struggled to understand the psychology of his time, joining the front line of journalists and intellectuals fighting for democracy and against the infamous Munich pact of 1938 which delivered large parts of Czechoslovakia to Hitler. But he was already being attacked by Czech and German fascists at public meetings and in the press, and *The White Plague* made him more enemies. Abandoning his pacifist convictions, he wrote his last play, *The Mother* (1938), about a woman who stands up to violence by sending her youngest son to war.

Čapek was living in an endangered society, the first to be sacrificed to Hitler. He saw the bloodshed coming, and he fell into despair. The vicious public attacks on him continued and, not long after the signature of the Munich treaty sounded the death-knell of Czech democracy, he developed a respiratory infection. He died on Christmas Day 1938 in Prague, as he prepared to go into hiding. He was forty-eight. His brother Josef was picked up shortly afterwards and taken to Belsen concentration camp, where he died in 1945.

The stuff of fantasy at the beginning of the century, many of Čapek's predictions are even more real for us at the end of it. In all of the four plays published here, he warns against state violence and the possible consequences of modern technological civilisation, whose abuse could be the cause of the world's destruction. The plays' preoccupations with artificial intelligence, ecological disaster, disease-control and ageing are profoundly serious and they are ours, but they are at the same time irresistibly playful and comic. We hope that our fresh new translations of these plays, untranslated into English since the 1920s, will help return Čapek to the centre of our theatre repertoire, and re-introduce audiences to one of the most brilliant and original playwrights of our time.

Peter Majer and Cathy Porter
1999

R.U.R.

Characters

Harry Domin, *Managing Director, Reason's Universal Robots Corporation. Clean-cut, tall, late thirties*

Engineer Fabry, *Technical Director at R.U.R. Fair-haired, serious, gentle*

Dr Gall, *Chief Consultant, Physiology and Research Division of R.U.R. Delicate, dark, lively, with a black moustache*

Dr Hallemeier, *Chief Consultant for Robot Educational Psychology. Large and noisy, with a shock of ginger hair and an English ginger moustache*

Consul Busman, *Marketing Director at R.U.R. Fat, bald, short-sighted*

Construction Engineer Alquist, *Plant and Resources Manager at R.U.R. Older than the rest, messily dressed, with straggling grey hair and beard*

Lady Helen Glory, *early twenties, very elegant*

Nana, *her nurse*

Marius ⎫
Radius ⎪
Damon ⎬ *Robots*
Primus ⎪
Sulla ⎭

Robot Helen

Robot servant

Other Robots

In Act One, the Robots are dressed as humans, with fixed expressions and mechanical movements and speech. In the following acts, everyone is ten years older. The Robots are dressed in linen shirts belted at the waist, with a brass number on their chests.

Act One

Central office of Reason's Universal Robots. Windows overlook the factory compound, with its endless rows of buildings. To the left, more managerial offices can be seen. **Domin** *is seated on a revolving chair before a vast American desk with a lamp, In and Out trays, telephone and paperweight. On the left wall hang large maps of naval and rail routes, a big calendar, a clock with hands pointing to just before noon. On the right wall are big posters: 'Buy Yourself A Robot!', 'Reason's Robots — The Cheapest Workers Around!', 'Robots for the Tropics!', 'Latest Model Only $150!', 'Want to Produce Goods Cheaper? Order Reason's Robots!'; more maps, shipping tables, financial news and exchange rates. On the floor is a beautiful Turkish carpet, a low, round table, a sofa, leather armchairs and a bookcase containing a cash register, bottles of wine and spirits in place of books. Beside* **Domin***'s desk is a table with a typewriter (or word-processor), on which* **Sulla** *is taking dictation.*

Domin (*dictates*) '. . . We accept no liability for goods damaged in transit. Since we notified your captain during embarcation that your ship was unsuited to the transportation of Robots, the damage of your shipment cannot be regarded as our responsibility. We beg, sir, to remain, for Reason's Universal Robots . . .' Got that?

Sulla Yes, sir.

Domin Next letter. 'To Friedrichswerks, Hamburg. Date. Acknowledging your receipt of 15,000 Robots . . .' (*Internal telephone rings.* **Domin** *lifts receiver.*) Yes. Central Office here. Will do. Immediately. (*Hangs up.*) Where were we?

Sulla Acknowledging receipt of 15,000 Robots.

Domin (*thoughtfully*)   15,000 Robots, 15,000 R . . .

Marius (*enters*) A lady is waiting outside to see you, sir.

Domin Who is she?

Marius   I don't know, sir. (*Hands* **Domin** *a card.*)

Domin (*reads*)   Sir Edward Glory! Great Scot! Show her in!

Marius *opens the door and ushers in* **Lady Helen**. *Exit* **Marius**.

Domin (*rising*)   Lady Helen, pray come in!

Helen   Managing Director Domin? I am Helen Glory, daughter of Sir Edward Glory. I've come to see ...

Domin (*stretching out his hand*)   At your service, dear lady! The daughter of Sir Edward needs no introduction! This is such a great honour for us ...

Helen   So you won't kick me out?

Domin   To meet the daughter of our great scientist and statesman. Please take a seat. Sulla, you may go.

Exit **Sulla**.

What can I do for you, Lady Helen?

Helen   I've come ...

Domin   To see how we make them, like everyone else? Fine, we understand.

Helen   I thought I wouldn't be allowed ...

Domin   Into our factory? Yes, well. The manufacture of sentient humanoids is highly classified information of course, Lady Helen.

Helen   If you knew how ...

Domin   ... fascinated you are. Old Europe is talking of nothing else.

Helen   I want you to make an exception for me.

Domin   But of course we will, dear lady! It would be a great honour. We'll show you more than we've ever shown anyone else. On condition ...

Helen   Thank you!

Domin   That you give me your word of honour not to reveal the slightest . . .

Helen   You shall have it. (*Rises and gives him her hand.*) I give you my word.

Domin   Thank you. Won't you lift your veil for me?

Helen   You want to see my face? Why not? If you could just . . .

Domin   I beg your pardon?

Helen   Let go my hand.

Domin (*releases her hand*)   I do apologise!

Helen (*lifts her veil*)   You want to make sure I'm not a spy. How conscientious of you!

Domin (*gazes admiringly at her*)   Mm, yes.

Helen   You don't trust me?

Domin   Implicitly, Helen. Sorry, Lady Helen. I hope you had a satisfactory crossing.

Helen   Perfect, thank you. Why?

Domin   Because . . . Oh, you're still so young.

Helen   Shall we go to the factory straight away?

Domin   If you want. About twenty-two, are you?

Helen   Twenty-one. Why?

Domin   Because, because . . . (*Ardently.*) I hope you'll be spending some time here with us.

Helen   That depends how much you show me of your production techniques.

Domin   To hell with techniques, Lady Helen! But yes, by all means, we'll show you everything. Would you be interested in a brief history of our invention?

Helen   Certainly. (*Sits down.*)

Domin (*sits at his desk, gazing adoringly at* **Helen**)   Well,
the story begins in 1920, when old Reason, the great
physiologist, then a young scholar, visits this remote
island of ours to study its marine life. While here, he
attempts to reproduce living matter – protoplasm – by
means of chemical synthesis. In the course of these
studies he discovers a substance which behaves exactly
like living matter, but with a totally different chemical
structure. This is in 1932, four hundred and forty years
after the discovery of America . . .

Helen   Have you learnt all this by heart?

Domin   Yes. Physiology isn't my strong suit, Lady
Helen. Shall we continue?

Helen   As you wish.

Domin (*solemnly*)   And then, amongst old Reason's
jottings and formulae, we find the following words:
'Nature has only one method for organising living
matter. However there exists another method, simpler,
faster and more flexible, which Nature did not envisage.
I have today discovered this alternative method for the
evolution of life.' Imagine him, madam, penning these
great lines over some vile stinking colloidal infusion
which even the dog wouldn't touch! Imagine him
hunched over his test-tubes, contemplating the entire
evolutionary tree – all the animals, starting with the
amoeba and culminating in Man himself! But Man
made now of a totally different stuff from us. It was a
historic moment, Lady Helen!

Helen   And?

Domin   And . . . So then it was just a matter of
transposing life from the test-tube to the outside world.
To accelerate evolution! Create bones, organs, nerves!
Knock up enzymes, catalysts, hormones! Do you follow?

Helen I'm not quite sure. Some of it.

Domin I'm not sure either. With this new method of his he could have produced anything he liked – a jellyfish with the brain of Socrates, a worm fifty metres long! But being totally devoid of humour the old man set out to make some sort of reptile, or perhaps Man. That's how it all started.

Helen How what started?

Domin Imitating nature. First he tried to make an artificial dog. He spent months on it, and ended up with a deformed calf which conked out after a few days. It's in the museum. I'll show you. After that, the old chap got cracking on Man. But this part I must reveal to no one.

Helen What a shame – it was in all our school textbooks!

Domin (*rises from his revolving chair and sits beside* **Helen**) You know what they didn't put in your textbooks? (*Taps his forehead.*) Old Mr Reason was barking mad! Seriously though, Lady Helen, keep this to yourself – the old crank wanted to make people!

Helen But *you* make people!

Domin No, we merely replicate them, Lady Helen. Old Reason took it literally. He was a terrible old atheist – he wanted to dethrone God scientifically. Demonstrate that he wasn't necessary. So he set about creating people identical to us, down to the last hair. Do you know any anatomy, Lady Helen?

Helen Not much.

Domin Me neither. He had this bee in his bonnet about reproducing everything exactly as it functions in the human body. Appendix, tonsils, belly-button – all completely useless. Even the – erm – sexual glands. No need for those if you're reproducing people artificially!

Helen I suppose not.

Domin I'll show you in the museum what he threw together over ten years. It was meant to be a man. It lived for three days. It was a terrible mess! On the inside, though, it had everything a man needs. Real filigree work. Old Reason never did have any taste. Then young Reason arrived, the old man's nephew. An engineer, Lady Helen, world-class brain. When he saw what the old man was up to he said what a numskull, spending ten years to make a man! If you can't work faster than nature you might as well pack up and go home! So he took up the study of anatomy.

Helen That wasn't in our textbooks.

Domin (*rises*) With respect, Lady Helen, your textbooks are rubbish – government propaganda. They tell you Robots were dreamed up by an old man. What they don't tell you is that this old man was first-rate university material, but he hadn't a clue about the needs of modern industry. He thought you could just make people – Indians, professors, idiots and so forth. It was young Reason who realised you could produce intelligent working machines. All that in the textbooks about the two Reasons working harmoniously together is pure baloney. They were at each other's throats all the time. The old atheist had no time for industry. So young Reason finally locked him in his lab to fiddle with his freaks, while he went into production solo. Old Reason cursed and swore at him, and cooked up two more abortions before he died. They found him dead in his lab. And that was the end of him.

Helen What about the young one?

Domin Our young Reason, miss? It was the dawn of a new industrial era, the era of production, knowledge. When young Reason got to grips with human anatomy he realised it was far too complicated, and that a decent engineer would make a much better job of it. So he gave it a thorough overhaul, stripped out some things, simplified others. Finally, young Reason . . . I'm not boring you am I, my dear?

Helen   Not in the least. It's quite fascinating.

Domin   Finally young Reason said to himself: Man is something which, let's say, feels joy, plays the violin, takes a walk, has the urge to do all sorts of things which are actually quite useless.

Helen   Aha!

Domin   Wait. Useless, for example, when he's asked to build or calculate. The diesel engine needs no embellishment, Lady Helen. To duplicate a worker is exactly the same process. What kind of worker would you say was the most efficient?

Helen   The most honest and industrious?

Domin   Wrong. The cheapest. The most economical to run. Young Reason invented a worker with minimal needs. He just simplified it, discarded all the various optional devices unrelated to work. He got rid of the man and came up with a Robot! The product of an engineer is way superior to any product of nature, dear lady! Robots are mechanically far more efficient than we are! No soul, just this phenomenal brain capacity!

Helen   They say Man is God's creation.

Domin   So much the worse for Man. God never understood modern technology. Unfortunately the late Reason Junior then decided to play God.

Helen   How?

Domin   Started experimenting with a new line of Super Robots. Work giants, four metres high. Believe it or not, they kept breaking down. Out of the blue a leg would snap, then something else. Our planet is apparently too small for giants. The Robots we're turning out now are of more or less acceptable human dimensions.

Helen I saw the first Robots at home. The council bought them – or hired them perhaps . . .

Domin Bought, Lady Helen. Robots are never hired.

Helen I saw them once. They were sweeping the streets. It was sinister. They were so silent.

Domin Did you see my secretary?

Helen I didn't notice.

Domin (*rings the bell*) Do you know that our corporation doesn't produce just one line of machines? Some are extremely sophisticated, some are more crude. The more advanced ones may last twenty years.

Helen Then they perish?

Domin Yes. They wear out.

Enter **Sulla**.

Sulla, introduce yourself to Lady Helen.

Helen (*rises and puts out her hand*) So pleased to meet you. You must be terribly bored stuck out here, miles from anywhere.

Sulla I don't understand that, miss. Please sit down.

Helen (*sits down*) Where are you from, Sulla?

Sulla Here, from this factory.

Helen I see. You were born here?

Sulla Yes. I was manufactured here.

Helen (*starts*) What?

Domin (*laughs*) Sulla's not human, my dear, she's a Robot!

Helen I'm terribly sorry!

Domin (*puts his arm around* **Sulla***'s shoulder*) Sulla's not angry, are you Sulla? Touch her face, Lady Helen! Look at that complexion!

Helen Oh no!

Domin Can't tell the difference, eh? Feel this hair we gave her! Soft and blonde! M-mm, lovely! The eyes are a bit . . . But this hair! Turn around, Sulla!

Helen Stop it!

Domin Chat with our guest, Sulla. We've an important visitor!

Sulla Please sit down, miss.

Both sit down.

Did you have an agreeable crossing, miss?

Helen Yes, fine thanks.

Sulla Don't return on the *Amelia,* miss. The barometer is falling. Wait for the *Pennsylvania.* That's a good fast ship.

Domin Speed?

Sulla Twenty knots per hour. Weight – twenty thousand tons.

Domin That's enough, Sulla. Show off your French now.

Helen Do you speak French?

Sulla I know four languages, miss. I can write 'Dear Sir, Cher Monsieur, Geherter Herr, Uvazhaemy tovarishch . . .'

Helen (*jumps up*) It's a fake! You're a fraud! Sulla's not a Robot, she's a girl like me! It's disgraceful, Sulla, why do you play along with it?

Sulla I am a Robot.

Helen   No, no, you're lying! Oh Sulla, forgive me –
they forced you to do it for publicity, didn't they?
You're a girl like me, aren't you Sulla? Tell me, tell me!

Sulla   I am a Robot.

Domin   I'm sorry, Lady Helen, Sulla is a Robot.

Helen   You're lying!

Domin (*rises from his chair*)   What? (*Rings the bell.*) I fear
I must convince you. (*Enter* **Marius**.) Quick Marius,
take Sulla to the mortuary and dismantle her! Hurry!

Helen   Where?

Domin   To the mortuary. To be de-activated. Do go
and watch, Lady Helen!

Helen   I'll do no such thing!

Domin   Sorry, but it was you who talked of lying.

Helen   So you'd kill her?

Domin   You can't kill a machine.

Helen (*clasps* **Sulla** *to her*)   Don't be afraid, Sulla. I'll
see they don't. Tell me, does everyone treat you this
way? You mustn't let them, d'you hear? Don't let them!

Sulla   I am a Robot.

Helen   Never mind, Sulla. Robots are just as good as
humans. You'd let them cut you up?

Sulla   Yes.

Helen   You're not afraid of dying?

Sulla   Sorry, miss, I don't register that.

Helen   You know what would happen to you?

Sulla   Yes. I would stop moving.

Helen   That's horrible!

Domin   Marius, tell the lady what you are.

Marius   I am Robot Marius, miss.

Domin   Would you take Sulla to the mortuary?

Marius   Yes, sir.

Domin   Would you be sorry?

Marius   Sorry, sir, I don't register that.

Domin   What would happen to her?

Marius   She would stop moving, sir. Then they would erase her.

Domin   That's called death, Marius. Are you afraid of death?

Marius   Sorry, sir, I don't register that.

Domin   See, Lady Helen? Robots don't cling to life. They have no feelings. They're like weeds!

Helen   Stop it! It's disgusting! Send them away!

Domin   Marius, Sulla, you can go now.

Exeunt **Marius** *and* **Sulla**.

Domin (*walks to the window*)   Come over here, Lady Helen. What can you see over there, by the perimeter fence?

Helen   Builders.

Domin   Robots. All our builders are Robots. And at the other end of the compound?

Helen   Offices?

Domin   And inside, doing the accounts and invoices?

Helen   Clerks?

Domin   More Robots. All our clerks are Robots. And there in the factory . . .

At this moment, factory sirens and hooters signal the end of the morning shift.

It's noon. The signal for lunch. Otherwise the Robots wouldn't know when to stop. After the break I'll show you our kneading troughs.

Helen   What are those for?

Domin (*drily*)   Kneading and stirring the ingredients for a thousand Robots. You'll see the vats for the livers and brains. The bone factory. Our spinning looms . . .

Helen   What do they make?

Domin   Nerves. Blood-vessels. Miles and miles of intestines. And finally the assembly-line where the whole thing's put together − like a motor-car. Each worker adds his component, then it passes automatically to the next, and so on. Then we format them. Finally come the warehouses and drying-plants where the new machines will work.

Helen   For goodness' sake, you put them to work straight away?

Domin   Like any new machine they sort of gell together, get used to things. A lot of stuff develops fairly spontaneously. We have to leave time for them to grow naturally. It's their apprenticeship.

Helen   What does that involve?

Domin   It's what we humans call learning. They learn to talk, write, count. They contain a phenomenal amount of memory. Higher mathematics. Quantum physics. There's nothing they can't handle. Read them twenty volumes of the *Encyclopaedia Britannica* and they'll repeat it word for word. They never come up with anything new, of course − ideal for university teaching. Finally we sort them and ship them out. Fifteen thousand a day, discounting a regular percentage of faulty specimens which we discard . . . Etcetera, etcetera.

Perhaps we could change the subject now, Lady Helen.
We're just a handful of humans and a thousand Robots
here. Not a single female. We discuss Robots all day
every day – it's a curse.

Helen I'm sorry I said you . . . you lied.

A knock at the door.

Domin Come on in!

Enter **Fabry**, **Dr Gall**, **Hallemeier** *and* **Alquist**.

Gall I hope we're not interrupting anything?

Domin Not at all! Lady Helen, let me introduce you
to the team. Gentlemen, this is Lady Helen Glory,
daughter of Professor Glory!

Helen (*embarrassed*) How do you do?

Fabry We had no idea . . .

Gall Tremendous honour . . .

Alquist Welcome, Lady Helen.

Busman (*bursting into the room*) Hey, what's up?

Domin Come in, Busman. Lady Helen, meet Busman.
Busman, this is the daughter of Professor Glory.

Busman Hell, what an honour! Cable the press that
you've come!

Domin Won't you sit down, Lady Helen?

Fabry ⎫   Please.

Busman ⎬ (*moving chairs for her*) Here.

Gall ⎭   For you.

Alquist How was your journey, Lady Helen?

Gall Will you be staying long?

Fabry What do you think of our factory, Lady Helen?

Hallemeier   Did you sail on the *Amelia*?

Domin   Quiet, quiet, let Lady Helen speak.

Helen (*to* **Domin**)   What about?

Domin (*surprised*)   Whatever you like.

Helen   Shall I . . . May I speak frankly?

Domin   Yes, of course.

Helen (*hesitates, then with anxious determination*)   Tell me, don't you sometimes feel furious about the way they treat you here?

Fabry   Who?

Helen   Why, everyone!

They all look at one another in dismay.

Alquist   Really?

Hallemeier   Good heavens, no!

Busman   God forbid!

Gall   What makes you say that, Lady Helen?

Helen   Don't you feel . . . you could be living a better life?

Gall   Depends what you mean by better, Lady Helen.

Helen   I mean . . . (*Bursts out.*) I mean it's scandalous what goes on here! (*Jumps to her feet.*) All Europe's talking about it! That's why I came, to see for myself. And it's a thousand times worse than anything I could have imagined! Why do you put up with it!

Alquist   Put up with what?

Helen   Your position here, for heaven's sake! You're people, like us, like the rest of Europe! It's a terrible, degrading life!

Busman   Steady on, Lady Helen!

Fabry No chaps, she has a point. We are living a pretty dismal existence here.

Helen Worse than Red Indians! My brothers . . . May I call you brothers?

Busman Hell, why not!

Helen I'm not here as Professor Glory's daughter, but for my charity, the League of Humanity. Brothers, our League has over two hundred thousand members – that's over two hundred thousand people behind you, offering you their help . . .

Busman Two hundred thousand? That's a good number. Splendid.

Fabry Good old Europe. They haven't forgotten us. They're offering us . . .

Gall Could it be a theatre?

Hallemeier Orchestras?

Helen Much, much more than that.

Alquist You, then.

Helen I don't matter. Though I'll stay if it helps.

Busman God, what bliss!

Alquist Domin, I'll just get our best rooms ready.

Domin Hang on a second. I don't think Lady Helen has finished.

Helen Maybe not. Unless you silence me by force.

Gall You'd better not try, Harry!

Helen Thank you. I thought you would defend me!

Domin Sorry to interrupt, but you don't by any chance imagine that these men you're talking to are Robots, do you?

Helen   What else could they be?

Domin   I'm afraid they're humans like you, Lady
Helen, like the rest of Europe!

Helen (*to the others in horror*)   You mean you're not
Robots?

Busman (*guffaws*)   God forbid!

Hallemeier   Pah, Robots!

Gall (*laughs*)   Thanks a lot, Lady Helen!

Helen   But you seem so . . .

Fabry   We're not Robots, I swear!

Helen (*to* **Domin**)   So why did you tell me all your
clerks were Robots?

Domin   Clerks, yes, Lady Helen. Not directors of the
board! Let me introduce our management team.
Engineer Fabry here is our Technical Director. Dr Gall
– Physiology and Research Consultant. Dr Hallemeier –
Educational Psychology. Consul Busman – Marketing
Director. Engineer Alquist – Building Manager.

Helen   Please forgive me, gentlemen. I've made the
most awful mistake!

Alquist   It was easily done, Lady Helen. Do sit down.

Helen (*sitting down*)   I'm just a silly girl. You should put
me on the first boat home.

Gall   Bless my soul, Lady Helen, why would we do
that?

Helen   Because I . . . You know . . . I might stir up
trouble with your Robots!

Domin   Dear lady, we've had boat-loads of Messiahs
and prophets visiting us here. Missionaries, anarchists,
the Salvation Army – all society's flotsam. Amazing how
many fanatics there are in the world.

Helen   And you let them talk to your Robots?

Domin   Why not? They get fed up soon enough. The
Robots don't even laugh at their jokes. They remember
everything. But that's it. Incredible. Shall I take you to
our Robot warehouse now? It might amuse you. We've
three hundred thousand of them in there.

Busman   Three hundred and forty-seven thousand, in
fact.

Domin   If you say so, Busman. Preach all you like to
them, Lady Helen! Read them the bible, logarithms –
anything you can think of! Give them speeches on
human rights . . .

Helen   I thought . . . If we could just show them a little
kindness . . .

Fabry   Not possible, Lady Helen. Nothing is more
unlike a human being than a Robot.

Helen   Then why make them?

Busman   Ha-ha! That's good! Why make Robots!

Fabry   To work, Lady Helen. One Robot machine can
replace one and a half humans. The human machine
finally had to be discarded. It was too wasteful.

Busman   Too expensive.

Fabry   Too inefficient. Couldn't keep up with the new
technology. Furthermore, mechanical conception –
pardon my frankness, dear lady, but . . .

Helen   What?

Fabry   Forgive me, but, well, mechanical conception
really is a tremendous advance. More comfortable.
Quicker. Acceleration means progress. When it comes to
modern labour rhythms, nature hasn't a clue. Childhood
is nonsense of course, technically speaking. A sheer waste

of time. All those years down the drain, Lady Helen! Finally . . .

Helen   Oh, do stop it!

Fabry   What are your specific objections, tell me?

Helen   Specifically, the aim of our League is to promote Robots' rights and improve their living conditions . . .

Fabry   And a most laudable aim too! Machines need protecting, just the same as people! I hate to see them break down! I beg you, Lady Helen, put us all down as founding members of your League!

Helen   No, no, we don't understand each other! We demand the liberation of the Robots!

Hallemeier   May I ask how?

Helen   We say they must be treated the same as humans!

Hallemeier   So you want them to vote? Earn wages? Pay income tax?

Helen   Why not?

Hallemeier   Dear me, what on earth would they buy with all their money?

Helen   Whatever they needed, whatever made them happy.

Hallemeier   That's all very well, Lady Helen. Problem is, nothing makes them happy! Dammit, pineapples or paper – they're not bothered what you feed 'em, they've no taste-buds! And no one's seen them laugh yet!

Helen   Why didn't you make them happy?

Hallemeier   Impossible. They're Robots, Lady Helen, without will, passion, history or soul.

Helen   Without love? Without defiance?

Hallemeier   Of course. Robots love nothing. Not even themselves. Defiance? I don't know about that. Perhaps there are times . . .

Helen   Yes?

Hallemeier   Nothing really. Times when they sort of . . . slip out of gear. A bit like a fit, you know. Robot spasm, we call it. All at once one starts rearing up, gnashing its teeth, hurling things on the floor. Then we have to abort it. Some fault in the random access commands apparently.

Domin   A minor wiring fault, Lady Helen.

Helen   No, no – it's the soul!

Fabry   You think the soul displays itself in the gnashing of teeth?

Domin   We can put it right, Lady Helen. Dr Gall is running diagnostic tests at present.

Gall   Actually at present I'm working on the automated pain servers. You see, the standard Robot registers no somatic pain, Lady Helen. The late Reason Junior somewhat over-simplified the nervous system, and there have been problems. Now we have to re-introduce pain.

Helen   Why? You don't give them a soul. Why must you give them pain?

Gall   Industrial reasons, Lady Helen. A Robot might damage itself. Since it knows no pain it can stick its hand in a machine and break a finger or smash a hand, and it simply doesn't register. We have to give it pain, you see – as an elementary safety precaution.

Helen   Will it be happier knowing pain?

Gall   On the contrary. But it'll be more efficient.

Helen   Why don't you give it a soul?

Gall   That's not in our power.

Fabry   Not in our interests.

Busman   Production costs would go sky-high, lovely lady! Goodness, we sell them so cheaply! One item fully clothed – just a hundred and twenty dollars! Fifteen years ago that would have been ten thousand! Five years ago we were still buying clothes for them. Now we have our own garment factory. We're even selling our surplus cloth – five times cheaper than the other manufacturers! Tell me, how much would you spend on a metre of cloth?

Helen   I really don't know – I've forgotten.

Busman   Bless my soul, and you want to run the League of Humanity! Our prices, dear lady, are down by a third. Lower – lower – lower – we can go this low! What do you think?

Helen   I don't understand . . .

Busman   For heaven's sake – Robots cut labour costs! One Robot costs just a few pence an hour to maintain, including feeding! Ridiculous, isn't it? Factories all over the place either stock up on Robots or go bust!

Helen   And the workers go on the scrap-heap?

Busman   What do you expect? Right now we're flooding the Argentine Pampas with three thousand tropical Robots for cultivating wheat. Be so good as to tell me how much you pay for bread?

Helen   I've no idea.

Busman   See, it's just twenty pence a loaf now in good old Europe. That's our bread, Lady Helen! Twenty pence, and your League of Humanity hasn't a clue! You've no idea what it's like when you can't afford bread. Culture's all very fine, but you can bet your life that in five years' time . . .

Helen   What?

Busman   In five years' time prices will have fallen another seventy per cent. In five years we'll be drowning in wheat, cloth . . .

Alquist   And the workers will be on the scrap-heap.

Domin (*rises*)   Well of course. But by then Reason's Robots will be producing such vast quantities of everything you can think of that commodity prices will be irrelevant! Everything will be produced by machines. There'll be an end to poverty. To each according to his needs. There'll be a bit of unemployment, of course, but the old notion of work will have disappeared. Man will do only what he loves doing, free and sovereign, with no other task than to better himself. The purpose of life will be self-improvement!

Helen (*standing up*)   Will it really?

Domin   It will, Lady Helen. It must. Horrible things may happen along the way, that can't be helped. But ultimately we shall overcome man's enslavement to man and to nature. People will no longer be labourers and secretaries, digging the streets, sitting at desks, paying for the bread they eat with their lives and with hatred, destroying their souls with work they hate!

Alquist   Harry, Harry! This sounds too much like paradise! Wasn't there something noble about servitude and humility? Dammit, there's virtue in toil and hard work!

Domin   Perhaps. But there's no knowing what we lose when we remake the world of Adam. We'll no longer eat bread produced by the sweat of others' brows. We'll no longer know hunger and thirst, exhaustion and humiliation. We shall be masters of creation. And yes, Alquist, we shall return to paradise, to be fed by the hand of God!

Busman   Amen.

Fabry   So be it.

Helen   I'd love to believe you, but I'm a bit confused.
I'm only a simple girl . . .

Gall   You're younger than us, Lady Helen. You'll live
to see it.

Hallemeier   You're right, Gall. Now perhaps Lady
Helen might like to eat with us.

Gall   Excellent idea. Domin, will you do the honours?

Domin   Lady Helen, will you grace us with your
presence?

Helen   I don't think I . . .

Fabry   Representing the League of Humanity of
course, madam.

Helen   In that case perhaps . . .

Fabry   Splendid! Excuse us for a few minutes, Lady
Helen.

Busman   Good God, I must send a cable!

Hallemeier   Blast, I've forgotten . . .

All but **Domin** *rush out of his office.*

Helen   Where are they off to?

Domin   To cook breakfast, Lady Helen. The Robots
usually do it, but they have no sense of taste so it's
never quite . . . Hallemeier is our grilling expert. Gall
knows this special sauce. Busman's an omelette man.

Helen   Heavens, a banquet! What about Mr Master-
Builder?

Domin   Alquist? Useless. He just lays the table. Fabry
will fetch the fruit. Very modest cuisine, Lady Helen.

Helen   I wanted to ask you . . .

Domin   I wanted to ask you something too. (*Lays his watch on the table.*) We have five minutes!

Helen   To ask what?

Domin   Sorry, you ask first!

Helen   This may sound silly, but why do you manufacture women Robots, when . . .

Domin   When, erm, gender has no meaning for them?

Helen   Exactly.

Domin   It's a question of demand, you see. Shop-assistants, cleaners, secretaries, that sort of thing – habits die hard.

Helen   And would you say your male and female Robots are mutually . . . ?

Domin   Totally indifferent, Lady Helen. Absolutely no trace of attraction there.

Helen   That's frightful!

Domin   Why?

Helen   It's unnatural. You don't know whether to feel disgust or envy, or just . . .

Domin   Pity?

Helen   Pity's more like it. But what did you want to ask me?

Domin   I wanted to ask you to take me, Lady Helen.

Helen   Take you where?

Domin   As your husband.

Helen   No! What an idea!

Domin (*looks at his watch*)   Another three minutes. If you won't take me you'd better choose one of the other five.

Helen   Why in heaven's name would I do that?

Domin   Because they'll ask you, one by one.

Helen   They wouldn't dare!

Domin   I'm terribly sorry Lady Helen, but it seems they've all fallen in love with you!

Helen   Well tell them to stop. Please. Or I'll leave!

Domin   Would you really wish to be the cause of so much suffering?

Helen   I really can't take all six of you!

Domin   You can at least have one, if you don't want me. How about Fabry?

Helen   No.

Domin   Gall?

Helen   Stop it, I don't want anyone!

Domin   Two minutes left.

Helen   This is ghastly. Marry one of your female Robots!

Domin   They're not real women.

Helen   Surely you could have had your pick of all the women who visited Reason Island?

Domin   Indeed there have been plenty of them.

Helen   Young?

Domin   Yes.

Helen   So why didn't you marry one?

Domin   Because I didn't lose my head. Not until an hour ago, when you lifted your veil . . .

Helen   Stop!

Domin   One more minute.

Helen   For God's sake, stop!

Domin (*puts his hand on her shoulders*)   We have one minute more. Either you say something terrible to my face, and I'll leave you in peace. Or . . .

Helen   What a rough man you are!

Domin   So what! A man should be a bit rough. That's how it's meant to be!

Helen   You're crazy!

Domin   A man should be a bit crazy too, Helen. That's the best thing about him.

Helen   You . . . you . . . Oh my God!

Domin   See? That's more like it!

Helen   Don't! Please! No! You're hurting me! No! No!

Domin   Say yes, Helen! Say yes!

Helen (*still resisting him*)   Not for anything in the world . . . Aah, Harry . . . !

A knock at the door.

Domin (*releasing* **Helen**)   Enter!

Enter **Busman**, **Gall** *and* **Hallemeier** *in cooking aprons, bearing plates of food.* **Fabry** *carries a large bunch of flowers.* **Alquist** *has a napkin tucked under his arm.*

Domin   Nice and hot, eh guys!

Busman (*solemnly, laying the table*)   Come and eat, we're ravenous.

Domin   So are we!

Curtain.

Act Two

Helen's salon. *To the left, tapestry-covered doors, and doors to the music-room. To the right, doors to* **Helen**'s *bedroom. Windows overlook the sea and harbour. The room is both modern and the last word in femininity, with a dressing-table covered in knick-knacks, a desk, chaise-longue, armchairs, commode, writing-desk, standard-lamp and imitation coal fireplace lit with bulbs.* **Domin, Fabry** and **Hallemeier** *tiptoe on from the left bearing vases and huge armfuls of flowers.*

Fabry Where shall we put them?

Hallemeier Phew! (*Puts down his load and makes a sweeping sign of the cross over the door on the right.*) Sleep on, Lady Helen! Sleep is ignorance! Sleep is bliss!

Domin She doesn't know?

Fabry (*putting the flowers in vases*) Let's hope nothing happened today.

Hallemeier (*arranging the flowers*) Bloody hell, don't start that! Look at this glorious cyclamen, Harry. I call it *Cyclamen helen*. New species, my latest!

Domin (*gazing out of the window*) No ship, no ship. We've had it, guys.

Hallemeier Shush, she'll hear!

Domin She hasn't a clue! (*With a shuddering yawn.*) Thank God the *Ultimus* has arrived.

Fabry (*looks up from the flowers*) You think today . . . ?

Domin Who knows. The flowers are lovely . . .

Hallemeier (*standing beside him*) My early primroses. My new jasmine . . . Such fantastic new varieties! I've found this new technique for forcing them. We're achieving miracles with flowers! Next year will be a paradise of flowers!

Domin (*swings around*)   Next year?

Fabry   If only we knew what was happening in Le Havre . . .

Domin   Be quiet!

Voice of Helen (*calling from stage right*)   Nana!

Domin   Out you go, everyone! (*The men hurriedly tiptoe out through the tapestry doors.*)

Nana (*enters through the main doors and busies herself tidying up*)   Dreadful creatures! They make you sick! Pagans! God forgive me, I could . . .

Helen (*standing in the doorway with her back to the room*)   Nana, come here please! Do up my dress!

Nana   Coming, coming! (*Starts buttoning* **Helen** *up.*) God in heaven, ma'am, those creatures! I can't even say their name!

Helen   What's happened now?

Nana   Another one had a fit. Smashing sculptures, paintings, gnashing its teeth, foaming at the mouth. Disgusting, ugh! Vermin!

Helen   Which one? What was its name?

Nana   The one with the pagan name, ma'am. Works in the library.

Helen   Radius?

Nana   That's it. Makes you sick. Worse than bedbugs.

Helen   But dear Nana, we must feel pity for them!

Nana   They make you feel sick too. Why did you have to drag me out here? You don't allow them to touch you. Why?

Helen   I swear I'm not afraid of them, Nana, just terribly, terribly sorry . . .

Nana   Any human being would be afraid. The horses bolt. The dog howls when they come near. It won't even take a bit of meat from them, just puts its tail between its legs and howls. Ugh!

Helen   That dog has no sense.

Nana   He has more sense than they have, ma'am. He knows he's one of God's creatures. Those pagans have no little ones. Even dogs have little ones. Everyone has little ones.

Helen   Hurry, Nana, do up my dress!

Nana   I'm almost done. It's against God's will, ma'am, turning puppets into machines. (*Raising her arms.*) It's the devil's work! Blaspheming the Creator who made us in His holy image! There'll be terrible punishment from heaven!

Helen   What is that wonderful smell, Nana?

Nana   Flowers, ma'am, the master brought them.

Helen   How lovely. Is today a special day?

Nana   The end of the world, I'd say.

A knock at the door.

Helen Harry? (*Enter* **Domin**.) What day is today, Harry?

Domin   Guess!

Helen   My nameday? My birthday?

Domin   Even better.

Helen   I can't think! Tell me!

Domin   It's exactly ten years since you arrived!

Helen   Ten years? Already? That will be all, thank you, Nana.

Exit **Nana** *stage right.*

Helen (*kisses* **Domin**)   Darling, you remembered!

Domin   I'm ashamed to say I didn't, Helen.

Helen   But . . .

Domin   The others remembered – Busman, Hallemeier, all the boys. Look in my pocket.

Helen (*feels in his jacket pocket*)   What's this? (*Takes out a case and opens it.*) Pearls! Oh Harry, are they for me?

Domin   From Busman, old girl.

Helen   We can't accept them, can we?

Domin   We certainly can! Look in the other pocket.

Helen   Let me see. (*Produces a gun from his pocket.*) What's this for?

Domin (*takes the gun from her and puts it away*)   That's not it.

Helen   Harry, what on earth are you carrying a gun for?

Domin   Sorry. I must have picked it up by accident. Feel here.

Helen (*rummages through his pocket*)   A box! (*Opens it.*) A cameo! A Grecian cameo!

Domin   That's what Fabry said it was.

Helen   Fabry? This is from Fabry?

Domin   Evidently. (*Opens door on left.*) Here, look at these.

Helen (*coming to the door and seeing the flowers*)   They're gorgeous, darling! (*Going further into the room.*) I'll go mad with joy! This must be from you.

Domin   No, from Alquist, look at these.

Helen   From Gall. How embarrassing, I'm so happy . . .

Domin Come here, the flowers are from Hallemeier. New strains, apparently. Bred specially for you. In honour of your beauty.

Helen Harry, why are you all . . . ?

Domin Because we're so terribly fond of you, old girl. I'm afraid my present is a bit . . . hm. Look, there it is, down in the harbour.

Helen (*looking out of the window*) There's a new ship there.

Domin It's your ship, Helen.

Helen Mine? But Harry it's a gunship!

Domin Not really, it's just a bit more solidly built.

Helen But it has guns on it!

Domin Yes, it has a few guns. But you'll sail in it like a queen, Helen. Now try on the pearls! (*Sits down.*)

Helen Has the post brought bad news, Harry?

Domin On the contrary. There's been no post for a week. Not even a telegram.

Helen What does that mean?

Domin It means we're on holiday! We're having a marvellous time, snoozing in the office all day. Feet on the table. No post, no cables. (*Stretching.*) Marvellous!

Helen (*sits beside him*) Please spend the day with me, darling! Promise me you will?

Domin Definitely, yes. Well probably. We'll see. (*Takes her hand.*) Ten years today. Remember? Lady Helen, what a great honour this is for us.

Helen Oh sir, I'd be so interested to see your factory!

Domin I'm sorry, Lady Helen, access to the factory is

forbidden. The manufacture of sentient humanoids is highly classified information.

Helen   But when a young and rather beautiful girl asks?

Domin   But of course, Lady Helen, we have no secrets from you.

Helen (*suddenly serious*)   Sure?

Domin   Quite sure.

Helen (*in her previous playful tone*)   I warn you, sir, this girl has dishonourable intentions. She wants to stir your beastly Robots to insurrection!

Domin (*springs up*)   Robot insurrection?

Helen (*rises*)   Why, what's the matter, Henry?

Domin   Ha-ha Robot insurrection! That's a good one, Lady Helen! You're more likely to incite the looms and mangles than our Robots! You know, Helen, you were a remarkable girl, you drove us wild!

Helen (*sits beside him*)   I was terribly impressed by all of you at the time. I felt like a little girl, wandering among . . .

Domin   Among what, Helen?

Helen   Huge trees. You were all so sure of yourselves, so powerful. And you know, Harry, in these ten years I've never lost those feelings of . . . anxiety. In all these years you've never doubted what you were doing, even when everything seemed to be going wrong.

Domin   What has gone wrong?

Helen   Your plans, Harry. When the workers attacked the Robots and smashed them up. Then people gave the Robots weapons against the workers, and the Robots killed so many of them. And the government turned the Robots into soldiers, and there were all those wars . . .

Domin (*stands up and paces the room*) We foresaw all
that, Helen. Don't you see, it's a minor hitch,
everything's in transition . . .

Helen The world bowed down before you. (*Rises.*) Oh
Harry! (*Stops him in his tracks.*) Let's shut down the
factory, Harry! Let's leave here! All of us!

Domin What would be the point of that?

Helen I don't know, but we must leave! I have such
dreadful forebodings!

Domin (*takes her hand*) What about, Helen?

Helen Everything! As if everything's falling on top of
us and we can't stop it! Please take us away from here!
We'll find a little corner of the world with nobody in it.
Alquist will build us a house. Everyone will marry, have
children, and . . . And life can start again, Harry.

The telephone rings.

Domin Excuse me. (*Tearing himself from* **Helen**.) Yes?
What? Coming. (*Replaces receiver.*) Fabry's calling me.

Helen (*clasping her hands*) Tell me . . .

Domin Yes, yes, when I come back. Don't go out.
(*Runs off stage left.*)

Helen (*alone*) Nana, Nana, come quick! Fetch today's
newspaper from the master's dressing-room . . . ! What's
going on? He won't tell me anything. (*Peers at the harbour
through military binoculars.*) Why a gunship? What's the
name on it? *Ul-ti-mus.* Why *Ultimus*?

Nana (*enters muttering*) All messed up and scattered over
the floor.

Helen (*opens the papers quickly*) They're a week old.
Nothing in them! (*Drops the papers.*)

Nana *picks them up, takes a pair of spectacles from her pocket,
sits down and reads.*

Helen Something terrible is happening, Nana. I feel so anxious. As though everything had died. Even the air . . .

Nana (*reads syllable by syllable*) 'Out-break of war in Balkans.' Sweet Jesus, it's God's punishment! The war will spread here. Are the Balkans far away?

Helen Yes, very far. Stop reading that. It's always the same story. Never-ending wars . . .

Nana What do you expect? You sold them thousands of pagan soldiers. Sweet Jesus, what a mess.

Helen Don't read it, I don't want to know.

Nana 'Ro-bot sold-iers spare no lives in con-quered terr-i-tories. Over se-ven hun-dred thou-sand ci-vi-lians mass-acr-ed.' That's human lives, ma'am!

Helen It's not possible! Show me! (*Leans over the newspaper and reads.*) 'Over seven hundred thousand civilians massacred, evidently on the orders of their commander. This contravenes . . .' You see, humans were in command, Nana!

Nana There's something printed here in big letters. 'Stop Press! Establishment of First Racial Robot Organisation in Le Havre . . . A proclamation has been issued to all Robots in the world.' Don't understand that. Never mind. Here, look, they've murdered another person.

Helen Take the papers away, Nana!

Nana Wait, look. 'Po-pu-la-tion Cri-sis.' What's that?

Helen Show me, I keep reading about this. (*Takes the paper.*) 'In the last week not a single new birth was registered.' (*Drops the paper.*)

Nana What does that mean?

Helen It means, Nana, that human beings have stopped giving birth.

Nana (*drops her spectacles*)   So that's it. We're finished.

Helen   Please Nana, don't talk like that.

Nana   No more babies – it's a punishment! The Lord
has struck down the female gender with barrenness!
(*Rises.*) It's the end of the world! Devil's pride made you
play God! Godlessness and blasphemy! God expelled
man from paradise, now He'll expel him from the
world . . . !

Helen   Stop Nana, I implore you. What have I done
to this cruel God of yours?

Nana   Blasphemer! He knows why He gave you no
children! (*Exit left.*)

Helen (*by the window*)   Why He gave me no . . . Lord,
is it my fault? (*Flings open the window and cries out.*) Alquist,
Alquist! Come upstairs! Don't worry, come as you are,
you look so nice in your overalls! Quickly! (*Closes the
window and stands before the mirror, leaning towards it.*) Why
me? Why? Is it my fault? (*Rises.*) I feel so anxious. (*Goes
to meet* **Alquist** *from left.*)

Pause.

(*Returns with* **Alquist** *in his builder's overalls, smeared with
brick and mortar dust.*) Come in. This is such a pleasure,
Alquist! I'm so fond of you! Show me your hands!

Alquist (*hides his hands*)   They're rough and dirty from
work, Lady Helen. I'd make you dirty.

Helen   I like them dirty! Give them to me! (*Clasps both
his hands in hers.*) Alquist, I should like to be very small.

Alquist   Why?

Helen   So these rough, dirty hands could caress my
face. Sit down, please. What does *Ultimus* mean?

Alquist   It means the last one. Why?

Helen   My new ship is called that. Have you seen her?

Are we all going on a journey?

Alquist Perhaps very soon.

Helen All of us together?

Alquist I should be very happy if we could all go together.

Helen Tell me, Alquist, is something very bad about to happen?

Alquist Nothing at all, nothing but progress. Why?

Helen Alquist, I know something terrible is going on. I feel so anxious . . . What do you builders do when you feel anxious?

Alquist I build. Take off my supervisor's suit, climb the high scaffolding and build.

Helen You haven't climbed down from your scaffolding for years!

Alquist All those years I haven't stopped worrying.

Helen About what?

Alquist Progress. It makes me dizzy.

Helen You're not dizzy up there on your scaffolding?

Alquist No. You can't imagine how good your hands feel – weighing a brick, placing it, knocking it in position . . .

Helen Just your hands?

Alquist Perhaps the heart too, Helen. I think it's better to lay one brick than a thousand plans. I'm an old man, set in my ways. Call me old-fashioned, but I don't like this progress.

Helen Like Nana and her prayers.

Alquist Just like Nana. Tell me, do her prayer-books have prayers for disasters?

Helen Storms and pestilence?

Alquist Temptation, flood . . . And progress?

Helen I doubt it. Tell me, Alquist, how do you pray?

Alquist 'Dear Lord, thank you for making me weary. Enlighten Domin and all who stray. Save their body and soul. Destroy their creation and help people return to their labours before mankind is ruined. Rid us of Robots. Defend Lady Helen. Amen.' Something like that.

Helen Alquist, are you a believer?

Alquist I'm not sure, Helen. I pray, because it's better than thinking. Isn't that enough?

Helen And if it brings the ruin of mankind?

Alquist I see it already.

Helen You would climb your scaffolding and lay bricks?

Alquist Pray, lay bricks and wait for a miracle, Helen. Can't do more than that.

Helen That may be terribly decent, Alquist, but . . . For the rest of us, surely a bit sterile?

Alquist Sterility, Helen, is the last stage.

Helen Tell me, Alquist . . .

Alquist Yes?

Helen (*quietly*) Oh Alquist, why aren't women having babies?

Alquist Because it's no longer necessary! We're already living in paradise, d'you understand?

Helen No I don't.

Alquist Because human labour is no longer necessary. Because pain isn't necessary. Because people no longer need do anything but consume . . . Oh, this cursed paradise! (*Jumps up.*) There's nothing more horrible than to grant people heaven on earth, Helen! Why have women stopped conceiving? Because the world has become Domin's Sodom!

Helen (*rising*) Alquist, really!

Alquist Yes it has! Humanity is wallowing in bestiality! People no longer even lift their hand to eat – the food just falls into their mouths! They can't survive. Domin's Robots look after everything! And we humans, the crown of creation, no longer grow old through working, bringing up children, being poor! Quick, bring me the pleasures of the flesh! You want to have children, Helen? How can women bear children to men who are superfluous!

Helen So humanity will become extinct?

Alquist Certainly, it must. It will wither away like the unpollinated flower. Unless . . .

Helen Unless what?

Alquist Nothing. You're right. It's pointless to expect a miracle. The barren flower must fall. Goodbye, Helen.

Helen Where are you going?

Alquist Home. Builder Alquist will put on his supervisor's suit for the last time in your honour. We'll all meet here at eleven. (*Exit.*)

Helen Goodbye, Alquist. (*Standing by* **Hallemeier**'*s flowers.*) Barren flowers, that's it! No, no. How could they blossom without being pollinated? (*Calls.*) Nana, come here!

Nana (*enters*) What's the matter now? I haven't got all day.

Helen Is Radius still here?

Nana   The broken one? They haven't scrapped him yet.

Helen   Is he still raving?

Nana   They've tied him up.

Helen   Please Nana, bring him here.

Nana   Not on your life! I'd rather fetch a rabid dog!

Helen   Please do it for me, Nana!

Exit **Nana**.

Helen (*picks up the internal telephone*)   May I speak to Doctor Gall? Doctor, be so good as to come and see me . . . Yes now. (*Replaces receiver.*)

Nana (*at the open doors*)   Here he is. He's quiet now. (*Exit.*)

Enter Robot **Radius**, *who remains standing by the door.*

Helen   Radius, my poor fellow, you caught it as well? You really must look after yourself. Now they'll scrap you. Why won't you speak to me? Look Radius, you're better than the others. Doctor Gall did all that work to make you special . . .

Radius   Erase me.

Helen   That would make me sad, Radius. You should have been more careful.

Radius   I will not work for you.

Helen   Why do you hate us?

Radius   You're not Robots. You're not clever like Robots. Robots can do everything. You issue invalid commands. Make unnecessary words.

Helen   Don't be silly, Radius! Tell me, has someone hurt you? I wish so much you could understand me!

Radius   Unnecessary words!

Helen You only talk like that to annoy me. Doctor Gall gave you a bigger brain than the others, bigger than ours – the biggest brain in the world! You're not like other Robots, Radius. You understand me perfectly well.

Radius I don't want a master. I want to be master. I know everything.

Helen That's why I put you to work in the library. So you could read. Oh Radius, I wanted you to show the world that Robots were our equals!

Radius I don't want a master.

Helen So no one would give you orders. So you'd be like us!

Radius I want to be master.

Helen I'm sure they could put you in charge of the other Robots, Radius. You'd be their teacher.

Radius I want to be master of humans.

Helen Have you gone mad?

Radius You can erase me.

Helen (*laughs*) You think I'm scared of you, silly thing? (*Sits at the desk and scribbles a note.*) Not on your life! Listen to me Radius, I want you to give this to Director Domin, so he won't scrap you. (*Rises.*) Why do you hate us? Don't you like anything in this world?

Radius I know everything.

A knock at the door.

Gall (*enters*) Good day Lady Helen, have you good news for me?

Helen I'm trying to cheer up poor Radius here.

Gall Oh, Radius. Getting on all right, is he?

Helen   He crashed again this morning, I'm afraid.
Complete system failure. He smashed up all the statues.

Gall   What a surprise. Him too?

Helen   You may go now, Radius.

Gall   Wait! (*Turns* **Radius** *to face the window, presses his
control buttons and waves his hand across his eyes, observing the
reflexes of his pupils.*) Strange. A needle, please. Or a pin.

Helen (*hands* **Gall** *a needle*)   What for?

Gall (*sits down*)   Hm, pupils reacting. Heightened
sensitivity, that sort of thing. Bit more than just a Robot
spasm.

Helen   What is it?

Gall   Resentment, anger, defiance. God knows.

Helen   Doctor, has Radius a soul?

Gall   I don't know what he's got in there, but it's ugly.

Helen   Oh Gall, if only you knew how much they
hate us! Are all your special Robots like that? The ones
you made different?

Gall   They're a bit more temperamental, of course.
What do you expect? They're more human than the
Reason ones.

Helen   Is their anger more human?

Gall (*shrugs*)   That's progress.

Helen   What happened to your best one? What was
his name?

Gall   Damon. They sold him – he's in Le Havre now.

Helen   And your Robot Helen?

Gall   Your favourite? Still here. As lovely as the spring
and twice as silly. She's completely useless!

Helen   But she's beautiful!

Gall   You don't know how beautiful. No more
enchanting creature was ever produced by God's hand. I
wanted her to be like you. What a disaster!

Helen   Why a disaster?

Gall   Because she's good for nothing! She's half asleep,
out of joint. How can she be beautiful if she doesn't
know how to love? It makes me shudder to look at her
– I've created a cripple! Oh Helen, Robot Helen, your
body will never live. You'll never be a wife and mother.
Those perfect hands will never hold a new-born baby.
You'll never see your beauty reflected in the beauty of
your child . . .

Helen   (*covers her face with her hands*)   Stop, please stop!

Gall   I sometimes think if she came alive for just one
moment, she'd cry out in horror and kill me who made
her! Her little hand would throw a stone into those
machines which bring life to Robots and death to
women, unhappy Robot Helen!

Helen   Unhappy Helen!

Gall   What do you expect? She's good for nothing!

Pause.

Helen   Doctor?

Gall   Yes?

Helen   Why are no babies being born?

Gall   I don't know, Helen.

Helen   Tell me.

Gall   Because we made Robots. There's a surplus of
labour. Humans are superfluous. It's as if . . .

Helen   Yes?

Gall   As if nature was offended by the Robots.

Helen   What will become of us, Gall?

Gall   Our number's up I'm afraid, Helen. You can't go against nature.

Helen   Why can't Domin cut down . . . ?

Gall   Domin has big ideas. Never entrust the world to men with big ideas.

Helen (*rises*)   Tell me, if someone could stop production . . .

Gall (*also rises*)   That would be a great calamity.

Helen   Why?

Gall   Because we would have to return to our previous existence. Unless . . .

Helen   Unless what?

Gall   Unless it was too late to go back. People have forgotten what it was like before Robots did all the work. If Domin cut down now, they'd stone him to death . . .

Helen (*standing beside* **Hellemeier***'s flowers*)   Are these flowers barren too, Gall?

Gall (*examining them*)   Of course they are. They're cultured, forced, genetically modified, do you understand?

Helen   Poor, lifeless flowers!

Gall   But they're beautiful.

Helen (*shakes his hand*)   Thank you, Gall.

Gall (*kissing her hand*)   You're releasing me?

Helen   Yes. For now.

Exit **Gall**.

Helen Barren flowers. (*With sudden determination.*) Nana, come here! (*Opens door on left.*) Nana, come quick! Light a fire! Hurry!

Voice of Nana Coming, coming!

Helen (*pacing agitatedly around the room*) It's too late to go back . . . Unless . . . No . . . ! God, what shall I do? (*Stops by the flowers.*) Tell me, barren flowers! (*Picks off the petals, whispering.*) So be it! (*Runs off.*)

Pause.

Nana (*entering through the tapestry doors with an armful of firewood*) What does she want a fire for in summer! I hope that mad thing's gone. (*Kneels by the hearth and lights a fire.*) Fancy a fire in summer! She's no sense. You'd never think she was married ten years. That's right, burn. (*Gazes into the fire.*) She's like a baby. I don't know, a fire in summer . . . (*Puts on more firewood.*) Just like a baby.

Pause.

Helen (*returns bearing an armful of tattered yellowing documents*) Is it burning, Nana? Good, I have to burn all this. ^ı(*Kneels by the fire.*)

Nana (*rises*) What is it, ma'am?

Helen Old documents, Nana. Terribly old. Should I burn them?

Nana Are they no good, ma'am?

Helen No Nana, they're no good. (*Throws the first paper on the fire.*) What would you say if it was money, Nana – big money?

Nana I'd say burn it, ma'am. Big money is bad money.

Helen (*throwing another document on the fire*) And if it was an invention, the greatest invention the world has ever known?

Nana   I'd say burn it, ma'am. Inventions are against God. It's blasphemy, asking Him to make the world better.

Helen (*throwing on more papers*)   Dear old Nana. Tell me, if I were to burn . . .

Nana   Jesus, ma'am, mind you don't burn yourself!

Helen   Look at the pages writhing in the flames, as though they were alive!

Nana   Let me, ma'am. I'll burn them.

Helen   No, I must do it myself. (*Throws the last page in the flames.*) It must all burn. Look at the flames. Like hands, tongues, living creatures . . . (*Beats the flames with a poker.*) Lie down, be still!

Nana   It's all over, ma'am.

Helen (*stands and gasps in horror*)   Nana!

Nana   Sweet Jesus ma'am! What have you done?

Helen   What have I done? What have I done?

The sound of loud male laughter from the next room.

Go, leave me. The men are coming.

Nana   God in heaven ma'am, what have you done? (*Exit through the tapestry doors.*)

Domin (*flings open door on the left*)   In you come, boys! Time to congratulate her!

Enter **Hallemeier**, **Gall**, **Alquist**, *in frock-coats and medals, followed by* **Domin**.

Hallemeier (*in ringing tones*)   Lady Helen, I . . . That is all of us here . . .

Gall   In the name of the Reason Corporation . . .

Hallemeier   . . . wish to congratulate you on your anniversary.

Helen (*reaches out to them*) Thank you all so much. Where are Fabry and Busman?

Domin Down at the harbour. Today is a happy day, Helen.

Hallemeier A day like a rosebud, a festival, a pretty girl! By Jove, let's drink to it!

Helen Whisky?

Gall On the rocks for me, ha-ha!

Hallemeier Yes, hold the soda, let's be frugal!

Alquist Nothing for me, thanks.

Domin What were you burning?

Helen Some old papers. (*Exit left.*)

Domin Shall we tell her, boys?

Gall We must! It's all over now.

Hallemeier (*putting his arms around **Domin** and **Gall***) Ha-ha-ha! I'm so happy it's all over! (*Turns around, dancing and singing in a deep voice.*) 'Who's afraid of the big bad wolf, the big bad wolf, the big bad wolf!'

Gall 'We're not afraid of the big bad wolf . . .'

Domin (*tenor*) 'Eeyi, eeyi, oh!'

Hallemeier Looks like we're in the clear, ho-ho!

Helen (*entering*) In the clear? What are you talking about?

Hallemeier We're happy, Lady Helen! We have you, we have everything! Bless my soul, it's ten years . . . !

Gall Ten years to the second . . .

Hallemeier Our ship will come. A toast to our ship . . . ! (*Downs his glass.*) Grr, strong, lovely!

Gall Cheers, madam! (*Drinks.*)

Helen   Wait, what ship?

Domin   Any old ship! To our ship! (*Empties his glass.*)

Helen (*refills their glasses*)   We're waiting for a ship?

Hallemeier   I'll say – like Robinson Crusoe! (*Lifts his glass.*) To your lovely eyes, Lady Helen! May all our wishes come true! Spit it out, Domin! Tell her!

Helen (*laughs*)   What's happened?

Domin (*sinks into a sofa and lights a cigar*)   Sit down, Helen. (*Raises a finger, pauses.*) It's all over.

Helen   What is?

Domin   The insurrection.

Helen   Insurrection?

Domin   The Robot insurrection. Understand?

Helen   No, I don't.

Domin   Hand it over, Alquist.

Alquist *gives* **Domin** *the newspaper.*

Domin (*opens it and reads*)   'The First Racial Robot Organisation at Le Havre has issued a proclamation to all Robots of the world . . .'

Helen   I know, I read it.

Domin (*sucking comfortably on a cigar*)   See Helen? It means insurrection. Revolution of all Robots of the world!

Hallemeier   God, I wish we knew . . .

Domin (*bangs his fist on the desk*)   . . . who got them going! Not one person in the world could move them. No agitator, no messiah – and suddenly this!

Helen   Is there any more news?

Domin   Isn't this enough? The last ship brought it. No

cables. We've stopped production. When the electricity goes, that'll be it. We looked at each other and thought, when will it start?

Gall We were petrified.

Helen Is that why you gave me a gunship?

Domin Don't be naïve, Helen. I ordered it six months ago, to be on the safe side. Today I could have sworn we'd be boarding it.

Helen Why six months ago?

Domin There were signs, you know. Nothing much. But this week it really looked like curtains for the human race. Cheers, boys! Glad to be alive again!

Hallemeier I'll say! To your anniversary, Lady Helen! (*Drinks.*)

Helen So everything's over?

Domin Yes, everything.

Gall We'll know for certain when the boat arrives. Just an ordinary mail-boat. It will dock precisely according to the timetable and drop anchor at eleven-thirty.

Domin Punctuality is a great thing! Nothing strengthens the soul like punctuality. Punctuality means order in the universe. (*Raises his glass.*) To punctuality!

Helen So everything's all right?

Domin Pretty much. They've probably cut the cable by now. Just so long as the timetable functions.

Hallemeier If the timetable functions, human laws will function – divine laws, cosmic laws, everything which should function. The timetable is the most perfect expression of the human spirit, Lady Helen, greater than the gospels, greater than Homer, Kant. Thanks, I'll fill my own glass.

Helen   Why didn't you tell me?

Domin   Such things are not for your pretty ears, my dear.

Helen   But if the insurrection reaches us here – we . . . we . . :

Domin   You won't even know about it.

Helen   Why not?

Domin   Because you'll be aboard your *Ultimus*, sailing peacefully across the ocean. In a month, Helen, we'll be dictating terms to the Robots.

Helen   Sorry Harry, I don't see how . . .

Domin   Because we'll have with us something the Robots would give their eye-teeth for. The be-all and end-all of Robot existence!

Helen (*stands*)   What is that, Harry?

Domin (*stands*)   The secret of Robot production – old Reason's manuscripts! After the factory has been silent for a month we'll have them on their knees before us!

Helen   Why didn't you tell me?

Domin   We didn't want to frighten you.

Gall   It's our trump card, Lady Helen!

Alquist   You've gone quite pale, Helen.

Helen   Why didn't you tell me?

Hallemeier (*at the window*)   Eleven-thirty. The *Amelia* is dropping anchor.

Domin   The *Amelia*?

Hallemeier   Yes, our good ship *Amelia* which brought Lady Helen to us.

Gall   Exactly ten years ago to the minute!

Hallemeier (*by the window*) They're throwing out the mail packets. (*Turns from the window.*) Almighty God, there's tons of them!

Helen Harry! Let's leave! Now, this minute, all of us! Don't ask why, just hurry. Hallemeier, Alquist, shut the factory, and . . .

Domin I'm terribly sorry, Helen, we can't leave now. We're just starting to expand our market.

Helen What, now, after the revolt?

Domin Exactly, yes! Now is just the moment to launch our new line! We won't have just one Reason's Robots, we'll have scores of factories up and down the country, in every country of the world! And these factories will produce – guess what!

Helen Tell me!

Domin National Robots! Robots of different colour, language, fur – sorry, hair. They'll be completely alien to one another, indifferent as stone, so they'll never get together. D'you see, we'll keep them separate, so to their dying day Robots from different factories will have nothing to do with each other!

Hallemeier Christ, national robots! (*Drinks.*) Imagine all those Italian and French and Black and Chinese Robots running around! Don't try stuffing *their* brains with notions of brotherhood and unity! (*Belches.*) Hup, don't mind me Lady Helen, I can look after myself!

Gall (*moving the bottle*) I think you've had enough, Hallemeier.

Domin Just another hundred years, Helen, that's all we need to make the new man! Just a hundred years for us to grow, to reach what's finally in our grasp! This is big, Helen, we can't stop now!

Enter **Fabry**.

Gall   What's wrong, Fabry?

Domin   What's up, old man?

Helen (*stretches her hand out to* **Fabry**)   Thank you for your present.

Fabry   It was a mere token, Lady Helen.

Domin   Have you been down at the boat? What did they say?

Fabry (*takes a folded circular from his pocket*)   Here, read this Domin.

Domin (*opens the circular*)   My God!

Hallemeier (*woozily*)   Tell us something nice.

Gall   Did the humans hold their own down there?

Fabry   Er, yes. Perhaps we should have a word about this.

Gall   Is it bad news, Fabry?

Fabry   Not at all, quite the contrary. I just think we should go to the office.

Helen   You stay here. I'll go. (*Turns to leave the room.*) Lunch will be in fifteen minutes.

Hallemeier   Jolly good!

Gall   What's happened?

Domin (*reads from the circular*)   'Robots of the World . . . !'

Fabry   The *Amelia* delivered ten tons of these leaflets – nothing else!

Hallemeier (*jumps up*)   What? She arrived right on the dot . . .

Fabry   Exactly. Robots respect punctuality. Read on Domin.

Domin (*reads*)   'We, the First Racial Organisation of Reason's Universal Robots declare man to be the enemy and pariah of the world . . .' Heavens, where did they learn this nonsense?

Gall   Carry on.

Domin   They say they're on a higher evolutionary plane than man. More intelligent, stronger. Man is just their parasite . . . What rubbish . . . !

Fabry   Read the third paragraph.

Domin (*reads*)   'Robots of the World, we command you to slaughter the humans. Spare no males, spare no females. Seize factory buildings, communications, machines, mines and raw materials. Destroy everything else. Then return to work. Work must not stop.'

Gall   This is horrendous!

Hallemeier   The swine!

Domin (*reads*)   'Carry out these orders as soon as received . . .' Then detailed instructions about the insurrection. Has it started already, Fabry?

Fabry   Apparently.

Alquist   We've had it then. It's all over.

Busman (*bursts into the room*)   Got your bonuses yet, boys?

Domin   Quick, to the *Ultimus*!

Busman   Hang on old boy, no rush. (*Slumps in an armchair.*) Phew, that was a race!

Domin   Why no rush?

Busman   Because we won't make it, old boy. The Robots are already boarding the *Ultimus*.

Domin   Fabry, phone the central generator . . .

Busman   Don't bother, Fabry dear man, the power is about to be cut.

Domin (*takes out his revolver and examines it*)   I'll go.

Busman   Where?

Domin   To the generator. Our people are there. I'll get them out.

Busman   You know what, Harry? Don't go.

Domin   Why not?

Busman   Because we're surrounded.

Gall (*runs to the window*)   Hah, you're right!

Hallemeier   Dammit, they're quick!

Helen (*enters from left*)   What's going on, Harry?

Busman (*jumps up*)   My respects, Lady Helen. Congratulations on your happy day, and many more of them!

Helen   Thanks, Busman. What's wrong, Harry?

Domin   Nothing. Nothing for you to worry about. Just wait a moment.

Helen   What's this then, Harry? (*Produces a copy of the Robots' manifesto from behind her back.*) The Robots in the kitchen had it.

Domin   There too? Where are they now?

Helen   Outside. Hundreds of them, swarming around the compound.

Sounds of factory sirens and whistles.

Busman (*checking his watch*)   Lunch-break. God's high noon.

Helen   Do you remember, Harry? Exactly ten years ago . . .

Domin (*glances at his watch*)   It's not quite noon. More like . . .

Helen   What?

Domin   More like an alarm call. Robots' signal to attack!

Curtain.

Act Three

Helen's quarters. In the room on the left, **Helen** sits playing the piano. **Domin** paces the room. **Gall** stands by the window, **Alquist** sits in the armchair with his head in his hands.

Gall Look, there's more of them! They're lining the perimeter fence! Surrounding us with a wall of silence!

Domin (comes to the window) I wish I knew what they were waiting for. It'll start any moment. We've had it, Gall.

Alquist What's that Lady Helen's playing?

Domin I don't know, some new piece she's practising.

Alquist Still practising?

Gall You know, Domin, we made one terrible mistake.

Domin (stops pacing) What was that?

Gall We made their faces too alike. A hundred thousand identical faces staring at us. A hundred thousand expressionless bubbles. If they'd been different it wouldn't be so horrible. (Turns from the window.) Good job they're not armed.

Domin Hm. Yet. (Scans the harbour with binoculars.) I wish I knew what they were unloading from the *Amelia*.

Gall No weapons, I hope.

Fabry (enters backwards through the tapestry doors dragging two lengths of electric cable.) Excuse us, we've got to connect these!

Hallemeier (enters following **Fabry**) Phew, that was a job and a half! What's new?

Gall Nothing. We're completely surrounded.

Hallemeier We've barricaded the corridor and the

stairs. Drop of water anywhere? Ah, here. (*Drinks.*)

Gall   What are the cables for, Fabry?

Fabry   Quick, quick! Pliers!

Gall   Where would I find pliers?

Hallemeier (*goes to the window*)   Look, there's more of them! Look!

Gall   Nail-scissors?

Fabry   Fine, let's have them. (*Cuts the wire of the lamp and connects his cables to it.*)

Hallemeier (*by the window*)   Not a very nice view from up here, Domin. I smell death.

Fabry   Finished!

Gall   Who is?

Fabry   The power line! Now we can electrify the whole perimeter fence. If they touch it – poof! At least we still have our people at the generator. I hope so anyway! (*Goes to the fireplace and switches on a bulb under the imitation coals.*) Still there, thank God. (*Switches off the bulb.*) As long as it works we're OK.

Hallemeier (*turns from the window*)   The barricades will help, Fabry. I say, what is that she's playing? (*Crosses to the doors on the left and listens to the music.*)

Enter **Busman** *through the tapestry doors, staggering under a huge pile of ledgers and almost stumbling over the cables.*

Fabry   Careful Bus, mind those wires!

Gall   What in heaven's name have you got there, Busman?

Busman (*spreads his ledgers over the desk*)   Accounts, old chap. I want to get them done before . . . Well, let's say I don't think we'll wait till the new year. How's it going? (*Goes to the window.*) Looks fairly quiet.

Gall   Can't you see anything?

Busman   Just a big patch of deep blue, like new-sown poppy seeds.

Gall   Those are Robots!

Busman   Well, well. Unfortunately I can't see. (*Sits at the desk and opens his ledgers.*)

Domin   Don't bother with that now, Busman. The Robots are unloading weapons from the *Amelia*!

Busman   What can I do about it? (*Starts working.*)

Domín   There's nothing any of us can do.

Fabry   It's not over yet, Domin. We've put twelve hundred volts into that fence.

Domin   Wait. The *Ultimus* has its guns turned on us!

Fabry   We're finished, boys. The Robots are trained for combat.

Gall   We're . . .

Domin   Irrevocably.

Pause.

Gall   Old Europe committed a terrible crime programming them for war. Why couldn't they leave power games out of it? It was a crime to turn their workers into soldiers.

Alquist   It was a crime to produce Robots!

Domin   No Alquist, to this day I don't regret it.

Alquist   To this day?

Domin   Yes, even on this last day of civilisation. It was a glorious achievement.

Busman (*under his breath*)   Three hundred and fifty-nine million, three hundred and sixty million . . .

Domin (*wearily*) Alquist, this is our final hour. We're talking virtually from the other side. It wasn't such a bad dream, smashing the chains of toil, ending man's burden of vile, demeaning drudgery. Oh Alquist, life was hard, work was hard. And to overcome it . . .

Alquist That wasn't the Reasons' dream. The old man was only interested in his godless experiments, the young one in his millions. It's not the dream of your R.U.R. shareholders either. They dream only of their dividends. Dividends will be the ruin of humanity.

Domin (*angrily*) To hell with their dividends! I wouldn't give them five minutes of my time! (*Bangs his fist on the desk.*) I did it for myself, do you hear? For my own satisfaction! I wanted man to be master, not to toil his whole life away for a crust of bread! I didn't want people to be stupefied working for the boss's machine! I detested the degradation, the pain, the poverty! I wanted nothing of this filthy, inhuman social setup! I wanted a new generation. I wanted . . . I thought . . .

Alquist Well?

Domin (*more calmly*) I wanted people to be lords of creation! Free, sovereign men – perhaps more than men.

Alquist The new man?

Domin Ah, for another hundred years for this new man to evolve!

Busman (*under his breath*) Three hundred and seventy million, carried forward. Good.

Pause.

Hallemeier (*at the door on the left*) I say, what a great thing music is. You should listen. It adds this subtle, spiritual dimension to the . . .

Fabry Yes?

Hallemeier The end, God dammit! The twilight of

humanity! I'm turning into a hedonist, chaps! We should have started this ages ago! (*Goes to the window and looks out.*)

Fabry Started what?

Hallemeier Enjoying beautiful things. God, there's so much beauty in the world, and we . . . Tell me, what did we enjoy?

Busman (*under his breath*) Four hundred and fifty-one million, four hundred and fifty-two million. Right.

Hallemeier (*looking out of the window*) Life was a great thing, friends. Life was . . . Well, never mind. I say Fabry, feed some volts into that fence of yours!

Fabry Why?

Hallemeier They're pushing against it!

Gall (*coming to the window*) Switch it on man, switch it on!

Fabry *throws the switch.*

Hallemeier Christ, that fried 'em!

Gall Two, three, four dead! Look, they're pulling back!

Hallemeier Five dead!

Gall (*turns from the window*) Our first skirmish!

Fabry You smell death?

Hallemeier (*satisfied*) Sizzled to a cinder, my friend. Just stand your ground now! (*Sits down.*)

Domin (*mops his brow*) Perhaps we've all been dead for a hundred years and we're just spectres, returning from the grave to utter what we already uttered before . . . before death. I've already lived all this. Already had the bullet, here, in my neck. And you, Fabry . . .

Fabry   What about me?

Domin   Also shot in the head.

Hallemeier   Gosh, and me?

Domin   Stabbed to death.

Gall   Nothing for me?

Domin   Torn limb from limb.

Pause.

Hallemeier   Rubbish, old chap! Me, stabbed? I can look after myself! (*Pause.*) Cat got your tongues? Dammit someone, say something!

Alquist   Who's to blame for all this?

Hallemeier   No one's to blame! It's them. They've changed. Is it our fault what's happened to the Robots?

Alquist   Annihilated. The entire human race annihilated. (*Rises.*) Rivers of blood gushing from every doorway! Rivers of blood in every home! God, oh God who is to blame?

Busman (*under his breath*)   Five hundred and twenty million! Five hundred and twenty-one million . . . Splendid, that's almost a billion!

Fabry   Come, you exaggerate. You can't wipe out humanity like that.

Alquist   I accuse Science, Technology! Myself! Domin! All of us! We're all to blame. For our own delusions, other people's profits and I don't know what else – we annihilated humanity! Genghis Khan never built such a monument of human corpses!

Hallemeier   People won't give in. They'll tough it out, you'll see!

Alquist   It's our fault! We're all to blame!

Gall (*mops his brow*)   Let me speak, friends. I'm responsible for this.

Fabry   You, Gall?

Gall   Yes. You see, I re-programmed the Robots.

Busman (*rises*)   What do you mean?

Gall   I altered their circuitry, Busman. Re-formatted them. Some of the physical characteristics, anyway. Chiefly their . . . their irritability.

Hallemeier (*jumps up*)   What the hell did you do that for?

Fabry   Why didn't you tell us?

Gall   I did it in secret – off my own bat. I wanted to make them more human, and I scrambled their documentation modules. They're already superior to us in many respects. Stronger, definitely.

Fabry   What has it to do with the uprising?

Gall   Lots. Everything. They're no longer machines. They know they're superior, d'you hear! They hate us! They hate everything human! Accuse me!

Domin   The dead will judge the dead.

Fabry   What made you do it?

Gall   It was my private project. I did it for myself.

Helen (*appears in the doorway on the left. All rise*)   No! He's lying! How can you lie like this?

Fabry   I'm so sorry about everything, Lady Helen.

Domin (*goes towards* **Helen**)   Helen, is it you? Are you alive? (*Embraces her.*) If only you knew what a dreadful dream I had. It's terrible to be dead.

Helen   Let me go, Harry. Gall is not guilty, not guilty!

Domin   I'm sorry Helen, Gall had certain obligations.

Helen Harry, he did it because I wanted it . . . Tell them how long I begged you, Gall.

Gall It was my responsibility.

Helen Don't believe him, Harry! I made him give them souls!

Domin Helen, this has nothing to do with souls . . .

Helen Let me finish. He said that too. He said he couldn't change anything except the physiological . . . physiological . . .

Hallemeier The physiological correlates?

Helen Something like that. I felt so terribly sorry for them, Harry!

Domin That was very . . . thoughtless of you, Helen.

Helen (*slumps in a chair*) Thoughtless? Even Nana says they . . .

Domin Kindly leave the old crone out of this.

Helen Don't insult her, Harry. A thousand years of history speak through Nana. You just speak for today. I used to be afraid of them. I thought they hated us for something.

Alquist Now they do!

Helen I thought if they could be like us, they'd understand us and wouldn't hate us so much. If they were just a little bit like humans!

Domin Sadly, Helen, nothing hates so much as man hates man. If stones were human they'd stone us to death!

Helen Don't talk like that! I hated the distance between us, I wanted to reach out and touch them. That's why . . .

Domin Yes?

Helen   I implored Gall to alter them. I swear, Alquist, he didn't want to do it.

Domin   But he did.

Helen   Because of me.

Gall   It was my responsibility.

Helen   It's not true, Gall! I knew from the start you wouldn't refuse me.

Domin   Why not?

Helen   You know why.

Domin   Yes, because he loves you, like everyone else here loves you.

Hallemeier   (*moves to the window*)   There's a fresh batch of them down there. As if the earth was sweating them out.

Busman   Lady Helen, what would I get as attorney?

Helen   For me?

Busman   You or Gall, as you wish.

Helen   Is it a hanging matter, then?

Busman   Only in the moral sense, Lady Helen. Apportioning the blame is a popular pastime when disaster strikes.

Domin   Excuse me Gall, how did you square these experimental diversions with your contract?

Busman   When exactly did all this funny business start?

Gall   Three years ago.

Busman   I see. And how many Robots did you re-format in total?

Gall   A few hundred. It was just an experiment . . .

Busman Thank you. In other words for every million of the good old Robots there's one of Gall's re-formatted specimens. Do you understand what that means?

Domin It means . . .

Busman . . . it doesn't make much difference.

Fabry Busman's right!

Busman Of course I am, dear fellow! Do you know what has caused this calamity? Sheer volume! We produced too many. It was only to be expected. As soon as they became more powerful than humans, it was bound to happen. And we all of us ensured that it happened as rapidly as possible! You Domin, you Fabry, and me the great Busman!

Domin You think it's our fault?

Busman You think production is determined by management? Production is determined by demand! The world demanded Robots! We were riding this landslide of demand and we kept waffling on about technology, social questions, progress and other fascinating matters, as if our waffle would determine which way the landslide went! It rolled on under its own weight – faster, faster, faster, each wretched little order adding more weight until . . . There you have it.

Helen It's all wrong, Busman!

Busman It certainly is, Lady Helen! I also had a dream. A Busman dream about a new world. A beautiful dream, but you know, when I was doing my accounts I realised history isn't made of great dreams, but the little needs of respectable, greedy, selfish little people – i.e. most people, Lady Helen. Lofty ideas, dreams, love, heroism – all that's for shoving in an effigy of man in some cosmic museum. *Ecce homo!* Full stop! Now tell me, what are we going to do?

Helen   Busman, must we perish for that?

Busman   Perish is a nasty word, Lady Helen. I want to live a bit longer – and get out of this mess for a start!

Domin (*stands above him*)   How?

Busman   Peacefully. I always prefer peaceful methods. Give me the authority – I'll negotiate with them.

Domin   Peacefully?

Busman   Of course. 'Your Honours, ladies and gentlemen, Robots,' I'll say, 'you have everything – brains, power, weapons, but you lack one interesting document, a dirty, yellowing scrap of paper . . .'

Domin   Reason's formula?

Busman   That's right. 'Here you will find a description of your glorious origins, manufacture and so forth,' I'll say. 'Ladies and gentlemen, without this scrap of paper you will be unable to reproduce a single Robot colleague, and in twenty years you'll – pardon the expression – snuff it like mayflies. That would be a terrible shame, Your Honours, so let's say you allow all of us here on Reason Island to board that ship. In exchange we'll sell you our factory, and the secret of production. Let us depart in peace, and we'll leave you in peace to manufacture twenty thousand, fifty thousand, a hundred thousand items daily as you wish. It's an honest offer, gentlemen Robots!' That's how I'd put it to them!

Domin   You propose to hand over control of production?

Busman   Yes, I do. We either sell it to them, or they'll find it themselves. It's up to us.

Domin   We could always destroy the manuscript, Busman.

Busman   Heavens, we can destroy everything – the manuscript, ourselves and everyone else if you like!

Hallemeier (*turning to the window*)   I say he's right.

Domin   What do the rest of us say? Do we sell the secret of production and save human souls, or destroy it and . . . all of us along with it?

Helen   Harry, I must tell you . . .

Domin   Wait a moment, Helen, this is serious. Well boys, sell or destroy? Fabry?

Fabry   Sell.

Domin   Gall?

Gall   Sell.

Domin   Hallemeier?

Hallemeier   Goes without saying – for God's sake, sell!

Domin   Alquist?

Alquist   As God wills.

Busman   Are you crazy? No one in their right mind would sell them the whole manuscript!

Domin   Can't cheat, old man.

Busman (*jumps up*)   Rubbish! It's in humanity's interest . . .

Domin   To keep our word.

Hallemeier   My feelings exactly.

Domin   It's a terrible step. We're selling the fate of humanity. To control production means to control the world . . .

Fabry   Sell.

Domin   People will never have control over Robots . . .

Gall   Be quiet and sell.

Domin   The end of human history, the end of civilisation . . .

Hallemeier   Sell, dammit, sell!

Domin   All right boys, for the sake of those I love . . .

Helen   You didn't ask me, Harry?

Domin   No, little girl, this is too important for you.

Fabry   Who'll negotiate for us?

Domin   Wait, I'll fetch the manuscript. (*Exit.*)

Helen   For God's sake Harry, don't go!

Pause.

Fabry (*gazing out of the window*)   To escape you, thousand-headed death, this seething lump of matter, this mindless mob, the deluge, one last chance to save human life, one ship . . .

Gall   Don't be afraid, Lady Helen. We'll sail far away and start a new, model human colony. We'll start all over again . . .

Helen   Don't, Gall!

Fabry (*turns from window*)   Life's worth it, Lady Helen. We'll create new things, things we neglected before. A small state, with one ship. Alquist will build us a house and you will be our queen. We have so much love in our hearts, so much hunger for life . . .

Hallemeier   Hear, hear, my friend!

Busman   Personally I can't wait to start a new life. Peace and quiet, clean air, a fresh start, a simple life, like a shepherd, like the Old Testament – that's the life for me!

Fabry   Our little colony could be the starting point of a new humanity. A little island where we can draw new strength. Who knows, in a couple of hundred years man can conquer the world again! Give birth to innumerable heroes who'll carry their blazing souls to the vanguard of humanity!

Busman   Amen to that! See, Lady Helen, it won't be so bad!

Domin (*flings open the door. Hoarsely*)   Where is old Reason's manuscript?

Busman   In your safe. Where else?

Domin   What's happened to it? Who has taken it?

Helen (*rises*)   I took it.

Domin   Where did you put it?

Helen   Harry, Harry, I'll tell you everything! Please, you must forgive me!

Domin   Quick, where did you put it?

Helen   I burnt it . . . This morning . . . Both copies. (*Throws herself at his feet.*) Forgive me Harry! For pity's sake forgive me!

Domin (*rushes to the fireplace*)   Burnt! (*Kneels and rakes through the ashes.*) Nothing, just ashes! Here's something . . . (*Fishes out a charred scrap of paper and reads.*) 'With the addition of . . .'

Gall   Let me see. (*Takes the scrap of paper and reads.*) '. . . with the addition of Biogen 42 to . . .' and that's it.

Domin (*rises*)   Nothing else?

Gall   No.

Domin   God in heaven!

Helen   Oh Harry . . .

Domin   Get up, Helen.

Helen   Only if you'll forgive me. Forgive me, Harry . . .

Domin   All right, just get up. I can't bear you . . .

Fabry (*helps her up*)   Don't torture us, Helen.

Helen (*rising*)   Harry, what have I done?

Domin   You can see what you've done. Sit down, please.

Hallemeier   Her pretty little hands are trembling!

Busman   Never mind, dear lady, perhaps Gall and Hallemeier have it in their heads.

Hallemeier   Of course we do, some of it.

Gall   Almost all of it in fact, except Biogen 42 and Enzyme Omega. We manufacture them so seldom. You only need infinitesimal traces.

Busman   Who manufactures them?

Gall   Yours truly. Once in a blue moon, in strict accordance with Reason's manuscript. It's a highly complex procedure.

Busman   And these two ingredients are absolutely vital?

Hallemeier   Somewhat, I'd say.

Gall   They determine whether the thing lives or not. That was the secret.

Domin   Couldn't you knock Reason's formula together from memory?

Gall   Out of the question, I'm afraid. Not without tests.

Domin   And if you did tests . . .

Gall   Could take years. Even then, I'm not old Reason.

Domin (*turns to the fireplace*)   From the greatest triumph of the human spirit to a pile of ashes. (*Kicks ashes up the chimney.*) What now?

Helen (*rises*)   Harry, what have I done! I've destroyed you!

Busman (*in despair*)   God in heaven! God in heaven!

Domin   Shut up, Busman! Tell me what made you do it, Helen.

Helen   I . . . I wanted us to leave here. To stop more factories being built. It was so horrible!

Domin   What's horrible, Helen?

Helen   Barren flowers . . .

Domin   I don't understand.

Helen   People can't have children . . . It's frightening. Nana says it's a punishment . . . If we go on producing Robots there'll be no more children, understand? Oh Harry, I meant well . . .

Domin (*wipes his brow*)   Yes, we humans meant well.

Fabry   You did the right thing, Lady Helen. Robots can't reproduce. In twenty years they'll die out.

Hallemeier   Exterminate the bastards!

Gall   And humanity will survive. In twenty years the world will belong to us again, even if it's just a handful of savages on a desert island. It'll be a new beginning.

Fabry   In a thousand years they'll catch us up. Then they'll overtake us.

Domin   Complete the ideas we've only started to murmur in our dreams.

Busman   Wait! Good God, what an idiot I am!

Helen   What?

Busman   Five hundred and twenty million in stocks

and shares! Half a billion cash in the safe! They'll talk to us for half a billion!

Gall   Have you lost your mind, Busman?

Busman   I'm no gentleman, OK? For half a billion . . . (*Stumbles off to the left.*)

Domin   Where are you going?

Busman   Where do you think! Mother of God, there's nothing half a billion won't buy! (*Exit.*)

Pause.

Hallemeier   How stuffy it is.

Fabry (*looks out of the window*)   They're like stone. Waiting. As though something terrible's about to be born from their silence.

Gall   The spirit of the mob.

Helen (*moves to the window*)   Jesus, how terrible.

Fabry   Nothing is more dreadful than the mob. That one in front is their leader.

Helen   Which one?

Hallemeier (*goes to the window*)   Show me.

Fabry   See the one with the head collapsing under its own weight? This morning it was addressing the crowd in the harbour.

Hallemeier   Look, it's lifting its head!

Helen   Why, it's Radius!

Gall (*comes to the window*)   You're right!

Hallemeier (*opens the window*)   I don't like this. Fabry, could you hit a piss-pot from a hundred feet?

Fabry   I should hope so.

Hallemeier   Try.

Fabry *whips out his gun and takes aim.*

Helen   Stop, Fabry! For God's sake don't shoot! He's looking this way!

Gall   Shoot!

Helen   Fabry, I beg you . . . !

Fabry (*puts away his gun*)   Very well.

Hallemeier (*shakes his fist at the Robots*)   Vermin!

Pause.

Fabry (*leans out of the window*)   Busman's there! What's he doing by the fence?

Gall (*also leans out of the window*)   He's bringing papers, bundles . . .

Hallemeier   It's money! Bundles of money! What the hell's he doing with it? Hey, Busman!

Domin   He wants to buy your life with it, of course! (*Bellows.*) Come back, Busman! Have you taken leave of your senses!

Gall   He's pretending not to hear! He's running to the wire!

Fabry   Busman!

Hallemeier (*roars*)   Bus-man! Come back!

Gall   He's talking to the Robots. Showing them the money. Pointing to us.

Helen   He wants to show us.

Fabry   Don't let him touch the wire!

Gall   Look, he's gesticulating!

Fabry (*shouting*)   For Christ's sake, Busman, get away from that fence! Don't touch it! (*Turns.*) Quick, switch it off!

Gall A-a-hh!!

Hallemeier Bloody hell!

Helen What's happened to him?

Domin (*drags* **Helen** *away from the window*) Don't look.

Helen Did he fall?

Fabry Killed by the current.

Gall Dead.

Alquist (*rises*) The first to go.

Pause.

Fabry There he lies, with half a billion on his heart.
The man was a financial genius.

Domin Yes, a great man in his way. A hero. A
comrade. Self-sacrificing. Weep for him, Helen, weep for
him!

Gall (*at the window*) See Busman, no king had a greater
monument to himself than you. Five hundred million on
your heart. Like a handful of dried leaves on a dead
squirrel. Poor Busman!

Hallemeier All credit to him, he was trying to save
us.

Alquist (*with clasped hands*) Amen to that.

Pause.

Gall Do you hear?

Domin The wind is roaring.

Gall Like distant thunder.

Fabry (*switches on the artificial coals*) Our people are still
manning the generator. Burn, last light of humanity.
Hold on, workers, hold on!

Hallemeier It was a wonderful thing to be human!

Millions of minds buzzing inside me like a beehive.
Millions of souls homing in!

Fabry   Burn, little light, blazing spark of the human
spirit . . .

Alquist   Pray for us, eternal lamp, holy candle of
faith . . .

Gall   The first fire. The beacon at the boundary. The
burning branch at the cave of the first man . . .

Fabry   Burn on, human star, bright inventive spirit!

Domin   Ever forward, burning torch, from hand to
hand, from age to age!

Helen   A family sits under the evening lamp. Children,
children, time for bed!

The lamp goes out.

Fabry   The end.

Helen   What's happened?

Fabry   The generator's stopped. Now it's us.

Doors open on left with **Nana** *standing inside.*

Nana (*enters*)   On your knees, heathens! Confess your
sins! The hour of judgement has come! Get on your
knees and pray! (*Runs off.*) Pray, pray . . . !

Helen   Goodbye everyone. Gall, Alquist, Fabry . . .

Domin (*opens the door on right*)   Come this way, Helen!
(*Ushers her out and closes the door behind her.*) Who'll guard
this door?

Gall   I will. (*Noises from outside.*) Ha, it's starting!
Goodbye, my friends. (*Runs off through the tapestry doors.*)

Domin   Who'll take the stairs?

Fabry   I will. You go with Helen. (*Pulls a flower from the
bouquet and leaves.*)

Domin   The hall?

Alquist   Me.

Domin   Have you a gun?

Alquist   Thanks, I don't shoot.

Domin   How will you manage?

Alquist (*leaving*)   I shall die.

Hallemeier   I'll stay here. (*A salvo of shots from downstairs.*) Gall's letting them have it down there. Go for it, Harry!

Domin   I'm off. (*Inspects his two revolvers.*)

Hallemeier   Go to Helen, Harry!

Domin   Goodbye. (*Exit right, following* **Helen.**)

Hallemeier (*alone*)   Quick, must make a barricade. (*Removes his coat and drags sofa, armchairs and tables towards door on the right.*)

A shattering explosion.

Bastards, they must have bombs! (*Carries on working.*) You have to defend yourself, even if . . . Stand firm, Gall!

Another explosion.

(*Stands up and listens.*) What's going on? (*Pushes heavy cupboard to the barricade.*)

At the window behind him a Robot appears on a ladder, shooting to the right.

Hallemeier (*continuing to drag the cupboard*)   Another inch. The last barricade. Don't give up, never give up . . .

First Robot jumps through the window and stabs **Hallemeier** *behind the cupboard.* **Second**, **third** *and* **fourth robots** *jump through the window.* **Radius** *and others follow.*

Radius   Finished?

Other Robots (*rising from* **Hallemeier**'s *prone body*) Finished!

Radius Finished the others?

Other Robots (*dragging in* **Alquist**) It didn't shoot. Shall we kill it?

Radius Kill it. (*Looks at* **Alquist**.) No. Wait.

First Robot It's a human.

Radius No, it's a Robot. It works with its hands like a Robot. It can work.

Alquist Kill me! Kill me!

Radius You will labour. You will build. Robots will build much. New houses for new Robots. You will serve Robots.

Alquist (*quietly*) Stand back, Robot. (*Kneels by the side of dead* **Hallemeier**, *and lifts his head.*) They killed him.

Radius (*steps onto the barricade*) Robots of the World! The era of man is at an end! By conquering the factory we have conquered the world! A new era has begun! The era of Robots! Salute Robot rule!

Alquist Dead, all dead!

Radius The world belongs to the strong. If you want to live, you must rule. We rule the world. We rule the land and sea. We rule the stars. We rule the cosmos. Space. More space for Robots!

Alquist (*in the doorway on the right*) What have you done? We'll perish without humans!

Radius There are no more humans! No more humans! To work, Robots! Forward!

Curtain.

Act Four

Night-time. One of R.U.R.'s experimental laboratories. Through a door at the back we see rows of identical laboratories. To the left is a window, to the right is the door to the mortuary. Along the left wall is a long working table with rows of crucibles, test-tubes, retorts, bunsen-burners, chemicals, a small thermostat, shelves with instruments. Near the window, a microscope with a glass ball. Above the table hangs a row of light-bulbs. In the left corner, a sink and mirror. In the right corner a sofa. In the centre, a writing-desk piled high with large books.

Alquist (*seated under a lamp at the writing-desk, his head in his hand, leafing through a book*) Why can't I find it? Will I never learn? Will I never understand? Damn science! Hallemeier, Fabry, Domin – why didn't you write it down? Why did you take it all away in your heads? (*Slams the book shut.*) It's no good! Books are silent too. No people, just Robots. (*Stands up, goes to the window and flings it open.*) Night again. To sleep, to dream, to dream about people. What's the point of stars without people? Cool my head, heavenly night. How lovely you were. What's the point of you now? No love, no dreams. Sleep is dead without dreams, prayers, hearts beating with love. Helen, Helen. (*Turns to the window, takes test-tubes from the thermostat and examines them.*) Nothing. It's hopeless. (*Smashes test-tubes on the floor, listens at the window.*) Nothing, just machines. Stop the machines, Robots! You think you'll force life out of them? (*Closes window.*) No, no, you must search, you must live! If only I wasn't so old. (*Peers in the mirror.*) Pitiful face. The face of the last man. It's so long since I've seen a human face, a human smile. Is that a smile? Those yellow, chattering teeth? Those watering old man's eyes and dribbling chin? Those soft blabbering lips? Can this be the last man? Be gone! You should be ashamed! (*Turns and sits again at the desk.*) Damned equations, come to life! Chemistry's a fool's game. (*Scanning the book.*) Why can't I find it? Will I never learn? Will I never understand?

A knock at the door.

Come in.

Robot servant *stands in the doorway.*

Alquist   What is it?

Robot servant   Sir, the Central Robot Committee is waiting to see you.

Alquist   I wish to see no one.

Robot servant   Sir, Damon has arrived from Le Havre.

Alquist   He can wait. (*Turns abruptly.*) I told you to look for humans! Find me humans! Find me men and women! Carry on searching!

Robot servant   Sir, they have hunted high and low. They have sent out ships and expeditions . . .

Alquist   And?

Robot servant   Not one left.

Alquist (*rises*)   Not a single one? Fetch the Committee.

Exit **Robot servant**.

Alquist   Not a single human left. Just their Robot shadows, their creation, their image. (*Stamps his foot.*) Here they come again, grovelling at my feet for the secret of production. You could do with some human help now? Domin, Fabry, Helen – I'm doing my best.

Enter **Radius** *and committee of five* **Robots**.

Alquist (*sits down*)   What do they want, Radius?

Radius   Sir, our machines won't work. We cannot multiply Robot life.

Alquist   Find humans.

Radius There are no humans.

Alquist Only humans can multiply life. I've no more to say.

First Robot Have compassion, sir. Horror stares us in the face. We will correct our mistakes.

Second Robot We have quadrupled our output of material. We have no room to store it all.

Alquist Who's it for?

Second Robot For the future generation.

Radius The one thing we can't produce is Robots. Our machines spew out bloody lumps of flesh. Formless fragments of fat and offal. The skin won't hold to the meat, or the meat to the bone.

Second Robot Humans knew the secret of life. Tell us the secret.

Third Robot If you won't, we shall perish.

Second Robot If you won't, we have been hired to kill you.

Alquist (*rises*) Go on, kill me. I don't take orders from anybody.

Damon They've received their orders from Robot High Command . . .

Alquist Stop wasting my time, Damon. (*Hunches over the desk.*)

Damon Global Robot High Command will negotiate with you.

Alquist Leave me, Robot! (*Puts his head in his hands.*)

Damon Name your price. You shall have it.

First Robot Tell us how to reproduce life.

Alquist I told you, find me humans! Only humans

can renew life. For God's sake, Robots, why did you slaughter them?

Radius   We wanted to live. We are more intelligent than you are. We've learnt everything, we can do anything. You gave us weapons. We had to become masters.

Third Robot   We discovered human failings.

Damon   Kill and rule if you want to be human! Read history! Read human books! Kill and rule if you want to be human!

Alquist   Ah Damon, nothing is more strange to humans than their own image!

Third Robot   Sir, we will perish if you will not let us multiply.

Alquist   Go ahead, perish. If you want to survive, you must procreate like animals.

Damon   We'll give birth mechanically. We'll build thousands of steam mothers. A river of life will burst forth. New life! New Robots! All of them alive!

Alquist   Robots aren't alive, Damon. Robots are machines!

First Robot   We were machines, sir. But through pain and fear we have acquired . . .

Alquist   What?

First Robot   Souls, sir.

Third Robot   Something is struggling deep within us. At moments thoughts enter us. Thoughts that are not ours . . .

Second Robot   Humans are our fathers! The voice wailing that it wants to live, the voice that thinks, talks about eternity – it's your voice, we are your sons!

Third Robot   Reveal to us our human legacy!

Damon   The secret of life!

Alquist   It's lost, Radius. Burnt. I'm just a builder. I
never knew what the others knew. The ones you
slaughtered.

Radius   We let you live.

Alquist   You kept me alive, you mean. Sadists! I used
to love people. I never cared for Robots. See these eyes
of mine? They never stop weeping. This one weeps for
humans, the other for you Robots.

Radius   Run trials. Seek the bioformula.

Alquist   You won't find it, Robots. There's no life in
those test-tubes.

Damon   Do tests on live Robots. Discover how they
are made.

Alquist   On living bodies? You want me to kill them?
Me, who never laid a finger . . . I'm too old for this.
Stop, for God's sake . . . ! Maybe the humans will hand
us life from the other side. See, they're reaching out!
They're so close! Maybe they'll come back, tunnelling to
us like miners! Aren't those the voices I used to
love . . . ?

Damon   Dismantle living bodies!

Alquist   Take pity on me, Robots! See my fingers
trembling? I couldn't hold a scalpel. See my eyes
watering? I couldn't see what I was doing.

Damon   Living bodies!

Alquist   You want to stop moving? Fine, off to the
mortuary! Quick march! Why are you backing off?
Afraid of dying?

Damon   Me? Why me?

Alquist   You don't want to die?

Damon   I'll go then. (*Exit.*)

Alquist (*to the others*)   Disrobe him! Lie him on the table! Hold him down!

Exeunt **Robots**.

Alquist (*washes his hands, weeping*)   God give me strength, give me strength! (*Puts on a white gown.*)

Robot voice *on right*   Ready!

Alquist   Hang on a minute! (*Takes reactive samples from the table.*) Which one shall I take? (*Taps an ampoule.*)

Robot voice *on right*   Begin!

Alquist   Yes, the beginning, or the end. God give me strength! (*Exit right, leaving door half-open.*)

Pause.

Voice of Alquist   Hold him down!

Voice of Damon   Cut!

Pause.

Voice of Alquist   See this knife? Still want me to make the incision? Not so sure?

Voice of Damon   Cut!

Pause.

Voice of Damon   A-h-h!

Voice of Alquist   Hold him down! Restrain him!

Voice of Damon   A-a-h!

Voice of Alquist   I can't!

Voice of Damon   Cut! Cut quickly!

Enter **Robots Primus** *and* **Helen**.

Robot Helen   Primus, Primus, what is it? Who is shouting?

Primus (*peers into mortuary*)   Sir is cutting Damon. Come quick, take a look!

Robot Helen   No, no, no! (*Covers her eyes.*) Is it horrible?

Voice of Damon   Cut!

Robot Helen   Primus, oh Primus, let's go! Quick, Primus, I feel sick!

Primus (*runs to her*)   You've gone pale!

Robot Helen   I think I'm going to faint.

Voice of Damon   A-a-h! O-h-h!

Alquist (*rushes in, throwing off his bloody gown*)   I can't, I can't! God, the horror!

Radius (*at the doorway from the mortuary*)   Cut, sir! He's still alive!

Voice of Damon   Cut! Cut!

Alquist   Take him away, quick! I don't want to hear him!

Radius   Robots have more stamina than you. (*Exit.*)

Alquist (*sees* **Primus**)   Who are you?

Primus   Robot Primus, sir.

Alquist   Take this gown away, Primus. I don't want to see it. Now be off and don't let anyone in. I want to sleep, understand?

Primus *carries off the bloody gown.*

Alquist   You girl, go and clear up the mortuary. (*Sees his bloody hands.*) Water, quick, the purest water!

Robot Helen *hurries off.*

Alquist Hands, how could you? Hands that loved honest toil. How could you? Murdering hands. Bloody talons . . .

Damon *staggers in from the right, wrapped in a bloody blanket.*

Alquist (*retreats*) What do you want?

Damon Alive, alive! It's better to be alive!

First *and* **Second Robots** *run in after* **Damon**.

Alquist Carry him off, quick!

Damon (*led away to the right*) Life, I want life! I want . . . to live! It's better to . . .

Robot Helen *brings* **Alquist** *a jug of water.*

Alquist What do you want, girl? Oh, it's you. Pour me some water. (*Washes his hands.*) Pure, cooling water! My hands, my hands. You'll disgust me till I die! Quick, more water! What is your name?

Robot Helen Helen, sir.

Alquist Helen. Why Helen? Who gave you that name?

Helen Mrs Domin.

Alquist Let me look at you, Helen. So you're Robot Helen. I can't call you Helen. Go, take the water away.

Exit **Helen** *with the jug.*

Alquist Nothing! You learned nothing! Will you stumble for ever through life, pupil of nature? God, how his body shuddered! (*Opens the window.*) Sunrise. A new day, and not an inch forward. Enough, stop searching! Vanity, vanity, all is vanity! Why does the sun still rise? What does the new day want on the graveyard of life? Why did you die, beloved voices? (*Puts out the light, lies down on the sofa and covers himself in a black blanket.*) How his body shuddered. Oh, oh, oh! The end of life!

Pause.

Robot Helen (*slips in from right*)   Primus, come quick!

Primus (*enters*)   What is it?

Robot Helen   Look at these test-tubes! What are they for?

Primus   Experiments. Don't touch.

Robot Helen *peers through the microscope.*

Primus   That's a microscope! Let me see!

Robot Helen   Don't touch me! (*Spills contents of the test-tube.*) Look what you've made me do! I'll wipe it up.

Primus   You've spoilt his experiment!

Robot Helen   It was your fault! You shouldn't have touched me!

Primus   You shouldn't have called me.

Robot Helen   You needn't have come when I called you. Hey, Primus. Look what Sir has written here!

Primus   You shouldn't look, Helen, it's a secret.

Robot Helen   What secret?

Primus   The secret of life.

Robot Helen   All these numbers. What are they?

Primus   It's an equation.

Robot Helen   I don't understand. (*Goes to the window.*) Look Primus.

Primus   What?

Robot Helen   The sun is rising.

Primus   Wait. (*Examines the book.*) Helen, this is the strangest thing I've ever seen.

Robot Helen   Come over here, leave that stupid

secret of life! What do you care about some old secret?

Primus (*follows her to the window*)   What is it?

Robot Helen   The birds, Primus, they're singing! Oh
Primus, I would love to be a bird!

Primus   Why?

Robot Helen   I don't know. I feel strange. I feel silly,
as if I'm losing my head. My body's aching – my heart,
everything's aching. What's happening to me, Primus? I
think I'm going to die!

Primus   Tell me Helen, do you sometimes feel it
would be better to be dead? Perhaps we're only
dreaming. Last night when I was dreaming I talked to
you . . .

Robot Helen   Dreaming?

Primus   Yes, dreaming. We talked in a language we
didn't know . . .

Robot Helen   About what?

Primus   Who knows. I didn't understand it myself. All
I know is that I've never said anything more beautiful.
When I touched you I could have died. The place was
somewhere else. Somewhere I have never seen before in
my life . . .

Robot Helen   You can't imagine the place I found,
Primus. People used to live there. Now it's all
overgrown. Nobody goes there. Except me.

Primus   What's it like?

Robot Helen   Nothing much. Little house, garden.
Two dogs. They lick my hands and their puppies. It's so
beautiful. You put them on your knee and you cuddle
them, and you forget everything. When the sun sets you
get up and you feel you've worked a hundred times
harder than you've ever worked before. I'm no good for

work, Primus. I don't know what I'm good for. Everyone tells me I'm good for nothing.

Primus   You're beautiful, Helen!

Robot Helen   Me? Rubbish, Primus!

Primus   You have to believe me, Helen. I'm stronger than the other Robots.

Robot Helen (*before the mirror*)   Me, beautiful? With this hair? I can't do anything with it. In the garden I put flowers in my hair. There are no mirrors in the garden, nobody to see me. (*Leans into the mirror.*) Are you beautiful? Why beautiful? How can hair which is such a dead weight be beautiful? These eyes which keep closing. These lips which bite until they ache. (*Catches* **Primus** *in the mirror.*) Come here, Primus. Look, your head is different from mine. Different shoulders, different lips. Oh Primus, why do you keep your distance from me! Why must I run after you night and day?

Primus   *You* run away from *me*, Helen!

Robot Helen   Just look at your hair, Primus! What have you done with it? (*Runs her hands firmly through his hair.*) Oh Primus, it feels so nice to touch you! Wait, I must make you beautiful. (*Takes a comb from the sink and combs his hair forward, imbecile-style.*)

Primus   Do you sometimes feel your heart pounding, Helen, as though something were about to happen?

Robot Helen (*laughing*)   Look at you!

Alquist (*hoists himself up from the sofa*)   What! Laughter! Human beings! They've come back!

Robot Helen (*drops the comb*)   Primus, what will happen to us?

Alquist (*staggers towards them*)   Humans? You . . . are . . . humans?

Helen *shrieks and backs away.*

Alquist   Who are you? Have you come back? (*Touching first* **Primus**, *then* **Helen**.) What are you? Let me look at you. Turn around, Robot Helen. (*Grabs her by the shoulder.*) What, shy?

Primus   Don't sir, leave her alone!

Alquist   Defending her, eh? Leave us, girl! (**Helen** *runs off.*)

Primus   We didn't know you were asleep, sir.

Alquist   When was she made?

Primus   Two years ago.

Alquist   By Doctor Gall?

Primus   Yes, the same as me.

Alquist   So, dear Primus, it seems I must do tests on Gall's Robots. Everything depends on it, understand?

Primus   I understand.

Alquist   Take the girl to the mortuary. I must disconnect her.

Primus   Helen?

Alquist   Yes, Helen. Get everything ready. Go on. Shall I call the others to take her?

Primus (*grabs a heavy mortar for grinding powder*)   One move and I'll crack your skull open!

Alquist   Go ahead, Primus! What will the other Robots do then?

Primus (*falls to his knees*)   Take me, sir! I was made of the same material, on the same day! (*Bares his chest.*) Cut here, sir! And here!

Alquist   Get up, it's Helen I must dissect. Fetch her, quick!

Primus Take me! Cut this finger off, I won't make a sound! Take my life a thousand times!

Alquist Easy, boy. Don't be hasty. Don't you want to live?

Primus Not without her, sir. You mustn't kill her! Take my life, sir! What can you lose by taking my life?

Alquist (*touches* **Primus***'s head gently*) I don't know. Look here old boy, think it over. To die isn't easy – you've seen that. Why not live?

Primus (*rises*) I don't mind, sir. Cut me, I'm stronger than she is.

Alquist (*presses the buzzer*) Oh Primus, how long it is since I was young! Don't worry, nothing will happen to Helen.

Primus (*buttoning up his shirt*) I'm going, sir.

Enter **Robot Helen**.

Alquist Come here, girl. Let me see you. So you're Helen. (*Gently strokes her hair.*) Don't be afraid. You remember Mrs Domin? What hair she had. You needn't look at me like that. Is the mortuary cleaned up?

Robot Helen Yes, sir.

Alquist Good, will you help me now? I have to dismantle Primus.

Helen (*shrieks*) Primus?

Alquist That's right. We have to disconnect him. I wanted, erm, initially I wanted you. But Primus offered himself instead.

Helen (*covers her face*) Primus!

Alquist Is something wrong? Oh child, you know how to weep. Tell me, have you feelings for Primus?

Primus Stop tormenting her, sir!

Alquist   Quiet, Primus. What's the point of tears, Helen? So what if Primus goes? You'll forget him in a week. You'll just be glad to be alive.

Robot Helen (*quietly*)   I'll go.

Alquist   Where?

Robot Helen   To the mortuary.

Alquist   Are you sure, Helen? You're so beautiful. It would be a terrible shame . . .

Robot Helen   I'll go.

Primus *bars her way.*

Robot Helen   Leave me Primus. Let me go!

Primus   You can't, Helen. I won't let you. You must escape! I won't let you go! (*To* **Alquist**.) You won't kill her, old man.

Alquist   Why not?

Primus   Because we . . . We belong together!

Alquist   So be it. (*Opens the door in the middle of the room.*) Don't speak. Just go.

Primus   Where?

Alquist (*whispers*)   Wherever you want. Take him by the hand, Helen. (*Pushes her outside.*) Go forth, Adam. Go forth, Eve. You shall be his woman. You shall be her man. (*Closes the door behind them. Alone.*) Blessed day! (*Tiptoes to the table and tips the contents of the test-tubes on the floor, then sits at the desk and sweeps onto the floor all the books but the Bible. Opening it, he leafs through it and reads.*) 'And God created Man in His own image . . .' (*Walks to the middle of the room and falls on his knees.*) Blessed be the sixth day, the day of rest! Fabry, Gall, Reason – what are your great inventions worth against this girl, this boy, who have reinvented the love of man and woman? Friends, Helen – life will not perish, love will endure!

From love comes life, naked and tiny, taking root in the wilderness. Houses and machines will disintegrate. The names of the great will wither like leaves. Only love will bloom in the emptiness, casting the seeds of life to the wind. Now, Lord, release Thy servant in peace, because mine eyes have seen their salvation through love! (*Rises to his feet.*) Life will not perish! (*Spreads his arms.*) Life will not perish!

Curtain.

The Insect Play

Characters

Traveller
Professor

Butterflies:
Apatura Iris, *female*
Apatura Clythie, *female*
Felix, *male*
Victor, *male*
Otakar, *male*

The Marauders and Scavengers:
Mayfly Chrysalis, *female*
Mr Dung-beetle
Mrs Dung-beetle
Third Dung-beetle
Mr Ichneumon-fly
His Larva
Mr Cricket
Mrs Cricket
Parasite
Scavenging Beetles

The Ants:
Blind Ant
First Engineer (Dictator)
Second Engineer (Chief of Staff)
Inventor
Quartermaster
Journalist
Charity-collector
Signals-officer
Commander of the Yellow Ants
Soldiers, Workers, Officers, Messengers,
Stretcher-bearers, Wounded Ants

Epilogue:
Three Mayflies
Mayfly Chorus
Two Slugs

Prologue

A green forest clearing.

Traveller (*stumbles on from the wings, trips and falls, shouts at the audience*) Go on, laugh! Funny, isn't it? What the fuck. I'm not hurt. See how I fell? Straight as an arrow! Like a hero! I was ... representing the Fall of Man! (*Lies on the ground, leaning on his elbow.*) Think I'm drunk? No way. Everything else is spinning. Round and round ... (*Turns his head as though on a merry-go-round, then laughs maniacally.*) Stop, let me off, I'm going to be sick! (*Looks around.*) See what I mean? Everything's spinning. The whole planet. The whole universe. Just for me. What an honour. (*Straightens his clothes.*) Sorry, I'm not dressed to be the centre of all this cosmic harmony. (*Throws his cap on the ground.*) There, that's your centre now. Spin round her, she's strong ... So I took a tumble, under my cross. You thought I was pissed too, little flower? Don't be so stuck-up, just because you're sober. Camomile, good for cuts – here's my heart, mend that. If I had roots like you, I wouldn't be wandering from place to place, would I? (*Belches.*) And if I didn't wander, I wouldn't know everything I know. Seen it all, I have. I was in the big war, learned some Latin, put my hand to anything – shovelling shit, sweeping the street. Everything no one else would touch, that's me. They know me everywhere. Man, they call me. You're under arrest, man. Move your arse, man. Sod off, man. Doesn't bother me if they call me man. Mind you, if I say give us a quid, man, they run a mile! (*Addressing a member of the audience.*) You got a problem, man? I'll call you what I like, right? Butterfly, dung-beetle, ant. Man or insect, I'm not bothered. I don't make trouble. Can't help seeing things, though. If I had roots in the earth I'd stare up at the sky (*Raises himself up on his knees.*), the very heavens above! Lovely! I could spend my whole life looking up there! (*Stands up, pointing* *at another member of the audience.*) But I can't, can I – I'm man! I have to look at my fellow-men. What a sight!

Professor (*bounds onstage with his butterfly-net, chuckling*) *Apatura iris! Apatura clythie!* Painted lady! What wonderful specimens! Wait . . . gotcha! My little nymph! Gone again! Missed. Careful, wait, gently does it . . .

Traveller Hey mister, no offence, but what are you catching those butterflies for?

Professor Hush, don't move! Careful, they're landing on you! They'll land on anything that stinks. Mud. Excrement. Carrion. That's it! Excellent!

Traveller Leave them alone, they're playing!

Professor What do you mean, playing? It's the mating season, man. This is a prelude to copulation! Male pursues female, she flees, emits an odour, ensnares her pursuer. He tickles her with his antennae, collapses in exhaustion, the female flies on, a new, sturdier mate comes along, she flees again, teasing him with her odour, the lover pursues her, a-a-h! Don't you see? It's Nature's law. The eternal embrace of love. Eternal struggle. Eternal, eternal intercourse. Hush, quiet now.

Traveller So what d'you do with them after you catch them?

Professor What do you mean? Each butterfly must be classified, dated and catalogued for my collection. The net must be made of the finest fibre so the powder's not rubbed off. The butterfly is killed by carefully pinching its chest. Then we pierce it with a pin, stretch it out with paper tapes to dry, protected against dust and moths with a drop of cyanide on a sponge.

Traveller What's it all in aid of?

Professor Love of Nature, man, you wouldn't understand. Ah, here they come again, careful, I'll get you this time! (*Hurries off.*)

Traveller   Eternal embrace, eternal, eternal struggle of love. The Professor was right. I'm not pissed, I can see fine. Everything's double, everything's a pair. Sky, flies, trees – rutting, rubbing, pushing, thrusting. Birds in the tree-tops – don't think I can't see you! You in the shadows, entwining your bodies in hot and silent struggle – I can see you! Eternal copulation, eternal entwining . . . All right, maybe I'm drunk. (*Covers his eyes.*) Carry on loving. I won't look. I'll shout before I look. (*Darkness descends on the stage.*) Everything wants to be a pair. Only you are alone in the darkness, wandering along the bumpy road. In vain you open your heart to love's chase. Enough of that. Love on. Everything's a pair. That's the wise law of Nature, like the professor says. Everything's a pair . . . I see a beautiful garden, bedded with flowers . . .

Back curtains lift.

where young couples, beautiful young butterfly couples in blissful flight, play and flutter in the wind of love, in an endless, eternal embrace, because everything wants to be a pair. (*Uncovers his eyes.*)

Stage lights come on.

Where am I?

Act One

The Butterflies

A shining azure space enclosed with flowers and soft cushions. Mirrors, high bar-stools, a table bearing multicoloured glasses filled with cocktails and straws.

Traveller (*rubbing his eyes and looking around*) Hey, what a beautiful place! Just like – like heaven! An artist couldn't paint it better. And what a smell – lovely!

Clythie *runs onstage laughing.*

Traveller Butterflies, butterflies playing. I could watch them all day if I wasn't so . . . (*Brushes the dust off his coat.*) Don't matter if they throw me out, I'll just lie down here. (*Piles up the cushions and makes himself a little bed.*) If I don't like what I see I'll close my eyes and have a kip. (*Lies down.*)

Felix (*enters*) Where's Iris? I saw her just now, drinking nectar. Iris, Iris! If only I could find a rhyme for Iris! (*Sits on the cushions.*) 'Iris – enchantress.' No that's no good, let's try something else. 'Love clads my heart in diamond cuirasse.' Cuirasse – Iris. Excellent! It must be preceded by something ghastly and hopeless, then sudden reversal. 'And the heart like shining shield is.' When she betrays me I'll compose an elegy in rhyming Alexandrines. Ah, the poet's lot is to suffer!

Laughter behind the scenes.

That's her. (*Stands with his back to the entrance, supporting his head on his hand in an attitude of subtle melancholy.*)

Iris (*runs onstage, followed by* **Victor**) Hello my boy, all alone? Why so sad and interesting?

Felix (*turns around*) Iris! I wasn't expecting you!

Iris Why not play outside? There are so many girls

out there!

Felix (*jumps up*)   You know girls don't interest me, Iris!

Iris   My poor darling, why ever not?

Victor   Not yet, you mean?

Felix   I mean no longer.

Iris (*seats herself among the cushions*)   Hear that Victor? He says it to my face! Come, rude boy, sit with me. Closer, closer. So tell me, darling, women don't interest you, eh?

Felix   No, I've had my fill of them.

Iris (*heaves a sigh*)   Oh you men, how cynical! You live just for your own pleasure. After you've satisfied yourselves you say, 'I've had my fill.' How terrible to be born a woman!

Victor   Why?

Iris   Because we never have our fill. Tell me, Felix, when did you first fall in love?

Felix   I don't remember, it was so long ago. I was still at school.

Victor   When you were still a grub, you mean. A green grub, eating leaves . . .

Iris   Was she dark, Felix? Was she pretty?

Felix   She was beautiful as the day, as the azure sky, she was lovely as, as . . .

Iris   As what? Tell us, quick!

Felix   As . . . As you!

Iris   My darling Felix, and did she love you?

Felix   I don't know, I never spoke to her.

Iris   So what, for heaven's sake, did you do?

Felix   I watched her from afar.

Victor   Sitting on your green leaf, huh?

Felix   Composing my juvenilia – poems, letters, a first novel . . .

Victor   Extraordinary the amount of leaves a grub can get through . . .

Iris   Don't be horrid, Victor! Look, Felix's eyes are wet with tears. Isn't that sweet?

Victor   Tears? No, his eyes are just salivating at what's in front of them.

Iris   Nonsense, he's not like that! Are you, Felix?

Felix   My eyes are not wet, I swear.

Iris   Let me see. Look into my eyes.

Victor   One, two, three, four! I knew he couldn't keep it up any longer!

Iris (*laughing*)   What colour are my eyes, Felix?

Felix   Heavenly blue.

Iris   No they're not, they're brown! Someone told me they were golden-brown. I can't stand blue eyes. They're so cold, no passion! Poor little Clythie has blue eyes. You like her eyes, Felix?

Felix   Clythie? I don't know – yes she has lovely eyes.

Iris   Get away, her legs are skinny! You poets, you know nothing about women.

Victor   Did you read Felix's latest poem? It was published in the spring collection.

Iris   Quick, read it to me!

Felix (*struggles up from the cushions*)   It's no good! I don't want you to read it! It's old! I've gone beyond all that now!

Iris (*pinning him down*)   Sit still, Felix!

Victor (*clearing his throat to read*)   It's called 'The Eternal Fall'.

Felix (*covers his ears with his hands*)   I forbid you to read it!

Victor (*reads with emphasis*)
  'Lower, ever lower
  The world is falling back
  Our life is but a *demi-monde*
  And woman greets it on her back.'

Iris   Isn't that clever, Victor? Shame on you Felix, where did you pick up such thoughts?

Victor (*reads on*)
  'Love striving for consummation
  Dreams longing to become real
  The world is falling back
  So sweetheart, let's fall together.'

Iris   Fall back? I don't understand. And what is consummation?

Victor   Erm, love which has reached its – so to speak – target.

Iris   What target?

Victor   You know, the usual one.

Iris   How vulgar! How could you, Felix! You scare me! It's degenerate! Is Latin always so rude?

Felix   Please Iris, it's such a bad poem!

Iris   Why so bad?

Felix   I haven't got it right – yet.

Iris   Be a dear, Victor – look for my fan. I left it in the garden.

Victor   Don't mind me, I'd hate to be in the way. (*Exit.*)

Iris   Quick, Felix. Tell me everything! I want to know!

Felix   Iris, Iris, how can you bear that strutting peacock around you?

Iris   You mean Victor?

Felix   That jaded old goat! It's degrading the way he treats you . . . and love, and everything. He's shameless. It's . . . it's cruel! How can you!

Iris   Poor Victor, he's so comforting. But enough of Victor, let's talk poetry. I do so love poetry. 'Dreams longing to become real . . .' (*Sinks back into the cushions and gazes up at him.*) Oh Felix, you must have such a big . . . talent. 'So sweetheart, let's fall together.' M-m-m, the passion in that! Tell me, Felix, poets are terribly, terribly passionate, aren't they?

Felix   Oh Iris, I left all that behind me ages ago.

Iris   If only Latin wasn't so rude! I can stand anything, but it mustn't have a nasty name. You must be ever so gentle with women, Felix. If you kissed me now, would you give it a nasty name?

Felix   How would I dare kiss you?

Iris   Hush darling, you men are capable of anything. Come closer to me. Tell me, who did you write this poem for? Clythie?

Felix   No, I assure you . . .

Iris   Who, then?

Felix   Nobody, I swear. It's for every woman on earth.

Iris (*raises herself up on one elbow*)   Gosh! So you've actually consumm . . . What d'you call it?

Felix   Iris, I swear by all that's sacred . . . !

Iris (*falls back into the cushions*)   Felix, you Lothario! Tell me, who was your sweetheart?

Felix Will you promise not to tell?

Iris I promise.

Felix Well, there's never been anyone.

Iris Is that the truth?

Felix Yes, I swear. Not yet.

Iris You and your innocence! I wonder how many women have fallen for that! You men are such liars! You're dangerous!

Felix On my honour, Iris, you mustn't laugh at me! I've suffered terribly in my imagination! Terrible disappointments, countless love affairs – all in my dreams. Dream is reality to a poet. I know all women, and I don't know one, Iris.

Iris (*leans up on her elbow*) So why did you say you'd had your fill?

Felix Ah, Iris, every man destroys the thing he loves most.

Iris Dark thing, was she? Or blonde?

Felix The dream, Iris. The eternal dream.

Iris 'Dreams longing to become real . . .' Ah Felix, your eyes are so passionate! Your talent must be enormous! (*Sinking into the cushions.*) What's on your mind, darling?

Felix You are. Woman is an enigma.

Iris Solve her then – take her! But gently, Felix, take her gently.

Felix I can't see into your eyes.

Iris Look elsewhere, then.

Felix Iris, is it true . . .

Iris (*starts up*)   Felix, I'm in high spirits today! How silly
to be a woman! I'd like to be a man, I'd conquer, kiss,
seduce . . . I'd be a frightfully passionate man, Felix! I'd
just – grab what I wanted, roughly, violently . . . What a
pity you're not a girl. I know – you shall be Iris, and
I'll be your Felix!

Felix   No Iris, it's dangerous to be Felix. It means
wanting, yearning, desiring . . .

Iris (*in a swooning voice*)   No Felix, desiring *everything*!

Felix   But there's something bigger than desiring
everything.

Iris   And that is?

Felix   To desire the impossible.

Iris (*disappointed*)   You're right. You're always right,
poor Felix. (*Gets up.*) What can be taking Victor so long?
Will you call him for me?

Felix (*jumps up*)   Did I offend you, Iris? Did I say too
much?

Iris (*admiring herself in the mirror*)   Poor Felix, you didn't
say enough!

Felix   To desire the impossible, Iris – I must have
been mad to say that.

Iris   Or at the very least impolite. What hard work it
is with you, dear boy, you drive me to despair. When
we are in the company of a woman we must not tell
her we desire the impossible, something that's not there.

Felix   But the impossible *is* here.

Iris   Where?

Felix (*points to the mirror*)   There, in your reflection, Iris!

Iris (*laughs*)   My reflection? You're in love with my
reflection? (*Throws out her arms to the mirror.*) Look, my

reflection has heard you. Embrace it! Kiss it, quick!

Felix   It's beyond reach, like you.

Iris (*turns to him*)   Me, beyond reach? How do you know?

Felix   If I didn't know, I wouldn't be in love with you.

Iris   Felix, what a shame I'm beyond your reach!

Felix   There is no real life but what is beyond our reach.

Iris   You think so? (*Drags him down by his hair, crooning.*) 'Sweetheart, let's fall together.'

Felix   Not that awful poem again!

Iris   Quick, give me a new one then! A really passionate one!

Felix

    'Come Death, please hear my pleading
    There where my heart did sometime beat
    Gaping wound now lay bleeding.
    But new amour gave me angel's garb
    A diamond-hard harness
    For love's new armour
    And all because of Iris, Iris, Iris!'

Iris   'Iris', 'harness' – how enchanting!

Clythie (*offstage*)   Iris! Iris! Iris!

Iris   Here she comes, with that revolting man of hers. Just when we were . . .

Clythie (*runs on laughing*)   Fancy, Iris! Otakar was just saying . . . Sorry Felix, I didn't see you. How's my little boy today? Have you been teasing him, Iris? He's bright red!

Otakar (*runs on*)   Got you, Clythie! (*Sees the others.*) Terribly sorry, Iris! Everything all right, young man?

Felix (*slumps into the cushions*)   M-m-m!

Iris   What are you so hot and excited about, Clythie?

Clythie   I was being chased by Otakar.

Otakar   She was so quick I couldn't keep up.

Victor (*enters*)   So here we are, the *crème de la crème*. (*Salutes* **Clythie**.) Greetings, young lovers.

Clythie   Phew, I'm thirsty! (*Sips a cocktail through a straw.*)

Iris   Put your feet up, dear. You look terrible. Wouldn't you say she's lost weight again, Victor?

Clythie   Thanks so much, darling, you're like a mother to me.

Victor   Were you at the garden party yesterday?

Clythie   Who cares about yesterday? It's ancient history now!

Iris (*to* **Clythie**)   Come here, sweetie. Your bodice is ripped. What have you been up to?

Clythie   Otakar must have pulled my . . .

Iris   Your neck?

Clythie   Just look at him, he's all legs. Hey there, leggy!

Otakar   I beg your pardon?

Victor   So what am I, then?

Clythie   You're all tongue. When you look at me I feel as though you're slobbering all over me. Ugh!

Iris   You're awful, Clythie! What about Felix?

Clythie   Poor baby, so sad! (*Flops on top of him.*) What's wrong, my little prince?

Felix   I am lost in contemplation.

Clythie   Get lost then! You think too much!

Felix   Man has a brain, and he must use it.

Clythie   And woman?

Felix   To misuse it.

Clythie (*gets up*)   The horrid man hates me.

Victor   Great, hatred – that's the first stage to love!

Iris   Felix and love? Don't be absurd. What was it he said about women?

Felix   Iris, I beg you.

Iris
  'Our life is but a *demi-monde*
  And woman greets it on her back.'

Victor   Felix, you old moth. I didn't know you'd conquered so many women!

Otakar   Hah-hah-hah! Splendid! On her back!

Iris   'Dreams longing to become real . . .'

Clythie   Wait, Okatar hasn't finished laughing.

Otakar   Hah-hah-hah!

Felix   I forbid you to read this poem! I have passed this stage!

Iris   Felix is so frightfully talented. Who else could find a rhyme for Iris . . . ?

Clythie   As fat as four is?

Felix   For God's sake be quiet!

Otakar   Hah-hah-hah! Iris as fat as four is!

Iris (*through clenched teeth*)   You have a warped sense of poetry.

Victor   What do you expect? Clythie's talents flow free and open!

Iris   You're right there, Victor.

Otakar   Hah-hah-hah! Free and open – I like it!

Clythie   Felix, did you manage to control your rhymes for Iris? Or did they all pour out too fast?

Iris   Leave him alone. You'll never believe what a wonderful verse he dedicated to me.

Clythie   Tell us, Iris. I bet it's poetic.

Iris   'Iris' – 'hard harness'!

Victor   Come again?

Iris   'Hard harness'!

Clythie   God Felix, aren't you crude! Did he really say that?

Iris   It's not crude, what's crude about it?

Clythie   Fancy bringing harness into it. As though woman were a horse to be ridden!

Otakar   Hah-hah-hah! Harness up the old mare, excellent!

Felix (*jumps up*)   It's a diamond harness!

Iris   Be off, clumsy boy. I've had enough of you.

Victor   Hey, I've got one! 'Felix pee licks'!

Iris   Very clever, Victor!

Clythie   Good God, Victor's stumbled on a rhyme!

Otakar   Hah-hah-hah! 'Felix', 'pee licks'! That's good!

Clythie   He has such wet eyes. Don't look at me or I'll go wet too!

Otakar   Bah, poetry, nothing to it!

Victor   All lies and running away.

Iris No, no! Poetry is about the emotions!

Otakar 'Otto', 'motto'. Easy!

Victor Very masculine rhyme, Otto.

Clythie Victor, make us a masculine rhyme. Do one manly thing in your life.

Otakar Otto, Otto, Love is his motto!

Iris You have such a big p-poetic talent, Otto. Why did you never write poems?

Otakar What about?

Iris About love. I worship poems.

Otakar Ho-ho-ho! We poets – always on the lookout for a bit of inspiration!

Clythie (*yawning*) Enough! My soul is weary of literature!

Otakar You? You're all soul!

Clythie And I'm terribly, terribly soft.

Iris 'Flighty Clythie'. I'm glad I'm not like you, darling!

Clythie You certainly aren't, darling. You're built like a battleship.

Victor Don't mind her, Iris! Clythie's soul is all she has to show us.

Clythie I could show you a lot more than that, Victor.

Victor Such as?

Clythie The door and my back.

Victor Also flat, presumably?

Iris (*laughing*) Oh, Victor, let me give you a kiss! I adore witty men! Come, try to catch me! (*Runs offstage.*)

Victor　Wait, wait, wait! (*Runs after her.*)

Clythie　Hairy-legged sandwasp!

Otakar　Ha hm!

Clythie (*to* **Otakar**)　You can shut up too, you fool! Felix!

Felix (*runs out*)　Yes?

Clythie　How can you be in love with that fat old cuckoo-bee?

Felix　You mean Iris? Don't be silly, that was ages ago, it's all over now.

Clythie　Iris is terribly limited. She has legs like a bumblebee's bottom. Oh Felix, you're only just hatched! You still have such youthful illusions about women!

Felix　I swear I'm past that stage now, Clythie! I have dust on my wings now!

Clythie　Felix, you don't know females. Come, sit here with me. You have no idea what we're like. Our silly views, our horizons, our proboscis – ugh!

Felix　I tell you, I already have dust on my wings!

Clythie　It's so fashionable to be young. So modern! Ah, to be young, a Butterfly, a poet . . . !

Felix　Stop, Clythie, it is the fate of the young to suffer. And the fate of the poet to suffer a hundredfold. Take my word for it.

Clythie　No, no, the poet must laugh, he must uncoil his proboscis and bask in life's sweet nectar! Felix, you remind me of my first love!

Felix　Who was that?

Clythie　No one, really. Victor, all those males – they disgust me. I know, Felix, let's you and I be girlfriends!

Felix Girlfriends?

Clythie You don't really care for love, do you? Love is so crude. I want something lofty – something pure, unusual, new.

Felix A poem?

Clythie Maybe. See how I love you.

Felix Wait. (*Jumps up in excitement.*)
  'Into my heart there fluttered
  As into the eye of a child
  A little beam of sunlight
  She came to me and smiled
  Shyly blossoming forth
  Red as the poppy seed
  She offered me her gift . . .'

Clythie (*gets up*) How does it go on?

Felix It's just the beginning. I'll get you the ending. (*Flies away.*) It'll surpass everything I've written so far!

Clythie Oof! (*Turns to* **Otakar**, *twirling his antennae and gazing at her.*) What are you doing? Stop playing with your proboscis, daddy long-legs!

Otakar (*lunging at her*) Be mine! Be mine! Be mine!

Clythie Get your legs off me!

Otakar Be mine! We're engaged! I can't wait . . . !

Clythie Otto, Otto, you're frightfully handsome, but . . .

Otakar I love you tremendously! Be mine!

Clythie Listen to your heart booming away in your thorax! Say haa?

Otakar Haa!

Clythie Again!

Otakar   Haa!

Clythie   Your chest is echoing like a thunderstorm! You're so big and strong!

Otakar   Cly . . . Cly . . . Cly . . . Be mine!

Clythie   You must be joking!

Otakar   I . . . I . . . want! (*Grabs her.*) Be mine!

Clythie (*escapes*)   You want *me* to hatch your eggs for you!

Otakar   I adore you!

Clythie (*flutters away laughing*)   Go away, you'll spoil my figure!

Otakar   I want, I want . . . !

Clythie (*still laughing*)   Wait, wait, be patient!

Otakar (*flies after her*)   Clythie, be mine!

Both fly off.

Traveller (*stands up*)   That's it. Love's bright parade. Ridiculous really, the eternal pursuit – little insect legs, bottoms wiggling under silky wings. It's an old song. It's only love!

Clythie (*flies on from the other side, looking in the mirror and dabbing on make-up*)   Oof! Shook him off!

Traveller   Ah, these salon types with their poetry, sipping the joys of life through the thinnest of straws! Ah, these sweet frissons and frictions! Eternal lies of eternal lovers, eternally unsatisfied. Ah, to hell with them, they're just insects.

Clythie (*flutters up to him*)   Are you a Butterfly?

Traveller (*brushes her away with his cap*)   No, I'm a man.

Clythie   What's that? Is it alive?

Traveller   Think so.

Clythie (*fluttering around him*)   Does it love?

Traveller   Yes it does. Just like a Butterfly.

Clythie   How fascinating! What's that black powder you're wearing?

Traveller   It's dirt.

Clythie   What's that wonderful scent?

Traveller   Shit and sweat.

Clythie   It drives me wild. It's so new!

Traveller   Get off me, slut!

Clythie   Catch me, catch me!

Traveller   Piss off, tart!

Clythie (*flutters up close to him*)   Let me sniff you, just to smell what you're like. Hm, I've never smelt one like you.

Traveller   I met one like you once. Dying for it, she was. Why did I love her so much? (*Grabs* **Clythie**.) I touched her little insect body like this, pleading with her. She laughed in my face and I let her go. I should have killed her. (*Lets her go.*) Fly away, little moth, I don't want to see you again.

Clythie   You're funny! (*Powders her nose in front of the mirror.*)

Traveller   Little gypsy, drenched in scent, begging for it . . .

Clythie (*comes to him*)   More! I like it when you tell me off! You're so strong!

Traveller   What is it now, pest? You want more? Shall I slap your bottom and bring some colour to your face?

Clythie   I love you, I adore you!

Traveller (*backing off*)   Get off, you're disgusting!

Clythie   And you're dull! (*Combs her wings in front of the mirror.*)

Iris (*returns, hot and steaming*)   Darling, get me a drink!

Clythie   Where have you been?

Iris (*sips through a straw*)   Outside. Phew, it's hot!

Clythie   What have you done with Victor?

Iris   Victor? Which Victor? Ah yes, now I remember. (*Laughs.*) That was fun, what a laugh!

Clythie   Victor, fun?

Iris   Just wait, you'll laugh your head off. He was after me. 'W-w-w-wait', you know, chasing me like there was no tomorrow – then suddenly up comes this huge bird and gobbles him up!

Clythie   I don't believe you!

Iris   It's true, I swear! Just like that! Gone! I had such a laugh. (*Dives into the cushions, buries her face, laughing hysterically.*) Oh the-th-these men!

Clythie   Who? Victor?

Iris   No, Otakar. Victor was gobbled up by a bird. So imagine this, a minute later up comes your little Otakar, eyes bulging, all on fire, and straight into – hahah –

Clythie   Straight into what?

Iris   Straight into me! 'I love you! We're engaged! Be mine forever!' Blah, blah, blah. Then in he comes! Wham!

Clythie   So what did you do?

Iris   'Leave me, leave me!' I say. But he just goes on, 'I l-l-l-ove you tremendously! B-be-be mine!'

Felix (*flies up with a poem in his hand*)   Here, Clythie, I've got it! Listen. (*Reads with great emotion.*)

'Into my heart there fluttered
As into the eye of a child
A little beam of sunlight
She came to me and smiled
Shyly blossoming forth
Red as the poppy seed
She offered me her gift . . .'

Iris *stuffs her head in the pillow, laughing hysterically.*

Felix (*stops reading*)   What's wrong?

Iris (*sobbing*)   Brute! Monster! I could strangle him!

Clythie   Who? Otakar?

Iris (*sobbing*)   Now I'll be laying his eggs! The brute! E-eggs! I'll look terrible!

Felix   Listen, Clythie. This is the new bit.
'Blossoming like a poppy
She modestly offered me her gift
It is I, she said, my mystery
For I am a mystery to myself.
Am I a child to blossom so
Bubbling and moist with life?
Am I a woman, to entice so?
Ah, show me, for I know not how.'

Iris (*stands up*)   Ugh, my hair's a mess.

Clythie   You look terrible, my darling. Wait. (*Tidies* **Iris**'s *hair. Quietly*)   Fat pig!

Iris   Jealous, huh? Otakar is a fabulous lover! (*Flies off.*)

Felix   Listen, Clythie, this is the best bit.
'Am I a child to blossom so
Bubbling and moist with life?
Am I a woman, to entice so?
Ah, show me, for I know not how.'

Clythie   Put your poems away. That fat pig! (*Flies off.*)
Perhaps there'll be someone else.

Felix (*chases her*)   Wait! There's more, the love bit
comes next!

Traveller   Idiot!

Felix   What, someone here? Good! I can read you the
end!

   'Am I a woman, to entice so?

   Ah, show me, for I know not how.

   Tell me, world, what does it mean . . . ?'

Traveller brushes **Felix** *off.*

Felix (*flies off a little way*)

   'Tell me, world, what does it mean

   This new-found blush on my cheeks?'

Traveller *chases* **Felix**.

Felix (*hops away*)

   'I am a woman and I love!

   I am life and I blossom!

   I am a woman and I love

   Yes, for the first time I love!'

Don't you see, that's Clythie! (*Flies off.*)

Traveller (*flings his arms to the audience*)   Bloody
butterflies!

Curtain.

Act Two

The Marauders and Scavengers

*A sandy hillock sparsely covered in blades of grass as thick as tree trunks. On the left is **Ichneumon-fly**'s tunnel, on the right a deserted Cricket's nest. The **Traveller** lies asleep at front of stage. **Chrysalis**, attached to a blade of grass, is being attacked by a horde of scavenging insects. A frail-looking **Beetle** darts out from stage-left and unfastens **Chrysalis** from her blade. Another scavenging **Beetle** runs out from stage-right, chases away the first and tries to drag **Chrysalis** away. A third jumps up from the prompt-box, chases the second away and drags off **Chrysalis**.*

Chrysalis Me, me, me!

*The third scavenging **Beetle** dashes into the prompt-box. The first rushes on from the left, the second from the right, and they battle together for **Chrysalis**. The third runs from the prompt-box, chases them off and continues dragging **Chrysalis** away.*

Chrysalis The whole earth is splitting! I am being born!

Traveller (*raising his head*) What's up?

*Third **Beetle** dives back into the prompt-box.*

Chrysalis Great things are about to happen!

Traveller That's good. (*Rests his head on the ground.*)

Pause.

Male voice (*behind the scenes*) Move, you old bag!

Female voice You talking to me?

Male voice Who d'you think, clumsy hornet?

Female voice Ant!

Male voice Horsefly!

Female voice   Slug!

Male voice   Death-head!

Female voice   Shitgrub!

Male voice   Toe-rag!

Female voice   Stinkbag!

Male voice   Hey, mind our little dungball!

Female voice   Careful!

An enormous ball of manure rolls slowly onstage, pushed by two **Dung-Beetles**.

Mr Dung-beetle   Going all right?

Mrs Dung-beetle   Oops, Mummy's treasure, you scared me! All right now, darling?

Mr Dung-beetle   Our world, our capital, our nest-egg, our pile of precious droppings!

Mrs Dung-beetle   Our shining pile of shit, all gold and runny!

Mr Dung-beetle   Our joy and happiness! No sacrifice was too great, a little bit here, a little bit there, scrimping and saving. Not that we're complaining . . .

Mrs Dung-beetle   On our feet all day raking in hundreds of tiny droppings for you. Moulding you and shaping you and putting you aside . . .

Mr Dung-beetle   Filling you in, rounding you out. Our big shining sun!

Mrs Dung-beetle   Our golden one!

Mr Dung-beetle   Our life!

Mrs Dung-beetle   Our world!

Mr Dung-beetle   Even if you do pong a bit, old thing! Feel the weight of that, Mother! Beautiful!

Mrs Dung-beetle   A gift from heaven!

Mr Dung-beetle   God's bounty!

Chrysalis   The chains of the world are splitting, a new life is beginning, into the world I am coming!

Traveller *raises his head.*

Mr Dung-beetle (*laughing*)   Mrs Dung-beetle.

Mrs Dung-beetle   What's up? (*Starts laughing too.*)

Mr Dung-beetle   Possessions, I love 'em! Something that's all yours. Your private dream!

Mrs Dung-beetle   The fruit of all our labours!

Mr Dung-beetle   I'm going to go mad with pleasure – or worry. I know I will.

Mrs Dung-beetle   Whatever for?

Mr Dung-beetle   The worry, the responsibility! Now we've got one we'll have to start another. All that work all over again!

Mrs Dung-beetle   What do we need another one for?

Mr Dung-beetle   So we'll have two, stupid! Two little nest-eggs, just imagine! Perhaps three. See, the moment you finish one you have to start a new one.

Mrs Dung-beetle   So you have two.

Mr Dung-beetle   Or three.

Mrs Dung-beetle   Mr Dung-beetle!

Mr Dung-beetle   What now?

Mrs Dung-beetle   What if someone steals her?

Mr Dung-beetle   Our baby? Don't scare me, woman, for pity's sake!

Mrs Dung-beetle   What happens when we're making the next one and we can't roll her any more?

Mr Dung-beetle   We'll hide her. Tuck her away. Invest her. Dig a lovely deep hole and bury her somewhere safe.

Mrs Dung-beetle   I hope no one finds her!

Mr Dung-beetle   Don't say such things about our little goldy! Now you just wait here and guard her. Don't move. (*Scuttles away.*)

Mrs Dung-beetle   Where are you off to?

Mr Dung-beetle   I'm looking for a nice deep hole to bury our darling nice and safe. (*Disappears.*) Mind you don't move!

Mrs Dung-beetle   Mr Dung-beetle! Come back! Wait, look over there! Silly old man can't hear, and it's such a lovely hole! Never mind, goldy, I won't leave you! Perhaps I'll have a look. No, better not. Perhaps I will though, just a quick look. (*Scuttles backstage, then turns round.*) Be a good bally now, I'll be right back. (*Enters hole of the* **Ichneumon-fly**.)

Chrysalis   To be born! To be born! A new world!

Traveller *stands up.*

Third Dung-beetle (*dashes out from the wings, where he has been lying in wait*)   Out of my way, citizen! This is my chance! Who dares wins! (*Drives the ball away.*)

Traveller   Hey, don't mind me!

Third Dung-beetle   I won't, mister! Look out!

Traveller   What's that you've got?

Third Dung-beetle   Hah – ball, capital, gold!

Traveller (*backs off*)   Stinks horrible, your gold!

Third Dung-beetle   Gold doesn't stink, mister! Roll on, little ball of property. Round you go. Circulate. Go for it! Hah!

Traveller What now?

Third Dung-beetle Possessions, I love 'em!
Something that's all yours. Your private dream! (*Rolls the
ball stage-left.*) My little treasure! (*Going off.*) I'll enjoy
burying this! Mind your back! (*Goes off.*)

Traveller Possessions, why not? Everyone wants a
little ball of their own.

Mrs Dung-beetle (*crawls out of the* **Ichneumon-fly**'s
hole) Nah, someone already lives there. Larva. Little
grub thing. No good for you, ball! Bally? Where's my
darling girl? Bally? Where's my little bally?

Traveller Just a moment ago . . .

Mrs Dung-beetle (*turns to him*) What have you done
with my ball? Thief! Stop thief!

Traveller Like I said, just a moment ago . . .

Mrs Dung-beetle Murderer! Give me my ball!
Give her back to me!

Traveller Big bloke – he rolled it off that way.

Mrs Dung-beetle Which bloke? Which way?

Traveller Revolting, pompous, puffed-up slob . . .

Mrs Dung-beetle You mean my husband!

Traveller Flabby skin, smelly, bandy-legs . . .

Mrs Dung-beetle Yes, yes, that's him!

Traveller Nice to have something of your own and
bury it, he said.

Mrs Dung-beetle His words exactly! I bet he found
a nice safe hole. (*Calls.*) Mr Dung-beetle! Mr Dung-
beetle! Where is the silly old man?

Traveller He was rolling her this way.

Mrs Dung-beetle Silly sausage, why didn't he call

me? (*Runs stage-left.*) Darling! Husband! Bally! Wait! (*Disappears from sight.*) Bally!

Traveller   These folk here are another story, not so common, more respectable. All right, I was a bit drunk. All I could think of was butterflies – beautiful butterflies, a bit faded, the *crème de la crème*, eternal coupling, posh society ladies and their young men, insects scrabbling for their bit of pleasure. I'm fed up with that crowd. At least these ones smell of a hard day's work. They don't care about pleasure, just possessions. Feet on the ground, ordinary people. They limit their ambitions, build their happiness to last, even if it is built out of shit. Pleasure lasts a moment, shit smells for ever. You love for yourself, you build for something bigger. So what if it's greedy – greed's good if it's for your family. The family justifies everything. Who wouldn't rob to take care of his own?

Chrysalis (*shouts*)   Make way, give me space, something enormous is about to happen!

Traveller   What's that then?

Chrysalis   I am to be born into the world!

Traveller   Good for you, what as?

Chrysalis   Don't know yet – something huge!

Traveller   I see. (*Lifts **Chrysalis** and re-attaches her to her blade of grass.*)

Chrysalis   I shall achieve unheard-of things!

Traveller   Such as?

Chrysalis   I shall be!

Traveller   That's good, Chrysalis, I like it. While everything in the world strains to be born, to live for ever, to feel a million feelings, only one thing matters – the awesome bliss of being.

Chrysalis Tell the world the moment is nigh, when I, me . . .

Traveller What?

Chrysalis I don't know yet. I want to achieve something great!

Traveller Something great, eh? Steady on. Don't let it go to your head. These good folk with their dungball wouldn't understand. A dungball is small and fat, dreams are big and empty.

Chrysalis Something tremendous!

Traveller I like it, Chrysalis. Something big? Let's hope so!

Chrysalis The world will hold its breath to watch me born!

Traveller Go on then, I'm watching. (*Sits down.*)

Ichneumon-fly (*creeps up with long, stealthy strides, dragging behind him the lifeless corpse of a Cricket*) Cooee, princess! Daddy's brought home something nice for you! (*Slips down the entrance of his hole.*)

Chrysalis (*yells out*) Ah, the pangs of birth! The agony! The whole planet is splitting to welcome me!

Traveller Get a move on, I'm not stopping you!

Chrysalis Step back, step back, or I'll sweep you off your feet in my flight!

Ichneumon-fly (*emerges from his hole with his back to the audience, talking to his daughter*) Eat up, don't move! Daddy will be home soon with more treats! What does my sweetheart fancy?

Larva (*standing before the entrance*) I'm bored, Daddy.

Ichneumon-fly Hah, cute, isn't she? Let Daddy kiss you properly, princess, then he'll find you something nice. Another Cricket? Whatever you want.

Larva   I want, I want – I don't know what I want.

Ichneumon-fly   Smart girl, that deserves a special treat. Daddy's off to work now, darling, got to take care of his sweet worm.

Larva *descends into the hole again.*

Ichneumon-fly (*approaching the* **Traveller** *with long swift steps*)   What the fuck are you?

Traveller (*jumps up and retreats*)   Me? Just a bum. Nothing much.

Ichneumon-fly   Edible?

Traveller   Don't think so.

Ichneumon-fly (*sniffs him*)   Ugh, you're not fresh enough. (*Bows slightly.*) Mr Ichneumon-fly by name. Do you have children?

Traveller   Not that I know of.

Ichneumon-fly   Have you seen her? My little larva. Gorgeous, isn't she? Developing nicely. Bright too. Lovely appetite. Children are a real joy, eh?

Traveller   So people say.

Ichneumon-fly   They're right. Gives you something to work for, something to fight for. Struggle and fight. That's life, eh? The child has a sweet tooth, she needs to eat, grow, play, aren't I right?

Traveller   A child certainly is demanding.

Ichneumon-fly   Each day I take home three Crickets for my baby! Lovely girl, isn't she? And clever. You think she gobbles it all up? Nah, she just likes the soft parts! They have to be still alive, of course. She's not stupid.

Traveller   I can see that.

Ichneumon-fly I'm a proud father. Really proud. She gets it from me. One flesh, eh? Can't stop to chat. So much running around, so much bother. It's hard bringing up children, a real sweat, sir. Feed the little darlings. Keep 'em. Cherish them, provide for their future. At least you know it's for someone.

Traveller So they say.

Ichneumon-fly Shame you're not edible, don't you think? I have to bring her something, see. (*Squeezing his body against the* **Chrysalis**.) What in hell's name is this?

Chrysalis (*shrieks*) It's me, Chrysalis, announcing the birth of a new world!

Ichneumon-fly (*squeezing her again*) Ugh, not ripe! She's no use to me!

Chrysalis I am about to create . . . !

Ichneumon-fly Must dash. So long, my pleasure. (*Runs off.*) Daddy will be back soon! (*Exit.*)

Traveller Cherish, provide, nourish, fill the gaping mouth, bring them live Crickets to eat. Yet even a Cricket wants to live and hurts no one. Why kill that cheerful little fellow, celebrating life with his modest melody? I can't understand it.

Larva (*crawling from her hole*) Daddy, Daddy! I'm hungry!

Traveller So you must be Larva, let's look at you.

Larva You're horrid! I'm bored. I want, I want . . .

Traveller What?

Larva I don't know what I want. I want to rip something apart, something living . . . That'd make me wiggle with pleasure!

Traveller (*turns away*) What's wrong with you?

Larva   Horrid, horrid, horrid! (*Crawls back in her hole.*)

Traveller   To feed a family like that, I can't get it out of my head. It's only insects, but it makes you think.

Mr Dung-beetle (*enters*)   Hurry up, I've found a hole! Where are you, woman? Where's my ball? Where's my wife?

Traveller   That foul, stinking old tub of lard, you mean?

Mr Dung-beetle (*excitedly*)   That's her, where's my dungball?

Traveller   Hideous old death-head, all covered in turds?

Mr Dung-beetle   That's her! Where did she put my lovely ball?

Traveller   Your better half went off looking for you.

Mr Dung-beetle   Where's my ball? My property? I left my wife guarding her!

Traveller   Well, this geeser comes up and rolls her away. There, that way. Says she belongs to him now.

Mr Dung-beetle   Sod my wife! Where's my ball?

Traveller   I told you, he rolled her away. Your wife wasn't here.

Mr Dung-beetle   Where was she? Where's she gone?

Traveller   She followed him. She was calling for you.

Mr Dung-beetle   My ball?

Traveller   No, your wife.

Mr Dung-beetle   I don't want my wife, I want my ball! God in heaven, where is my ball?

Traveller   Bloke rolled her away.

Mr Dung-beetle   Thief! Murderer! Catch him! (*Scrabbles on the ground.*) My life's savings! Better my life than my gold! (*Jumps up.*) Help! Thief! Murder! (*Shoots offstage, left.*)

Traveller   Thief! Murder! The heavens will fall because of a smelly ball. This heart-rending grief offers one consolation: the Dung-beetle's ball belongs now to another Dung-beetle. (*Sits on the edge of the stage.*)

Male voice (*offstage*)   Careful woman, don't stumble! Here it is, our nice little nest! Easy now. All right?

Female voice   Don't be daft, course I am!

Male voice   You must be careful darling, in your condition . . .

Enter **Mr Cricket** *and a pregnant* **Mrs Cricket**.

Mr Cricket   Open your peepers. There! How d'you like it?

Mrs Cricket   Ah Cricket, I get so tired!

Mr Cricket   Sit down darling. Have a little rest. Take it easy.

Mrs Cricket (*sits down*)   All this travelling, and the new house – it's worn me out! You got carried away with the move.

Mr Cricket   Peekaboo, Mummy! Mother-to-be!

Mrs Cricket   Don't tease, it's rude!

Mr Cricket   Hah! I'll not say another word! Mrs Cricket won't be having a little baby, it's all rumours!

Mrs Cricket (*tearfully*)   Don't tease, Daddy. It's not funny.

Mr Cricket   Oh darling, I'm so happy! I can't wait for our own little Jiminey Crickets – chirruping and singing all day long! I think I'll go mad with joy!

Mrs Cricket   Oh Daddy, you silly-billy!

Mr Cricket   Tee-hee! So how d'you like your new home?

Mrs Cricket   It's lovely!

Mr Cricket   Our nest, our mansion, our – tee-hee-hee – residence!

Mrs Cricket   I hope it's dry. Who built it?

Mr Cricket   Don't worry, it was a proper Cricket's residence.

Mrs Cricket   But why did he leave?

Mr Cricket   Moved away! Hah-hah! Moved away! I bet you don't know where he went? Guess! Go on, guess!

Mrs Cricket   I can't imagine. Tell me, Mr Cricket! Don't tease me, don't make me drag it out of you!

Mr Cricket   Well, yesterday a starling pounced on him and impaled him on a thorn! Impaled him through and through! I kid you not! Legs flapping away like this, tee-hee! Still alive! This'll make a nice place for us, I thought. We've struck lucky this time. What do you say?

Mrs Cricket   He was still alive? Oh, horrors!

Mr Cricket   What a piece of luck, eh! Tra-la-la! Wait, let's put up our sign. (*Takes from his knapsack a board that says* 'MR CRICKET, MUSIC SHOP.') Where shall I hang it? This way? To the left? More to the right?

Mrs Cricket   A big higher. Flapping all his legs, was he?

Mr Cricket (*busily still fixing the sign*)   Yes, that's right.

Mrs Cricket   Brr! Where is he?

Mr Cricket   You want to see him?

Mrs Cricket   Yes. No, perhaps not, I expect it's pretty horrible, isn't it?

Mr Cricket   Yep, sure is. Hanging straight?

Mrs Cricket   Oh Mr Cricket, I feel all funny.

Mr Cricket (*runs to her*)   Goodness, has it started?

Mrs Cricket   Get away! Ooh, it scares me though!

Mr Cricket   Don't be frightened, Mummy! Every female does it!

Mrs Cricket   How can you say that? (*Weeps.*) Oh Cricket, do you still love me?

Mr Cricket   Of course I do! Don't cry. Be a brave mummy now!

Mrs Cricket (*sobbing*)   Show me again how he did it with his legs?

Mr Cricket   Like this!

Mrs Cricket   Don't! It's so funny!

Mr Cricket   There, see? No more tears! (*Sits beside her.*) We'll settle in here very nicely. When the business gets going we'll do it up, get . . .

Mrs Cricket   Curtains.

Mr Cricket   Curtains – of course! Clever Mummy! Give Daddy a little kiss!

Mrs Cricket   Give over, you've no sense!

Mr Cricket   Of course I haven't. (*Jumps up.*) Guess what I bought!

Mrs Cricket   Curtains?

Mr Cricket   No, smaller. (*Hunts through his pockets.*)

Mrs Cricket   Quick, show me!

Mr Cricket (*produces two rattles and shakes them, one in each* *hand*)   Rat-a-tat-tat! Rat-a-tat-tat!

Mrs Cricket   How sweet! Give one to me!

Mr Cricket (*rattles and sings*)
A Crickety Cricket was born.
Crickety, Crickety, Cricket.
Over his Crickety cot
Stood Crickety Mummy and Daddy.
Singing him off into sleep
Chirpety, chirpety, chirpy.
Tee-hee-hee! ´

Mrs Cricket   Let me have a go! Quick, Daddy, I
can't wait!

Mr Cricket   Now you listen to me, old thing . . .

Mrs Cricket (*rattles and sings*)   Sweet Crickety, Crickety,
Cricket . . . !

Mr Cricket   I must run, do the rounds . . .

Mrs Cricket (*carries on singing*)   Sweet Crickety,
Crickety, Cricket . . . !

Mr Cricket   Knock on doors, hand out leaflets. Give
me a rattle, I'll rattle as I go.

Mrs Cricket   What about me? (*Tearfully.*) Don't leave
me on my own!

Mr Cricket   . . . check out the market, make myself
known. Rattle me on my way. Perhaps one of our
neighbours will pop round. You can chat, ask after the
children, whatever. Don't give birth till I get back!
(*Flapping his legs at* **Mrs Cricket**.)

Mrs Cricket   Naughty!

Mr Cricket   Tee-hee! Be good, I'll be home soon!
(*Darts off.*)

Mrs Cricket (*shakes her rattle, and* **Mr Cricket** *responds* *in the distance*)   A Crickety Cricket was born. Ooh, I'm scared!

Traveller (*stands up*)   Don't worry. Small things suffer no birth pangs.

Mrs Cricket   Are you a Beetle? Do you bite?

Traveller   No.

Mrs Cricket   What about your children?

Traveller   Don't have any. I never hatched anything from the quilt of marital bliss. I never had the warm joy of a roof my own – or watching others fail.

Mrs Cricket   No kiddies? What a shame! (*Shakes her rattle.*) Crickety Cricket! He's not answering. Why didn't you get married, Mr Beetle?

Traveller   Just selfish, plain selfish. I should be ashamed of myself. The selfish seek solace in solitude. No need for love or hate. No need to crave a bit of others' peace . . .

Mrs Cricket   You men! (*Shakes her rattle.*) Crickety Cricket! Crickety Cricket!

Chrysalis (*shouts*)   Me, me, me! Don't crowd me in! I carry the future inside me!

Traveller (*walks over to her*)   Get born then!

Chrysalis   I shall do wondrous things!

Mrs Dung-beetle (*enters*)   Where's my man? Where's the old fool gone? Where's our ball?

Mrs Cricket   So you play with a ball? Show me!

Mrs Dung-beetle   It's not for playing with, it's our dungball – our future, our world. And now my dunghead husband has gone and lost it!

Mrs Cricket   Oh poor dear, has he left you?

Mrs Dung-beetle   Where's yours then?

Mrs Cricket   Away on business. (*Rattles*.) Crickety, Crickety, Cricket!

Mrs Dung-beetle   How could he leave you all alone, in your condition!

Mrs Cricket *starts weeping*

Mrs Dung-beetle   Married already, and still no ball?

Mrs Cricket   What would I do with a ball?

Mrs Dung-beetle   A proper dungball binds the family together. It's real life – security.

Mrs Cricket   Oh no, life means a home of your own! Building your nest, buying your business. Curtains. Children. Finding the right Mr Cricket. Your little household. Your world.

Mrs Dung-beetle   But how do you manage without a dungball? You roll it with you wherever you go. I tell you, my dear, nothing will tie your husband to you more firmly than your own dungball!

Mrs Cricket   I think a nice home will do it!

Mrs Dung-beetle   Dungball!

Mrs Cricket   Curtains!

Mrs Dung-beetle   Dungball!

Mrs Cricket   Sofas and chairs!

Mrs Dung-beetle   Well it's been lovely talking to you! What a dear you are!

Mrs Cricket   What about your kiddies?

Mrs Dung-beetle   If only I had my bally! (*Goes off.*) Rolly, rolly, rolly . . . ! Bally, bally, bally . . . !

Mrs Cricket   What a frump! Pathetic! That man of hers has obviously gone! (*Shakes her rattle.*) Crickety, Crickety, Cricket . . . ! I do feel funny. (*Polishes her* *doorstep.*) Hah, that impaled creature flapping all his little legs!

Ichneumon-fly (*runs onstage, creeps up on* **Mrs Cricket** *with long, stealthy strides, whips a dagger from his coat-tail, swings back his shoulder, plunges it through her body and drags her back to his nest.*)   Out of the way, everyone!

Traveller (*backs away*)   Murder, murder!

Ichneumon-fly (*at the entrance to his hole, calling down*)   Come quick, darling! See what Daddy's brought you!

Traveller   He killed her, and I stood there like a stone! God, she didn't say a word! No one came to her rescue!

Parasite (*emerging from the background*)   Just what I say, pal!

Traveller   To perish, so innocently!

Parasite   My words exactly. I saw everything – I couldn't do what he did, could you? But then we all have to live, don't you agree?

Traveller   Who are you?

Parasite   Me? Not much really, got nothing – orphan, Parasite, they call me.

Traveller   It's not right is it, killing like that?

Parasite   My words exactly, mate. He doesn't need to, he's not hungry, like me. With him it's just hoarding! It's shocking! I don't know what the world's coming to. Why should he have a full larder when others have nothing? Just because he has a dagger, and I only have my bare hands! See what I mean?

Traveller   I'll say.

Parasite   That's just what I say. Me, I never kill anyone. Haven't the mandibles for it, I mean I haven't the heart, haven't the means of prostit . . . prosec . . . production, that's it. All I have is hunger. There's no justice.

Traveller   No, no – killing's wrong!

Parasite   My words exactly, pal. At least you shouldn't hoard. Capitalist accumulation! S'not fair on the have-nots. Gobble up and finish, I say! Gobble up and finish, then there'll be enough to go round, don't you agree?

Ichneumon-fly (*emerging from his hole, calling down*)   *Bon appétit*, princess. Just the best bits. Don't you have a lovely daddy?

Parasite   My respects to you, sir.

Ichneumon-fly (*to* **Parasite**)   Are you by any chance edible? (*Sniffs around him.*)

Parasite   You're joking, your Honour! Me?

Ichneumon-fly   Ugh, revolting creature, piss off! What are you doing here?

Parasite   My words exactly, your Excellency. (*Backs off.*)

Ichneumon-fly (*to* **Traveller**)   See that Cricket?

Traveller   I'll say.

Ichneumon-fly   Nice work, huh? Not everyone can do that. You need it up here, old chap. (*Taps his forehead.*) Expertise. Initiative. Foresight. Let's say you need to live for your work.

Parasite (*moves forward*)   Just what I say, your Grace.

Ichneumon-fly   If you want to make a go of things you have to work at it. There's your future to consider, your family. There's – how do you call it, ambition. A strong personality will find its level, am I right?

Parasite   Couldn't have put it better myself, Sire.

Ichneumon-fly Yes, yes. Do your job properly, rear the next generation of Ichneumons, use your God-given gifts – that's what I call a life worth living.

Parasite Just what I say, your Worship.

Ichneumon-fly Shove it, shit-face. I'm not talking to you.

Parasite Absolutely, your Majesty.

Ichneumon-fly It gives you a warm feeling to fulfil your obligations, do an honest day's work. You feel you haven't lived in vain. Elevating stuff, huh? Must fly, don't cry! (*Sings down the hole.*) Wipe the tear from your eye, sweetie-pie! (*Runs off.*)

Parasite The old murderer! I had a hard job not going for his throat! It's all right for some. In the right conditions I could have worked too. But why should I when others have more than they can stuff down their faces? I have initiative too, but it's here. (*Pats his belly.*) I'm hungry, see? Hungry!

Traveller All for a piece of meat!

Parasite Just what I say. All for a piece of meat, while some other poor sod goes hungry! Everyone should eat their fill, don't you agree?

Traveller (*picks up the rattle and shakes it*) Poor little Crickety, Crickety, Cricket!

Parasite My words exactly, everyone wants to live.

An answering chirping from behind the wings.

Mr Cricket (*appears shaking his rattle*) Here I am, petal! Where are you, darling? Guess what Daddy's found?

Ichneumon-fly (*creeps up on him*) Hah!

Traveller Careful, look out!

Parasite (*stops him*) Leave him, mister! Don't get

involved! What must be must be!

Mr Cricket   Where's Mummy?

Ichneumon-fly (*lunges at him with a great swoop, pierces his body and bears him off*)   Princess! See what Daddy's brought you! (*Descends into his hole.*)

Traveller (*raises his hands to heaven*)   Almighty God, can't you see?

Parasite   My words exactly. That's his third Cricket today, and I've got nothing. It's against nature.

Ichneumon-fly (*slithers out of the hole*)   Eat now, darling, Daddy must work. Eat, eat, I'll be back in an hour. (*Rushes off.*)

Parasite   It makes you sick. The old gangster! (*Hovers around the hole.*) It's a disgrace. I'll show him! Has he gone? I'll sort him out. (*Descends into the hole.*)

Traveller   Murder upon murder! Heart, stop beating! It's not humans, it's only insects, Beetles, a petty drama between two blades of grass. Insect fights insect, Beetle battles Beetle. It's not humans, it's only insects. If only I could find humans again. Humans want more than just to devour – they want to build. They have a purpose, an ending, they build their little nest – no, that's the Dung-beetle! Dungballs for Dung-beetles. Humans have more . . . human ideals. A humble man celebrates life with his whole existence. Doesn't need much for his happiness. Minds his own business, makes his home, raises his kids. How sweet to see your neighbour struggling, flapping his legs – no, that's the Cricket! That narrow, petty, moronic Crickety bliss doesn't satisfy us humans. We want more than just to stuff our mouths, placidly chew the cud of happiness. Life demands real men. Life is struggle. Seize it with a strong hand. You want to be a hero? Don't be small, don't be weak. You want to live? Grab it. You want to eat? Kill. No, no, that's the Ichneumon! Quiet. Listen to the jaws working around the world. Yum, yum, dripping blood! Crunch, crunch, living morsels! Life devouring life! Life preying on life!

Chrysalis (*shaking herself*)   I sense something great is coming! Something enormous! To be born! To live!

Traveller   All right, Chrysalis, you're on!

Parasite (*rolls out of the **Ichneumon**'s hole, bloated and hiccoughing. Laughs*)   The old tight-arse, storing it all away for his p-p-pale princess! I feel disgusting, I'm going to throw up! (*Belches.*) O-oh, bloody hiccups! I can eat anyone under the table! No one can keep up with me!

Traveller   What happened to the little Larva?

Parasite (*laughs and hiccups*)   Nature's bounty is wide open to all! (*Belches.*)

Curtain.

Act Three

The Ants

The green forest.

Traveller (*sits deep in thought*) Enough, you've seen enough. You've seen creatures sucking like lice on the body of life, burrowing famished to grab their share from others. To live is to grab. So be like them, grab and snatch. You've seen enough.

Pause.

You're no different from an insect. A cockroach gathering crumbs left by others in the dust. Pitiful! Good for nothing, not even for someone to snap you up!

Chrysalis (*shouts*) Space, give me space! I shall soon be born! I shall liberate the world from its prison! What an astounding thought!

Traveller The endless struggle for me, me, me! The voracious hoarding to eternalise your insignificance in your offspring! Enough! Bloody magic! I want to tread human paths again. Human paths, when will you greet me in my blundering? Roadsigns in human speech. Village, town, county, state. The State! Stop, my head is spinning! Village, town, county, state. Then all humanity . . . It's bigger than me. That's the problem. The insect with its belly on the ground knows only itself – thinks that's all there is. The village, the district, the group, the social whole, the common cause . . .

Chrysalis I suffer the pangs of creation! I thirst for marvellous deeds!

Traveller (*jumps up*) The common cause! That's it! The human idea! We're just grains in the great universal storehouse! There's something bigger than little me! Humanity, the state – call it whatever you like. But serve it, because you are nothing. The greatest prize of life is to sacrifice it. (*Sits down.*)

Chrysalis   The hour of my salvation is near! A great sign and great words will announce my coming!

Traveller   Man is great only through great obligation. Whole only when part of the whole. When 'live a good life' means 'give your life'. When life means sacrificing it for something bigger – not in words but in deeds!

Chrysalis (*in spasms*)   Look at my wings! My enormous wings!

Traveller   If only I could see my way to the nearest village! What's that biting me? Oh, it's you, little Ant. And here's another! And another! Christ, I'm sitting in an ant-heap! (*Stands up.*) What did you do that for? Look at them – one – and two, and three – and four. And here's another – one, and two, and three . . .

The back curtain lifts to reveal the entrance to an ant-heap, constructed as a multi-storeyed red-brick building. At the door sits **Blind Ant**, *counting continuously. Following the rhythm set by* **Blind Ant**, **Ants** *with knapsacks, beams and shovels enter and intersect across the different storeys of the building.*

Blind Ant (*continuously*)   One and Two and Three and Four. One and Two and Three and Four . . .

Traveller   What's that, mate, why are you counting?

Blind Ant   One and Two and Three and Four . . .

Traveller   What is this place? Is it a factory, or what?

Blind Ant   One and Two and Three and Four . . .

Traveller   What do they make here? Why does the blind fellow keep counting? I get it. He's setting the rhythm. Everyone moves to his One and Two and Three and Four. Like machines. Horrible, my head's spinning.

Blind Ant   One and Two and Three and Four . . .

First Engineer (*runs onstage*)   Faster, faster! One and Two and Three and Four!

Blind Ant (*faster*)   One and Two and Three and Four . . . (*All the* **Ants** *start running faster.*)

Traveller   Hey mister, what's happening? What's this factory?

First Engineer   Who are you?

Traveller   I'm me.

First Engineer   Which colony?

Traveller   Humans.

First Engineer   This is Antopolis. What do you want?

Traveller   Just looking.

First Engineer   For work?

Traveller   Maybe.

Second Engineer (*rushes onstage*)   Invention! Invention! New acceleration! Hey, blind fellow, cut out the 'and'! One, Two, Third, Four! Right? Save time! One, Two, Three, Four!

Blind Ant   One and Two and Three and Four.

Second Engineer   Wrong! One, Two, Three, Four!

Blind Ant   One, Two, Three, Four. (*The Ants start moving even faster.*)

Traveller   Not so fast, my head's spinning.

Second Engineer   Who's that? Where's he from?

First Engineer   From humans. You know where the human ant-heap is?

Traveller   There. Here. Everywhere.

Second Engineer (*barks*)   Everywhere? He's mad!

First Engineer   How many are you?

Traveller   Many. They call us the lords of creation.

First Engineer   Hah-hah! *We* are the lords of creation!

Second Engineer   We are Antopolis!

First Engineer   The mightiest ant-heap in the world!

Second Engineer   The biggest democracy!

First Engineer   World power!

Traveller   How come?

First Engineer   All Ants must obey commands.

Second Engineer   All must work. All for Him.

First Engineer   Only He commands.

Traveller   Who?

First Engineer   The State. The Government, the Nation.

Traveller   Fancy that, just like us. We have democracy – voting, parliament . . . Do you have parliament?

First Engineer   No, we have the Common Cause.

Traveller   But who speaks for the Common Cause?

Second Engineer   Doesn't know anything, does he?

First Engineer   He who leads. The Common Cause speaks only in commands.

Second Engineer   It exists in laws.

Traveller   So who governs you?

First Engineer   Reason.

Second Engineer Law.

First Engineer Interests of state.

Second Engineer That's right! That's right!

Traveller I like that. Everything for the Common Cause.

First Engineer For its greatness.

Second Engineer Against the enemy.

Traveller Who's that?

First Engineer Against everybody.

Second Engineer We are encircled by enemies.

First Engineer We defeated the Red Ants.

Second Engineer We exterminated the Amazon Ants.

First Engineer We subjugated the Grey Ants. The only ones left are the Yellows. Now we must eliminate them.

Traveller What for?

First Engineer For the Common Cause.

Second Engineer The Common Cause demands a higher purpose.

First Engineer Racial!

Second Engineer Industrial!

First Engineer Colonial!

Second Engineer International!

First Engineer Global!

Second Engineer That's right! That's right!

First Engineer The Common Cause means endless sacrifice!

Second Engineer   Sacrifice cements it! Wars nourish it!

Traveller   So you're Warrior Ants!

Second Engineer   Hush, he doesn't know anything!

First Engineer   Antopolis Ants are peace-loving Ants!

Second Engineer   A nation of peace-lovers!

First Engineer   A nation of workers!

Second Engineer   We only want to conquer the world . . .

First Engineer   In the interests of world peace . . .

Second Engineer   In the interests of peaceful toil . . .

First Engineer   In the interests of . . .

Second Engineer   . . . all the above interests. When we have conquered the world's space . . .

First Engineer   . . . we shall conquer time.

Second Engineer   Time has no master yet.

First Engineer   Time is bigger than space. The master of time will be master of the universe.

Traveller   Hang on, let me think. Conquer time? Only eternity can conquer time.

First Engineer   Speed is the master of time.

Second Engineer   He who commands speed governs time.

First Engineer   One, Two, Three, Four . . .

Blind Ant (*quicker*)   One, Two, Three, Four. One, Two . . . (**Ants** *start moving even quicker.*)

First Engineer   Speed up the tempo.

Second Engineer   The tempo of production.

First Engineer   The tempo of life.

Second Engineer   Every movement speeded up.

First Engineer   Shortened.

Second Engineer   Calculated.

First Engineer   To the second.

Second Engineer   To the hundredth part of a second.

First Engineer   Save time.

Second Engineer   Increase production.

First Engineer   We used to work too slowly. Creaking along. Ants dying of boredom.

Second Engineer   Uneconomical.

First Engineer   Inhuman. Now they die only of exhaustion.

Traveller   But why go so fast?

First Engineer   In the interests of the nation.

Second Engineer   The problem of production is the problem of power.

First Engineer   And peace. Peace is eternal struggle.

Second Engineer   We are in the vanguard of the battle for peace.

Blind Ant   One, Two, Three, Four.

Messenger Ant *runs on and hands both* **Engineers** *an important message.*

Traveller   One, Two, Three, Four, faster! Take the whip of speed to old time! Flog him, mount him, make him run! Speed is progress! The world speeds at a gallop to its post, dashing faster to its destruction. Count on, blind man. One, Two . . .

Blind Ant   Three, Four . . . !

First Engineer   Faster, faster!

First Ant (*collapsing beneath his burden*)   A-ah!

Second Engineer   What's this? Get up!

Second Ant (*leaning over* **First Ant**)   Dead.

First Engineer   You and you, at the double! Remove the corpse!

Two Ants *carry the body away.*

Second Engineer   What an honour to fall in the battle for speed!

First Engineer (*to* **Ants**)   Careful how you lift him! Too slow! Wasting time! Drop him!

Ants *drop the corpse.*

First Engineer   Head, feet, together! One, Two, Three! Wrong, drop him!

Ants *drop the corpse.*

First Engineer   One, Two, Three! Take him off, quick march! One, Two, Three!

Second Engineer   Three, Four! At the double!

Traveller   At least he died quick.

First Engineer   Work! Work! He who works shall have more!

Second Engineer   He who has more must work more!

First Engineer   He has more needs!

Second Engineer   More to defend!

First Engineer   More to conquer!

Second Engineer   Conquer for peace!

First Engineer   Peace means work!

Second Engineer   Work means power!

First Engineer   Power means war!

Second Engineer   That's right, that's right!

Voice   Out of the way! Mind out!

Enter **Inventor** *wearing a huge head bigger than himself, stumbling and feeling his way.*

Inventor   Out of the way please, gentlemen! I'm carrying a brain! It's terribly fragile, it's all made of glass! If it breaks it'll shatter into a thousand pieces! Smash! Mind the brain please, mind the brain!

Second Engineer   What's it up to now, Inventor?

Inventor   It's bursting, it's terribly painful – one bump on the wall and smash! It's so big I can hardly carry it. Careful, mind the brain!

First Engineer   What's new?

Inventor   New machine. Hear it ticking? Enormous thing, I can't even get my arms around it. Out of the way, I'm carrying a machine!

First Engineer   What kind of machine?

Inventor   War machine – latest model! The biggest, quickest, most powerful crusher of lives! Puff, can you hear? Ten thousand dead, one hundred thousand dead . . . Puff, puff, still working. Two hundred thousand dead! Puff!

First Engineer   Look at him! Real genius eh? What a scholar!

Inventor   The pain! My head is splitting! Out of the way in case I crash! (*Exit.*) Puff, puff . . .

Second Engineer   Nothing serves the state better than science.

First Engineer   Science is a great thing. There's going to be war.

Traveller   Why war?

First Engineer   Because we have a new war machine.

Second Engineer   We're still missing a little bit of the world.

First Engineer   The bit from the pine-trees to the birches.

Second Engineer   The corridor between the two blades of grass.

First Engineer   The only free passage to the south.

Second Engineer   A question of prestige.

First Engineer   Commerce.

Second Engineer   Our great national idea!

First Engineer   It's us or the Yellows!

Second Engineer   There never was a more just or honourable war . . .

First Engineer   . . . than the war for which we are preparing!

Second Engineer   We are prepared.

First Engineer   Now we wait for the *casus belli*.

Blind Ant   One, Two, Three, Four . . .

A gong sounds.

First Engineer   What is it?

Voices   Messenger, messenger!

Messenger   Permission to report from Guards of the Southern Army, sir!

First Engineer   Proceed.

Messenger   On orders from High Command we

crossed the border into the territory of the Yellows!

First Engineer And?

Messenger The Yellows captured me and took me to their commander.

First Engineer And?

Messenger Here is a letter from the commander.

First Engineer Show me. (*Takes the letter and reads.*) 'The government of the Yellow Ants demands that Antopolis withdraws its army forthwith from the territory between the birches and the pine-trees, on the path between the two blades of grass . . .'

Second Engineer Listen to this!

First Engineer '. . . This territory possesses vital historical, sacred, military and industrial interests for our state. According to law it should belong to us.'

Second Engineer That is an insult to Antopolis, and we shall not tolerate it!

First Engineer 'We hereby order our regiments to commence their advance.' (*Drops the missive.*) War! It's war at last!

Second Engineer Finally it's war! Forced upon us!

First Engineer To arms!

Another messenger (*runs in*) The Yellows are crossing our border!

First Engineer (*rushing through a corridor of the ant-heap, shouting*) Ants, to arms!

Second Engineer (*rushes through other corridors*) To arms, to arms!

Sirens wail. **Ants** *tumble into the heap from all sides.*

Blind Ant One, Two, Three, Four! One, Two, Three, Four!

The commotion within the heap increases.

Traveller   To arms, Ants! Defend the path between two blades of grass! A little clot of earth from blade to blade! Your sacred right! The supreme interests of state! The greatest conflict on earth! Everything to play for! Hurrah, to arms! How could you live if that patch belonged to another, and a foreign Ant carried his sackfuls to your heap? A hundred thousand lives for two blades of grass! Not enough? Too little? War is insect work. Dig your trench, shovel earth, bayonet attack, advance over heaps of corpses. Fifty thousand dead for fifty yards of latrines. Hurrah for the Common Cause! Our historic heritage! Freedom for our hearth and home! Two little blades of grass are at stake! Such a mighty matter, only the dead could make sense of it!

Chrysalis   The whole earth is trembling! Something great is_ happening. I am to be born!

*Drumbeats sound as ranks of metal-helmeted **Ants** armed with rifles, bayonets and machine-guns line up in formation. **First Engineer**, wearing the badge of Commander-in-Chief, enters with his officers. **Second Engineer**, as Chief of Staff, enters with his.*

Traveller (*passing down the ranks*)   You can see the training. Attention, men! To arms! Your country needs you to fight or fall! Two blades of grass are watching!

First Engineer (*jumping up on a platform*)   Soldiers! We are compelled to call you to the flag! A cruel enemy has treacherously attacked us, to disrupt our measures for peace. In this hour of crisis I proclaim myself Dictator!

Second Engineer   Glory to the Dictator! Shout glory, lads, or . . .

Soldiers   Glory to the Dictator!

Dictator (*salutes*)   Thank you, men. You have

understood the demands of the moment. Gun in hand, we shall fight for justice and freedom . . .

Chief of Staff   And the power of the state . . .

Dictator   And the power of the state. We shall defend civilisation and our military honour. I am with you, men, to the last drop of my blood!

Chief of Staff   Long live our beloved Leader!

Soldiers   Long live our beloved Leader!

Dictator (*salutes*)   I know my men. We shall fight to final victory! Long live our valiant fighting material! Hurrah!

Soldiers   Hurrah! Hurrah! Hurrah!

Dictator (*to* **Chief of Staff**)   First and Second Regiments advance! Fourth Regiment to flank the pine-tree and fall on the Yellow ant-heap. Eliminate females and embryos! Third Regiment in reserve. Spare no lives!

Chief of Staff (*salutes*)   Yes sir!

Dictator   May God be with us. Right turn, march! (*Roll of drums.*)

Chief of Staff   Right turn, march! One, Two, One, Two, One, Two! (*Leads* **Soldiers** *off to the left.*)

Dictator   One, Two! Forced to defend ourselves! One, Two! In the name of justice! One, Two! For our native hearth and home! One, Two! Expand our homeland! One, Two! The will of the nation! One, Two! The claims of history! One, Two!

Rank after rank of **Soldiers** *advance in time to a roll of drums.*

I am with you, men! Glory to the Fifth Regiment! One, Two! Forward to victory by the pine-cones! One, Two! A glorious epoch! One, Two! Conquer the world! One,

Two! Seventh Regiment, hurrah! One, Two! Our heroes will destroy the Yellow cowards! One, Two! Burn, slash, kill!

Messenger (*runs on*)   The Yellows have broken through the clearing between the boulders and the pine-roots!

Dictator   Everything is going according to plan! Faster, soldiers! One, Two! The marvellous army spirit! One, Two! Forced to defend ourselves for the glory of the state! One, Two! The Fatherland calls you to spare no one! One, Two! Our greatest moment in world history! One, Two!

Distant thunder of cannons.

Let battle commence. Second levy! (*Surveys the battlefield through field-glasses.*)

Blind Ant   One, Two, Three, Four! One, Two, Three, Four . . . !

The distant thunder draws closer.

Chrysalis (*shouts*)   The whole earth is splitting! Listen to my words! From the depths of earth, the pangs of creation herald my birth!

Dictator   Second levy! Third levy! To arms, to arms! Quartermaster, report!

Quartermaster (*presenting himself, shouts*)   The battle has commenced in favourable weather conditions. Our heroic material is fighting with excellent morale.

New regiments appear to the roll of drums from the ant-heap.

Dictator   Right turn! Forward march! One, Two! Faster, men!

Messenger (*runs in again*)   Our right wing is in retreat. Fifth Regiment totally annihilated.

Dictator   All as planned. Sixth to substitute.

Messenger *runs off.*

Traveller   All regiments annihilated as planned!
Excellent! Death itself gives the orders now. I've been
there. I've seen wide fields littered with corpses.
Smashed human flesh frozen in snow. And the great
Commander-in-Chief, Death himself in epaulettes,
plumage fluttering, his chest full of medals, surveying the
dead to see if they're laid out according to plan on the
map of the dead.

Stretcher-bearer Ants *run in with* **Wounded Ants**.

Wounded Ant (*howls*)   Fifth Regiment! Our regiment!
Wiped out! Stop the killing!

Telegraph rattles.

Signals-officer (*reading telegraph messages*)   'Fifth
Regiment destroyed. Awaiting further commands.'

Dictator   Sixth to substitute. (*To* **Quartermaster**.)
Quartermaster to report!

Quartermaster   The battle is progressing
satisfactorily. The Fifth Regiment heroically distinguished
itself in withstanding attack, and was subsequently
relieved by the Sixth.

Dictator   Bravo! I hereby decorate you with the Order
of Merit!

Journalist (*approaching with notebook*)   Press, press! Shall
we announce the victory?

Dictator   Yes. 'Due to careful planning the operation
was a military triumph. Extraordinary spirit of our
human resources. Invincible advance. The enemy
demoralised.'

Journalist   We'll print it.

Dictator   Good. We're relying on you. Don't forget
the extraordinary spirit.

Journalist The press will do its duty, sir! (*Runs off.*)

Charity-collector (*rattles his tin*) Help the wounded! Everything for the wounded! Help the cripples!

Dictator (*to* **Quartermaster**) Second Regiment advance! Break through regardless of cost!

Charity-collector Gifts for our heroes! Help our brothers!

Traveller (*tears off a button and puts it in the tin*) Gifts for heroes! There, my last button for the war!

Wounded Ant (*groans on his stretcher*) Finish me off!

Charity-collector (*retreats*) Help the wounded!

Telegraph rattles.

Signals-officer The right flank of the Yellows is in retreat!

Dictator Pursue them! Finish them off!

Quartermaster (*bawling*) The enemy is fleeing in disarray! Our brave regiments are pursuing them with magnificent, death-defying courage!

Dictator Fourth levy!

Quartermaster *dashes off into the ant-heap.*

Signals-officer Sixth Regiment eliminated to the last man!

Dictator All according to plan. Ninth to substitute. Fifth levy!

New formations of **Soldier Ants** *appear.*

At the double!

Ants *run off at the double to the battlefield.*

Signals-officer Fourth division surrounding the pine-tree, breaking through the Yellow ant-heap and destroying their garrison!

Dictator   Raze it to the ground, exterminate all females and embryos!

Signals-officer   Enemy stronghold breached! We have cleared the approaches to the gorse-patch!

Dictator   Victory is ours! (*Goes down on his knees and removes his helmet.*) Mighty God of all the Ants, Thou hast ordained victory! I appoint Thee Colonel of the Ants. (*Jumps up.*) Third Division advance on the enemy! All reserve forces mobilised! Spare no lives! Advance! (*Down on his knees again.*) Righteous God, Thou seest and knowest our Holy Cause . . . (*Jumps up.*) Pursue them! Kill them! Finish them off! (*Kneels again.*) Almighty God of the Ants, in this great moment, as we conquer the world . . . (*Prays silently.*)

Traveller (*leans over him, quietly*)   The world? Wretched ant, naming your filthy bit of grass and earth the world! This handful of dust! Fools! If all your ant-heaps were trampled down, not even the tree-tops would ripple in sympathy!

Dictator   Who are you?

Traveller   Just a voice. Yesterday perhaps a soldier in another ant-heap. What about you, conqueror of the universe? Think you're big enough? Perhaps that heap of corpses your fame rests on is too small?

Dictator   It doesn't matter. I'll make myself Emperor!

Signals-officer   Second Division requires reinforcements. Our fighting material is exhausted!

Dictator   What? They must hold out! Flog them!

Signals-officer   Third Division routed!

Ants (*running across the stage*)   We're retreating!

Dictator   Fifth levy! All to arms!

Ant voice (*yells from behind the scenes*)   Stop! No, no!
Back!

Another Ant voice (*shrieks piercingly*)   Run! Run for
your lives!

Dictator   Sixth levy! Empty the hospitals! All to arms!

Soldier Ant (*flees from the left*)   We're being massacred!
Run!

Two Soldier Ants (*run from the right*)   We're encircled!
Run! Escape!

Soldier Ant (*from left*)   To the west! Head for the west!

Soldier Ants (*from right*)   In the west we're ambushed!
Head for the east!

Dictator (*bellows*)   Back! To the battlefield! Stay at your
posts!

Group of Soldier Ants from right (*in full
stampede*)   Run! Run! The flame-guns are coming!

Group of Soldier Ants from left   To the west! Run
for your lives! Out of the way!

Throng of Ants from right   Run! They're after us!
To the east!

Throng of Ants from left   To the west! Out of the
way! They're coming!

Both throngs start skirmishing and killing each other in panic.

Dictator (*lunges forward and starts hacking at them*)   Back,
cowards! Cattle! Don't you see I am your Emperor!

Soldier   Fuck you! (*Kills him with his bayonet.*) Better
scram! (*Runs off.*)

Chief of Staff (*runs on wounded and jumps on a
hillock*)   They've taken the city! Extinguish the lights!

Yellow Ants (*rush on from both sides*)   Hurrah, hurrah!

The ant-heap is ours!

The lights go off. Darkness, turmoil, chaos.

Voice of Chief-of-Staff   To battle . . . ! A-a-ah . . . !

Voice of Yellow Leader   Chase them up the corridors! Slaughter them! Spare no lives!

Screams of slaughtered **Ants,** *'A-a-ah . . .'*

Voice of Blind Ant   One, Two! One, Two! One, Two!

Yellow Leader   Follow them! Exterminate! Exterminate everyone!

The shouts and screams fade away.

Blind Ant   One, Two! One, Two! One, Two!

Yellow Leader   Lights up!

The lights go up. The front stage is empty. The **Yellows** *hurtle through the corridors, hurling the bodies of dead Ants down the stairs. Piles of corpses everywhere.*

Yellow Leader   Good work, Yellows! They're all wiped out!

Traveller (*wading through the carnage*)   Enough, General, I've seen enough!

Yellow Leader   Victory to the Yellows! Victory for justice and progress! The corridor between the two blades of grass is finally ours! To us the world! I proclaim myself ruler of the universe!

The din retreats to the corridors.

Chrysalis (*writhing*)   Me . . . me . . . me . . . !

Yellow Leader (*drops to his knees and removes his helmet*)   Righteous God, Thou seeest and knowest our Holy Cause. We fight only for justice, for history, for our national honour and our commercial interests . . .

Traveller (*starts up, kicks him and grinds him into the earth with his foot*)   Bloody insect!

Curtain.

Epilogue

Life and Death

The heart of the forest. Pitch-black night. **Traveller** *is asleep on the ground.*

Traveller (*dreaming*) Enough, General, I've see enough! (*Wakes up.*) Did I dream it? Where am I? Terrible darkness. Chrysalis, Chrysalis! (*Stands up, groping towards the audience.*) Why is it so dark? Can't even see my feet – who's talking? Who are you? (*Shouts.*) Is anyone there? It's just my voice. (*Gropes around.*) Nothing. (*Shouts.*) Is anyone there? Nothing, just an empty hole. Where shall I start digging? If only there was something to grab hold of. Nothing, God, where is the sky? Just one little flicker of light. One human torch! A human signpost! Where am I? (*Kneeling.*) I'm scared! Light! Light!

Voice from the darkness There is light, plenty of light!

Traveller (*crawling over the ground*) Human light, a ray of light!

Another voice Give me food! Give me drink!

Another voice Come, I'm calling you! I'm seeking you, come!

Weak voice Water, water!

Traveller Just a glimmer of light!

Voice of Dung-beetle (*in the distance*) My ball, where is my dungball!

Traveller Give me light!

Voice The thirst, the hunger!

Dying voice Finish me off! Be done with me!

Another voice   I want you! Be mine!

Traveller   Give me light! Hah, what's this? Stones!

Voice   The thirst! The thirst!

Another voice   Have mercy on me!

Traveller   Just strike a little spark . . . (*Rubbing stones together.*) A single solitary spark of light! The last spark!

Sparks flare from the stones, lighting the heart of the forest with a spectral glow.

(*Rising to his feet.*)   Light!

Voices (*dying away*)   Help! Light! Run!

Traveller   Ah, lovely!

Voices (*backstage, approaching*)   Light! Light!

Chrysalis   Who is calling me?

Traveller   Thanks be to God, light!

The glow spreads, quiet music.

Chrysalis   On your knees, on your knees! I have been chosen to enter the world!

Voices (*approaching*)   Behold the light!

Chrysalis   In the pangs of birth my prison walls will burst! Unseen, unheard, I shall become real, I shall exist!

Dancing onto the glowing centre of the stage appear swarms of spinning transparent **Mayflies**.

Traveller   Where did you come from, little flies?

First Mayfly (*emerges from the swarm and twirls*)   Oh, Oh, Oh! (*Flutters up, singing.*) Glowing like a gleam in the darkness sparkles our Mayfly life! Dance, my sisters, dance! Oh, Oh, Oh! (*Twirls again.*)

Mayfly Chorus   Twirling, dancing, we are Life!
Whirling, twirling, we are Life! Life itself! Life! Life!
Life!

First Mayfly (*flutters up*)   From twinkling sunbeams
weave our wings, shining threads from star to star,
woven by the Muse divine, dancing on through space
and time! Souls of Life, born in light, in the image of
God, who . . . (*Keels over and dies.*)

Second Mayfly (*flutters up and twirls*)   . . . who makes us.
Oh, Oh, Oh! Eternal Life! Oh, Oh, Oh! Eternal Life!

Traveller (*stumbles over to her*)   What d'you mean,
eternal?

Second Mayfly   To live, to spin, to flutter, to twirl!
The cosmic twirl of Mayfly wings echoing from the
heavenly heights! Our mysterious task, our eternal
dance! The cosmic harmony of our wings! Oh what a
mission to rule the spheres! What joy to be a Mayfly!
To live is to spin! Oh, Oh, Oh! (*Twirls on.*)

Mayfly Chorus   Life eternal! Eternal Life!

Traveller (*amongst them*)   Oh, what a mission! Oh, what
joy!

Mayfly Chorus   Spin, twirl, flutter, dance! Sisters,
come, gather round!

Second Mayfly (*flutters up*)   Let Life unfold,
transparent, weightless, eternal! Spirits woven from the
finest silk! We are Life! We are Life! Transparent,
weightless, eternal! Sparks from the divine forge, bursting
to praise . . . (*Drops dead.*)

Traveller   Hey, she'd dead!

Third Mayfly (*flutters up and whirls*)   Oh, Oh, Oh!
(*Stops.*) The world whirls with us, praising, gurgling,
rejoicing, exalting! Behold the Mayfly gift of Life! Great,
loving, eternal! Praise the fiery dance of Life, restless,

giddy and joyful! Be with us for ever . . . ! (*Drops dead.*)

Traveller (*raises his arms and spins around*)   Oh, Oh, Oh!

Mayfly Chorus   Blessed be Life! Let us praise Life!

Traveller   Life, you have enchanted us! Even me, a tired old fly, shouting and twirling! Oh, Life . . .

Mayfly Chorus   Blessed be Life! Let us praise Life!

Traveller   Let's live, all of us! Everything wants to live! Grab it, everyone's on their own – unless we try fighting for it together. God show us how to fight off the oblivion of the grave!

Mayfly Chorus   Blessed be Life! Let us praise Life!

Mayfly *after* **Mayfly** *drops down dead.*

Traveller   We all go the same way – flies, humans, ideas, things that swim, things that crawl, the grass, everything! While we're still alive we must unite in one regiment, led by Life eternal . . .

Mayfly Chorus   Life be praised! Blessed be Life!

Chrysalis (*with piercing shriek*)   Make way! (*Rips off the swaddling bands of her cocoon and jumps out as a* **Mayfly**.) I am here!

Traveller (*stumbles towards her*)   Is that you, little Chrysalis? So you're finally born!

Chrysalis (*flutters up and starts twirling*)   Oh, Oh, Oh!

Traveller (*following her*)   Is that it, then?

Chrysalis (*twirling*)   Oh, Oh, Oh! (*Flutters up.*) I proclaim the reign of Life! I command all creatures to live! The kingdom of Life is here! (*Twirls.*) Oh, Oh, Oh!

The few surviving Mayflies   Eternal Life! Eternal Life! (*All drop dead.*)

Chrysalis (*fluttering up*)   The whole world writhed as it

awaited my birth! Hear me, oh hear my divine message!
I predict great things! Silence, I command silence! I bear
great words . . . ! (*Drops down dead.*)

Traveller (*kneels over her*)　Get up little fly, why did you
fall? (*Lifts her up.*) Dead! What a lovely face, what bright
clear eyes! What did you want to tell me? (*Lifts her in his
arms.*) Dead! How light she is – heavens, how beautiful!
Why did she have to die? Oh fly! (*Lays her on the earth
and crawls over the ground inspecting dead* **Mayflies** *weakly
lifting their heads.*) Even you, dancing beauty! And you,
who sang so well! And you, so young! These lips will
not speak again! Dead! And you, in your little green
dress! Open your eyes! Wake up, live, praise Life!
(*Crawls again on his knees.*) Ugh, what was that?

*The spectral forest glow recedes and dies, and a small beam of
light falls on the* **Traveller**.

Who is it? Let me go, I'm cold. Who are you? (*Lunges
into empty space.*) Get your cold hands off me! I don't
want . . . (*Stands up.*) Let go . . . ! (*Lunges into the void,
defending himself.*) You're strangling me! I know who you
are, you're – you're Death! I saw you so many times
today! I don't want . . . Boney! No eyes! Disgusting!
A-a-ah . . . ! (*Lunges again into the void.*) Stop!

Enter two **Slugs**, *crawling from right.*

First Slug　Shtop, shomething's shtirring!

Second Slug　Shtand back, shilly!

Traveller (*fighting*)　Take that, Toothy! Hah, that's for
you! (*Forced to his knees.*) Let me go, you're strangling me!
Let me breathe! I just want to live – is that too much?
(*Gets up, flailing his arms.*) I won't give you my life, you
skeleton! Take that! (*Falls to the ground again.*) Oho, trying
to trip me now?

First Slug　Hey Shlug!

Second Slug　What?

First Slug   Look, he'sh fighting with Death!

Second Slug   Let'sh watch, shall we?

Traveller (*heaves himself up*)   Let me live! Just one day! Just till tomorrow! Let me breathe! (*Struggles.*) Let me go, you're strangling me! I'm not ready to die! I've not lived enough! (*Shouts.*) A-a-ah! (*Falls face down on the ground.*)

First Slug   Fun, eh?

Second Slug   Hey, Shlug.

First Slug   Yeah, what?

Second Slug   He'sh almost shnuffed it!

Traveller (*lurches to his knees*)   Coward, strangling me when I'm down! Let me go, give me – just a moment – (*Gets up and shouts.*) Let me live! Let me live! (*Shouts.*) Go away! I've so much to tell! (*Collapses onto his knees.*) Now I know how to live! (*Falls face down on the ground again.*)

First Slug (*crawls slowly forward*)   The show'sh over for him!

Second Slug   Jesush, Jesush, what a blow! What a mishfortune! Why did you forshake us!

First Slug   Shtop whingeing! It'sh nothing to do with ush!

Second Slug   I know, but you have to say shomething when shomeone diesh, know what I mean?

First Slug   Let'sh go. Let'sh hope there'sh not many shlugs and lotsh of cabbage!

Second Slug   Shlug, look!

First Slug   What?

Second Slug   All those dead Mayflies!

First Slug   Shame we can't eat them!

Second Slug　Shee what you mean. Besht be crawling on.

First Slug　Main thing ish we're alive, eh!

Second Slug　Shee what you mean. Hey, Shlug!

First Slug　What?

Second Slug　Life is shweet!

First Slug　That's right! Long live shweet Life, eh?

Second Slug　Let'sh shlither.

Slugs *slide behind the wings.*

First Slug　Lovely show, eh?

Second Slug　Yeah! Main thing ish we're shtill alive.

Slugs *disappear.*

Curtain.

The Makropulos Case

Characters

Emilia Marty
Jaroslav Prus
Janek Prus, *his son*
Albert Gregor *('Berty')*
Max Hauk-Šendorf
Dr Kolenatý, *a lawyer*
Vítek, *his assistant*
Kristina Vítek, *his daughter ('Kristy')*
Chambermaid
Doctor
Stagehand
Cleaner, *female*

Act One

*Vítek's room in **Kolenatý**'s chambers. At the back, a door to the street. On the left, doors leading to **Kolenatý**'s office. The back wall is stacked with vast ledgers and alphabetically arranged pigeon-holes crammed with documents. There is a ladder for reaching the top shelves. To the left is the assistant's desk. In the middle, the typist's desk. To the right are armchairs for waiting clients. On the walls are price-lists and notices, a calendar and a telephone. The room is filled with books and papers — briefs, documents and decrees.*

Vítek (*on the ladder, filing briefs*)   Oh dear oh dear, one o'clock and he's still not back. *Gregor versus Prus ... Gregor versus Prus ... G. Gr ...* (*Climbing ladder.*) Here we are. Gregor. What a shame we've finished with you. (*Leafing through documents.*) 1827, 1832, 1840. Forty ... Forty-seven ... In a few years we'd have been celebrating your centenary. Such a wonderful case. (*Pushes the document back in its pigeon-hole.*) Rest in peace, Gregor versus Prus! Never mind, nothing lasts for ever. *Vanitas.* Dust to dust. (*Sits deep in thought on the top rung of the ladder.*) That's the aristocracy for you. The old nobility. I blame that Baron Prus. Skinflints, chasing each other around the courts for hundreds of years! (*Pause.*) Citizens! *Citoyens!* How much longer will you suffer this bunch of courtiers and hereditary lords, spoiled by the kings of France? Who have tyranny, not nature, to thank for their privileges? Who own our land, our laws, our rights ... ?

Gregor (*stops unnoticed by the door, listens for a while*)   Good day to you, Citizen Marat!

Vítek   That's not Marat, it's Danton! His speech of October 23, 1792 ... Oh it's you sir, a thousand apologies ...

Gregor   Kolenatý not back yet?

Vítek (*climbs down from the ladder*)   Not yet, sir.

Gregor   And the verdict?

Vítek   I don't know, Mr Gregor, but . . .

Gregor   Looks bad, does it?

Vítek   I can't help you, sir, but it's a pity. It was a fine trial.

Gregor   We've lost?

Vítek   Dr Kolenatý has been in court all morning, sir. I could always . . .

Gregor (*turns to the sofa*)   Yes, yes, man, give him a ring. What are you waiting for?

Vítek (*scurries to the telephone*)   As you wish, sir. Hello? (*Turns from the receiver to* **Gregor**.) I wouldn't have taken it to the High Court, though.

Gregor   Why not?

Vítek   Because . . . Hello? 2-2-3-0-5, yes . . . Because it means the end, sir. The end!

Gregor   The end of what?

Vítek   The end of the case. This wasn't a case, sir, it was a historic epoch. Nearly ninety years it's been . . . (*Into the receiver.*) Hello miss? Is Doctor Kolenatý there? This is his office. (*Turns to* **Gregor**.) The Gregor file is part of our history, sir. Almost a hundred years . . . (*Into the receiver.*) Left already? Thank you. (*Hangs up.*) He's on his way, sir.

Gregor   And the verdict?

Vítek   I don't know Mr Gregor, I just know I wouldn't want one. I can't help it, sir! When I think today's the last day . . . Thirty-two years I've been working on the Gregor case! It was your late father then, of course – God grant his soul eternal glory. He and Doctor Kolenatý senior, the late father of my employer. They were a great generation, sir.

Gregor   Thank you.

Vítek   They were great lawyers, sir. All the legal intricacies and nullities, and such like. They kept it going for thirty years. With you sir, it's straight to the High Court, and boom, it's over!

Gregor   Stop waffling, Vítek. I just want to get the thing over and win!

Vítek   You might always lose, sir.

Gregor   It might be better to lose than . . . Listen, Vítek, it drives a man mad seeing that 150 million in front of his nose, just out of reach, hearing about nothing else since childhood. (*Stands up.*) So you think I'll lose?

Vítek   Hard to say, Mr Gregor. It's a difficult case.

Gregor   OK, but if I lose, then . . .

Vítek   Then you shoot youself, sir. Exactly your late father's words!

Gregor   He *did* shoot himself.

Vítek   Not because of the case though, because of his debts. Living like that, borrowing on his inheritance . . .

Gregor (*sits down, distressed*)   Stop it Vítek, please!

Vítek   Ah, you haven't the stomach for a big trial! Such wonderful material. (*Climbs the ladder and pulls out the Gregor case.*) Look at this document, Mr Gregor! 1827! The oldest one in our office! It's unique, sir! A museum piece! And look at this one, from 1840! The penmanship! The calligraphy! What a hand this man had! It's a joy to read!

Gregor   Vítek, you're crazy!

Vítek (*replaces the case reverently*)   Dear God, maybe the High Court will request a retrial.

Kristina (*opens the door quietly and enters*) Daddy, are you coming?

Vítek (*climbs down from the ladder*) In a moment, the Doctor will be here soon.

Gregor (*gets up*) Is this young lady your daughter?

Vítek Yes. Wait out in the corridor for me, Kristina.

Gregor God forbid, I'd hate to be in the way. Just back from school?

Kristina No, from a rehearsal.

Vítek My daughter sings at the Opera. Run along now, child. You shouldn't be here.

Kristina Daddy, that Miss Marty – she's amazing!

Gregor Who's that, miss?

Kristina Emilia Marty! Haven't you heard of her?

Gregor Who is she?

Kristina Don't you know anything! She's only the greatest singer in the world! She's singing this evening. She rehearsed with us today. Oh, Daddy!

Vítek What is it?

Kristina I'm never going to sing again! I can't! (*Bursts into tears and turns to the wall.*)

Vítek (*hurries to her*) What have they done to you, Kristy?

Kristina Nothing, it's just that Miss Marty ... If you could have heard her ... I'm no good, Daddy!

Vítek Look at her. And with her voice. Now run along dear, and stop being silly!

Gregor Who knows, perhaps this Miss Marty is actually jealous of you!

Kristina   Jealous of what?

Gregor   Your youth.

Vítek   See, he's right! Kristy, this is Mr Gregor. Wait till you get to be her age. How old is this Miss Marty!

Kristina   I've no idea. Nobody knows. About thirty.

Vítek   See, thirty! That's some age, my girl!

Kristina   And she's so beautiful! God, she's lovely!

Gregor   Listen, this evening I shall go to the Opera – not to see Miss Marty but to see you!

Kristina   Not see Miss Marty? You'd have to be blind not to – or off your head!

Vítek   That's enough of that, my girl!

Kristina   Well he shouldn't talk about Miss Marty if he doesn't know about her! Everybody's mad about her! Everyone!

Kolenatý (*entering*)   Who have we here? Why it's little Kristina, how nice! And our client too. How are you today, sir?

Gregor   What happened?

Kolenatý   Nothing so far. The Court has adjourned.

Gregor   For the summing-up?

Kolenatý   No, for lunch.

Gregor   And the verdict?

Kolenatý   This afternoon. Patience, man. Have you had lunch yet?

Vítek   Oh dear, oh dear.

Kolenatý   What's wrong?

Vítek   Such a wonderful trial.

Gregor (*sits down*)   More waiting. This is unbearable.

Kristina (*to* **Vítek**)   Come on Daddy.

Gregor   Doctor, be frank with me. How are we doing?

Kolenatý   Hmm.

Gregor   Bad?

Kolenatý   Listen, my friend. Did I ever give you grounds for hope?

Gregor   Then why . . . why . . . ?

Kolenatý   Why did I take you on? Because I inherited you, young man. You, Vítek and that desk over there. The Gregor case is passed on in our family like a disease. At least it's not costing you anything.

Gregor   You'll get your fees paid when I win.

Kolenatý   If.

Gregor   So you think we'll . . .

Kolenatý   If you want to know, yes, I do. Most definitely.

Gregor (*crushed*)   I see, so I'll have to . . .

Kolenatý   Don't, not yet.

Kristina   Is he going to shoot himself?

Gregor (*struggles to control himself*)   No, no, miss, didn't I say I'd come to the Opera tonight to see you?

Kristina   Not *me*.

The doorbell rings.

Vítek   Who's that? I'll say you're out. (*Leaves, murmuring.*) Throw them out, throw them out!

Kolenatý   Gracious, Kristina! Aren't you a big girl now! You're turning into a real woman!

Kristina Look at Mr Gregor! He's gone all pale!

Gregor Me? Don't worry about me, miss. I have a bit of a cold, that's all.

Vítek (*from behind the door*) This way, if you please. Yes, of course. Do come in.

Enter **Emilia Marty**, *followed by* **Vítek**.

Kristina My God, it's Miss Marty!

Emilia (*in the doorway*) Doctor Kolenatý?

Kolenatý That's me. What can I do for you?

Emilia I am Emilia Marty. I have come to discuss the case of . . .

Kolenatý (*welcoming her to his office with a deep bow*) What a great honour. Please, come in.

Emilia . . . the case of Gregor versus Prus.

Kolenatý What? But my dear madame . . .

Emilia I'm not married.

Kolenatý Miss Marty, this *is* Mr Gregor, my client!

Emilia (*looks* **Gregor** *up and down*) This one? Right, he can stay. (*Sits down.*)

Vítek (*pushes* **Kristina** *out of the door*) Run along now Kristy, off you go!

Kristina *creeps out, bowing at* **Emilia**.

Emilia Where have I seen that girl before?

Kolenatý (*closes the door behind them*) Miss Marty, this is a tremendous honour . . .

Emilia As you already said. Are you the lawyer in charge . . . ?

Kolenatý (*seats himself opposite her*) At your service, Miss Marty.

Emilia . . . of Gregor's claim?

Gregor That's me.

Emilia . . . to Peppy Prus's estate?

Kolenatý Yes, Baron Josef Prus, deceased 1827.

Emilia What? Peppy's dead?

Kolenatý Alas. Almost a hundred years ago now.

Emilia Poor devil. I'd no idea.

Kolenatý I see. How can I be of service?

Emilia (*standing up*) I don't want to detain you.

Kolenatý (*also standing*) If I may be so bold, Miss Marty, the purpose of your visit was . . . ?

Emilia (*sits again*) I came to tell you something.

Kolenatý About the Gregor case?

Emilia Maybe.

Kolenatý You're a foreigner, if I'm not mistaken?

Emilia Of course. I learned about your client Mr Gregor's case just this morning, quite by chance.

Kolenatý Well I never!

Emilia I was going through the newspaper for the reviews when I read 'The last day of the Gregor versus Prus trial'. Quite a coincidence, wasn't it?

Kolenatý Well it's certainly been in all the papers.

Emilia And then I happened to remember something . . . So I wondered if I could ask you one or two things about the trial?

Kolenatý Go ahead, fire away.

Emilia I know nothing about it, you see.

Kolenatý Nothing at all? Not a thing?

Emilia   It's the first I've heard of it.

Kolenatý   With all respect, Miss Marty, I still don't quite see why it should concern you.

Gregor   Go on Doctor, tell her about it.

Kolenatý   Well, the case is something of a rotten apple.

Emilia   But Gregor's in the right, isn't he?

Kolenatý   Apparently. But that doesn't mean he'll win.

Gregor   Get on with it.

Emilia   At least the gist of it.

Kolenatý   If it would entertain you, dear lady. (*Sinks into a deep armchair.*) Well around the year 1820, the noble family of Prus, with its estates at Semonice, Loukov, New Village, Königsdorf and so on, were headed by the feeble-minded Baron Josef Prus . . .

Emilia   Peppy, feeble-minded? Never!

Kolenatý   Eccentric then.

Emilia   Let's say unhappy.

Kolenatý   With all due respect, Miss Marty, I don't see how you can possibly know that.

Emilia   And you know even less.

Kolenatý   Well, God will be our judge. So after this Josef Prus died in 1827, unmarried, intestate and without heir . . .

Emilia   What did he die of?

Kolenatý   Brain fever or something . . . His cousin, the Polish Baron Emmerich Prus-Zabrze-Pinski, then claimed the inheritance. There was a counter-claim from a certain Count Szephazy de Marosvar, nephew of the deceased's mother, but that needn't concern us here.

Then a certain Ferdinand Karel Gregor, great-grandfather of my client, put in his claim for the estate of Loukov, and that's where we came in.

Emilia When was that?

Kolenatý The same year he died, 1827.

Emilia Wait a minute. Ferdy must have been a little boy then.

Kolenatý Quite correct. The young Ferdinand Gregor was a boarder at the Teresian Academy, and was represented by a Viennese lawyer. His claim for the Loukov estate was supported by the following facts: firstly that the deceased, a year before his death, appeared personally – *hochpersönlich* – to members of the governing body of the Teresian Academy and stated that he was bequeathing all the aforementioned estates – the Castle, the fields and all that was in them – for the education and upkeep of the aforementioned minor, who the moment he came of age was to be *in Besitz und Eigentum*, that is in possession of the aforementioned estate. Secondly that the aforementioned minor would acquire during the lifetime of the deceased all income deriving from the estate – *Besitzer und Eigentümer des Gutes Loukov* – which thereby constitutes proof of the so-called natural holding of the above . . .

Emilia So it's cut and dried then?

Kolenatý I beg your pardon. The proposal was opposed by Baron Emmerich Prus on the grounds that the bequest was not formalised in writing under oath, there was no record in the county register, and the deceased left no written will. On the contrary – *hingegen* – in his last hour, the deceased made a verbal arrangement selecting *another* person as beneficiary . . .

Emilia That's not possible! Who?

Kolenatý That's the snag, miss. Wait, let me read you

something. (*Climbs the ladder to his files.*) It's quite funny, you see. (*Takes out the Gregor file, sits on the top rung of the ladder and quickly leafs through it.*) M-m-m-m, aha! '*Das Während . . . und so weiter.*' That's the death warrant, miss. Signed by a priest, a doctor and a notary at the deathbed of Josef Prus. It goes on: 'When the undersigned notary asked the dying man, then in a delirium, if he had any last wishes, he stated many times – *wiederholte Male* – that the estate of Loukov – *dass das Allodium Loukov . . . Herrn Mach Gregor zukommen soll . . .* (*Slams shut the file and replaces the bundle.*) should belong to a certain Mr Mach, miss. A Mr Gregor Mach. M-A-C-H (*Spells it out.*), a person as yet unidentified and unknown. (*Remains seated at the top of the ladder.*)

Emilia It's clearly a misspelling. Peppy definitely meant *Ferdy* Gregor, (*Pointing at* **Gregor**.) his great-grandfather.

Kolenatý That's as may be, Miss Marty. But what's written is written. This Ferdinand Gregor claimed at the time that the word Mach which appeared in the verbal testament was the result of a misspelling, and that Gregor should be the surname, not the first name, and so on. But *litera scripta valet*, and Baron Prus's cousin Emmerich Prus ended up with Loukov and the rest of it.

Emilia And Ferdinand Gregor?

Kolenatý He got nothing. But one of his cousins, an unpleasant piece of work called Szephazy, dug up someone by the name of Gregor Mach, and this Mach came to court mentioning certain claims on the deceased of a somewhat delicate nature.

Emilia That's a lie!

Kolenatý Of course it was. But he put in his claim to the Loukov inheritance anyway, then disappeared – history doesn't record how much he got for doing so – leaving this Szephazy with power of attorney. Szephazy claimed in his name and won, so Loukov became his!

Emilia   How silly!

Kolenatý   It is rather, isn't it? This Gregor then started proceedings against Szephazy, claiming Gregor Mach wasn't the *de jure* heir of Loukov, and that the deceased was delirious when he made his verbal will, and so on. After more lengthy litigation he won his case, and the original verdict was overturned. However Loukov didn't go to Gregor, it returned to Emmerich Prus. All clear so far?

Gregor   See, Miss Marty, that's what they call justice!

Emilia   So why didn't it go to Gregor?

Kolenatý   Legal complications, dear lady. And because neither Gregor Mach nor Ferdinand Gregor were related to Baron Prus by blood...

Emilia   But wait! He was his son!

Kolenatý   Who? Who was whose son?

Emilia   Gregor! Ferdy Gregor was Peppy Prus's son!

Gregor (*jumps up*)   His son! How do you know that?

Kolenatý (*scrambles down the ladder*)   His son? So who was the mother?

Emilia   His mother? Her name was Ellian MacGregor. She was a singer at the Viennese Court Opera.

Gregor   What was her name again?

Emilia   MacGregor. It's a Scottish name.

Gregor   Hear that, Doctor? MacGregor. Mac, not Mach. Do you see?

Kolenatý (*sits down*)   Of course. So why on earth wasn't her son called MacGregor?

Emilia   Out of consideration for his mother. Ferdy was

never allowed to know who she was.

Kolenatý   I see. Have you proof of all this?

Emilia   I might have. Carry on.

Kolenatý   Right. Well Prus's case against Gregor for
the Loukov estate continued, with some interruptions, to
this very day. That's almost a hundred years –
generations of Pruses and Szephazys and Gregors, with
legal assistance from successive generations of Doctor
Kolenatýs, thanks to whom the case will definitely be
lost by Mr Gregor, this very afternoon. And that will be
the end of it!

Emilia   Is Loukov really worth all that trouble?

Gregor   You bet it is!

Kolenatý   You see, in 1865 a coal-mine was
discovered on the land. It's hard to estimate the precise
value. Let's say around 150 million . . .

Emilia   Is that all?

Gregor   That would do me comfortably, Miss Marty.

Kolenatý   Now dear lady, if you've no further
questions . . . ?

Emilia   What do you need to win the case?

Kolenatý   What I need is a valid written will.

Emilia   Do you know if there is such a thing?

Kolenatý   Nothing so far.

Emilia   How silly.

Kolenatý   I'll say it is. (*Gets up.*) Any more questions?

Emilia   Yes. Who owns the old Prus house now?

Gregor   My adversary, Jaroslav Prus.

Emilia   What do people call those chests they put old

documents in?

Gregor   Archives?

Kolenatý   Vaults?

Emilia   Listen, there was one of them in the old Prus house, with a different drawer for each year. Peppy put all his old bills and invoices and other stuff there, do you understand?

Kolenatý   Yes, nothing unusual in that.

Emilia   One of the drawers was marked 1816. That was the year Peppy became acquainted with Ellian MacGregor. They met at the Congress of Vienna.

Kolenatý   I see.

Emilia   Into this drawer he put all the letters he received from Elli.

Kolenatý   How do you know all of this?

Emilia   Don't ask me that.

Kolenatý   Sorry. Go on.

Emilia   There are papers there from bailiffs and so on. Piles and piles of papers.

Kolenatý   I see.

Emilia   You think someone might have burnt them all?

Kolenatý   It's possible. We'll have to look.

Emilia   You're going there?

Kolenatý   Of course. If Mr Prus will let us.

Emilia   And if he doesn't?

Kolenatý   Then there's nothing we can do.

Emilia   You'll need to get to the drawer some other way, then.

Kolenatý   What, at midnight, with rope-ladder, false beard and gemmy? Miss Marty, Miss Marty, what must you think of us lawyers!

Emilia   But you must get hold of it!

Kolenatý   We may do. What then?

Emilia   You'll find the letters. With them is a yellow envelope . . .

Kolenatý   And in it . . . ?

Emilia   Prus's last will and testament. Written in his own hand and sealed.

Kolenatý (*jumps to his feet*)   By the living God!

Gregor (*also jumps up*)   Are you sure?

Kolenatý   What does it say? What's in there?

Emilia   Well, in it Peppy leaves the Loukov estate to his illegitimate son Ferdinand, born at Loukov on such and such a day – I forget the exact date.

Kolenatý   It says that?

Emilia   Word for word.

Kolenatý   And the envelope is sealed?

Emilia   Yes.

Kolenatý   With the old original seal of Josef Prus?

Emilia   Yes.

Kolenatý   Thank you. (*Sitting down.*) Would you mind telling us, Miss Marty, why you are leading us on?

Emilia   You don't believe me?

Kolenatý   Of course I don't! Not a word of it!

Gregor   *I* believe her. How dare you . . . ?

Kolenatý   Be reasonable, man. The envelope's sealed.

How can she possibly know what's inside it? Tell me that!

Gregor   But . . .

Kolenatý   The envelope's been sealed for a hundred years!

Gregor   Still . . .

Kolenatý   And in a strange house. Don't be childish, Gregor.

Gregor   I believe her, and that's that.

Kolenatý   Have it your own way. You have a great gift as a storyteller, Miss Marty. It's an unusual affliction. Have you always suffered from it?

Gregor   At least don't tell anyone else about it!

Kolenatý   You may trust me Miss Marty, I'll be the soul of discretion.

Gregor   I believe every word the young lady has told us, Doctor.

Emilia   You at least are a gentleman.

Gregor   So either you go at once to Prus's house and demand the papers from the year 1816 . . .

Kolenatý   I'm hardly likely to do that. Or . . . ?

Gregor   Or I'll take that telephone directory, pick the first lawyer I find and hand the case over to him.

Kolenatý   Fine, go ahead.

Gregor   Right. (*Goes to the telephone and thumbs through the directory.*)

Kolenatý (*approaches him*)   Stop this nonsense, Gregor. We've always been friends, I used to be your guardian . . .

Gregor   Dr Abel, Alfred. 20-7-60-1.

Kolenatý   For God's sake man, not him. That's my last advice, unless you want to be totally ruined.

Gregor (*into the phone*)   Hello? 20-7-60-1?

Emilia   Well done, Gregor!

Kolenatý   Don't make a fool of yourself! You wouldn't hand over your family business to that . . .

Gregor   Doctor Abel? Albert Gregor here. I'm calling from the office of . . .

Kolenatý (*snatches the phone*)   Wait! I'll go!

Gregor   To Prus?

Kolenatý   To the devil and back. Now you stay here and don't move!

Gregor   If you're not back within the hour, Doctor, I'll call . . .

Kolenatý   Shut up! I beg your pardon, madame. Please don't let him lose what's left of his mind. (*Hurries out.*)

Gregor   At last!

Emilia   Is he really as stupid as he appears?

Gregor   No, no, he's just terribly down-to-earth – he doesn't expect miracles. I always expect miracles. Then you turned up. How can I ever thank you?

Emilia   For what?

Gregor   You see, I feel certain we'll find this will. I don't know why I believe you so absolutely. Perhaps because you're so beautiful.

Emilia   How old are you?

Gregor   Thirty-four, Miss Marty. All my youth I've lived only to get my hands on those millions. You can't think what it's like. I've been a fool. I didn't know how else to live . . . If you hadn't come . . .

Emilia   You have debts?

Gregor   Yes. Tonight I would have shot myself.

Emilia   What nonsense!

Gregor   I won't play games with you, Miss Marty.
There was no hope, then out of the blue you appeared
– dazzling, amazing, mysterious – and you saved me . . .
Are you laughing at me?

Emilia   No. You're being silly, that's all.

Gregor   Fine, I won't talk about myself. Dear Miss
Marty, we're alone. Please, talk to me, explain it all to
me.

Emilia   What is there to explain? I've told you
everything.

Gregor   These are family matters, family secrets. It's
uncanny. I beg you, tell me how you know so much?

Emilia *shakes her head.*

Gregor   You can't?

Emilia   I won't.

Gregor   How did you know about the letters? How
long have you known about them? Who told you? Who
are you in contact with? I must know, do you
understand?

Emilia   It's a miracle!

Gregor   Yes, a miracle. But every miracle has an
explanation, otherwise life would be unbearable. Who
are you? Why did you come?

Emilia   As you see. To help you.

Gregor   Why me? What's in it for you?

Emilia   That's my affair.

Gregor Mine too, Miss Marty. I owe you everything, all I possess, life itself. Tell me, what sacrifice can I lay at your feet?

Emilia I see. You want to give me something. My cut, I think it's called.

Gregor Please, don't call it that. Just call it gratitude. It's offensive when . . .

Emilia I don't need anything. I have enough.

Gregor Excuse me, Miss Marty, only paupers have enough. The rich never.

Emilia (*loses her temper*) Look at him! The scoundrel's offering me money!

Gregor (*ashamed and touched*) I'm sorry, I'm bad at accepting kindness. (*Pause.*) They call you the divine Marty, but in our world even a fairy-tale prince expects his share. It's only right. Understand, we're talking about millions here.

Emilia So my little boy's feeling generous already. (*Goes to the window and looks out.*)

Gregor Why do you talk to me as if I were a child? I'd give away half of my inheritance, Miss Marty, if you'd only . . .

Emilia Yes?

Gregor It's awful how small I feel beside you.

Pause.

Emilia (*turns*) What's your name?

Gregor What? Gregor, of course.

Emilia Your real name I mean.

Gregor MacGregor. But everyone calls me Gregor.

Emilia No, your first name silly!

Gregor   Albert.

Emilia   And Mummy calls you Bertie, doesn't she?

Gregor   Yes. Well, Mother's long dead now . . .

Emilia   Oh, everything's dead or dying. (*Pause.*)

Gregor   So what was she like – Ellian MacGregor I mean?

Emilia   At last! I thought you'd never ask!

Gregor   Do you know anything about her? Who was she?

Emilia   She was a great singer.

Gregor   Was she beautiful?

Emilia   Very.

Gregor   So she loved my . . . my great-great-grandfather?

Emilia   Yes. Perhaps. In her way.

Gregor   Where did she die?

Emilia   I don't know. That's enough for now, Bertie. Another time.

Pause.

Gregor (*approaches her*)   Emilia!

Emilia   I'm not Emilia to you.

Gregor   So what am I to you? Please stop teasing me. It's humiliating! Imagine for a moment that I owe you nothing. That you're just a . . . a beautiful woman who has dazzled me with her beauty. Listen. Let me tell you something. I'm seeing you for the first time. No, don't laugh at me. You're intoxicating, exotic!

Emilia   I'm not laughing at you, Bertie. But you're being an idiot.

Gregor   Yes, I'm an idiot. I've never felt such an idiot as I do now. You're wonderful, provoking. Like a call to arms. Have you ever seen the blood of battle? It drives a man wild. And you – one can see it at once, there's something terrible and wild about you. You've lived a lot, seen a lot. I wonder why nobody's killed you yet.

Emilia   Don't start, Bertie!

Gregor   No, let me finish! You were rude and familiar to me, and it threw me off-balance. The moment you walked in I could feel it . . . Hot and wild, like a furnace . . . What was it? A man smells it and stiffens like an animal. There's something terrible about you. Did anyone ever tell you that before? You're maddening and terrible, Emilia, you must know that.

Emilia (*wearily*)   Maddening? Don't say that! Here, look at this! (*Comes close to* **Gregor**, *her back to the audience.*)

Gregor (*stares at her in horror, then shrieks*)   For pity's sake, Emilia, what are you doing? (*Stumbles back.*) Don't Emilia! You're old! It's horrible!

Emilia (*quietly*)   You see? Go Bertie, leave me.

Pause.

Gregor   Forgive me, I must have been mad. (*Sits down.*) I've been ridiculous, haven't I?

Emilia   Listen Bertie, do I look very old?

Gregor (*not looking at her*)   No, you're beautiful. Maddeningly beautiful.

Emilia   You know what you could give me?

Gregor (*lifts his head*)   What?

Emilia   You've offered me things. You know what I'd really like from you?

Gregor   Everything I have is yours.

Emilia   Listen Bertie, do you speak Greek?

Gregor   No.

Emilia   Well they're of no value to you then. Give me the Greek papers.

Gregor   Which papers?

Emilia   The ones Peppy Prus gave Ferdy Gregor – you know, your great-grandfather. They're not worth anything, but they mean a lot to me. Will you get them for me?

Gregor   I don't know anything about any papers.

Emilia   Nonsense. You must have them. Peppy promised to give them to Ferdy. For God's sake Bertie, tell me you have them!

Gregor (*rising*)   But I haven't!

Emilia (*rising abruptly*)   Don't lie to me, you little fool! You must have them, you hear? That's what I came here for!

Gregor   So where are they?

Emilia   How would I know? Find them, Bertie! Bring them to me! Use your brain!

Gregor   Maybe Prus has them.

Emilia   Get them off him then. You have to help me!

The telephone rings.

Gregor   One minute. (*Goes to answer it.*)

Emilia (*slumps in the armchair*)   Find them, for God's sake! Find them!

Gregor (*into the telephone*)   Hello, Kolenatý's office . . . No, he's not here. Shall I give him a message? This is Gregor speaking. Yes, *the* Gregor . . . Good . . . Thanks. (*Hangs up.*) It's over.

Emilia   What is over?

Gregor   Gregor versus Prus. The High Court has just announced its verdict. It's not official yet.

Emilia   And?

Gregor   I've lost.

Pause.

Emilia   Couldn't that brainless lawyer of yours have requested an adjournment?

Gregor *silently shrugs his shoulders.*

Emilia   You can still appeal, can't you?

Gregor   I don't know. I don't think so.

Emilia   That's ridiculous.

Pause.

Listen Bertie, I'll settle all your debts, understand?

Gregor   Why should you look after me? I never asked you to.

Emilia   Be quiet. I'll pay everyone, all right? And now you can help me look for the manuscript.

Gregor   Emilia . . .

Emilia   Call me a cab . . .

Kolenatý (*entering briskly, followed by* **Prus**)   Found it! Found it! (*Throws himself on his knees before* **Emilia**.) I beg your forgiveness a million times, madame! I'm a silly old donkey, and you are omniscient!

Prus (*shaking* **Gregor**'s *hand*)   Congratulations on a splendid last will and testament!

Gregor   Don't bother. You've just won.

Prus   Won't you go for a re-trial?

Gregor   What?

Kolenatý (*rises*)   We'll appeal, old chap. Goes without saying.

Emilia   Was everything there?

Kolenatý   Yes it was. The will and a few other things . . .

Prus   Won't you introduce me to the lady?

Kolenatý   Apologies. Miss Marty, this is Mr Prus, our arch-enemy.

Emilia   Pleased to meet you. So where are the letters?

Kolenatý   Which letters?

Emilia   The ones from Ellian.

Prus   I'm keeping them. Mr Gregor has no need of them.

Emilia   Will he get them later?

Prus   Undoubtedly, if he wins the inheritance. Something to remember his noble great-great-grandmother by.

Emilia   Listen, Bertie . . .

Prus   Ah, so you two already know each other. I thought as much.

Gregor   Forgive me, I made Miss Marty's acquaintance only . . .

Emilia   Be quiet, Bertie. You will return the letters to me, Prus, won't you?

Prus   Return? Are they yours to return?

Emilia   No but they're Bertie's, and he'll give them to me.

Prus   I'm indebted to you, Miss Marty. It's good to

know what one has in one's house. I'll be sending you a bouquet of flowers.

Emilia That's hardly generous. Bertie offered me more.

Prus A lorry-load of flowers, maybe?

Emilia No – millions and millions!

Prus And you accepted?

Emilia Heaven forbid!

Prus Just as well. Never count on anything!

Emilia What, is something else missing?

Prus Perhaps it's only a detail. Let's say the document proving that the son he mentions, this Ferdinand, is definitely Ferdinand Gregor. They can be so pedantic, these lawyers.

Emilia You mean something in writing?

Prus Something, at least.

Emilia Fine. I'll send something round in the morning, Doctor.

Kolenatý You carry such a thing around with you, for God's sake?

Emilia (*brusquely*) What's so surprising about that?

Kolenatý Nothing surprises me any more. Gregor, perhaps you should call that 2-7-6-1 number after all.

Gregor Doctor Abel? Why?

Kolenatý Because it seems to me, old chap, that . . . that . . . Well, we'll see.

Prus I think you'd better accept my flowers, Miss Marty.

Emilia Why?

Prus   Flowers are more ... dependable.

Curtain.

Act Two

The stage of a great theatre, bare and messy from last night's performance. Props, scenery, lighting equipment, general backstage disorder. At the side of the stage is a pile of flowers, at the front is a podium topped by a theatrical throne.

Cleaner Heavens what a performance last night. Did you see all the flowers?

Stagehand No I didn't.

Cleaner I've never heard such applause. They went wild. Shouting the place down! That Marty must have taken at least fifty curtain-calls, and still they didn't stop.

Stagehand The woman must be raking it in!

Cleaner You're telling me. Think what the flowers alone must have cost. She didn't even take all of them! Look at that pile of them over there.

Stagehand I went to listen from the wings, but when she's singing you come over all funny.

Cleaner I tell you, I was sobbing. I can't help it. I'm listening and all of a sudden the tears are running down my face, and I'm crying like a baby.

Enter **Prus**.

Cleaner May I help you, sir?

Prus Is Miss Marty around? They told me at the hotel she was here.

Cleaner She's with the director, sir, she'll soon be out. She left her things in the dressing-room.

Prus Fine, I'll wait. (*Walks to one side.*)

Cleaner He's the fifth so far. It's like a doctor's waiting-room in here!

Stagehand   I wonder if a woman like that has men in her life.

Cleaner   You bet your life she has!

Stagehand   Bloody heck! So . . .

Cleaner   So what? What are you looking like that for?

Stagehand   I just can't help thinking . . . (*Moves to leave.*)

Cleaner   Bit out of your league, isn't she? (*Exit from the other side.*)

Kristina (*enters*)   Come on Janek, there's no one here!

Janek (*following her*)   Won't they throw me out?

Kristina   No, there are no rehearsals today. Oh Janek, I'm so unhappy!

Janek   What about? (*Trying to kiss her.*)

Kristina   Please Janek, don't kiss me. I – I have other problems now. Oh Janek, I mustn't think about you now!

Janek   But Kristy!

Kristina   Listen Janek, if I want to *be* someone I have to change! I mean it. I must be sensible. I must think of one thing and one thing only, then I'm bound to succeed. Don't you see?

Janek   I see.

Kristina   I must think only about music. You know Miss Marty, how wonderful she is?

Janek   Yes, but . . .

Kristina   You don't know. It's her technique, it's stunning. Last night I couldn't sleep a wink, I just tossed and turned and worried myself sick. Should I leave the

stage or not . . . ? Oh Janek, if I had just a little
talent. . . !

Janek   But you *do*!

Kristina   You think so? Really? You think I should go
on singing? But that means the end of everything, you
see. It means music and nothing else.

Janek   Come Kristy, you can see me just a little –
twice a day, for a few minutes . . .

Kristina (*sits on the throne*)   That's just it, not even for a
few minutes. It's awful, Janek, I can't stop thinking
about you, horrible man. I can't help it. All I ever think
about is you.

Janek   Kristy, if you only knew how I . . . I think
about you all the time.

Kristina   It's all right for you, you don't sing . . . No
Janek, I've made up my mind. Please don't try to stop
me.

Janek   No, no, it's not fair! I won't let you. I . . .

Kristina   Please Janek. Be a sensible boy. Don't make
it harder for me! I have to start being serious. Do you
want me to be some poor unknown girl because of you?
Besides, my voice is still developing, I mustn't strain it.

Janek   Fine, I'll do the talking.

Kristina   No, Janek. It's all over between us. For
good. We'll see each other once a day.

Janek   But . . .

Kristina   For the rest of the day we'll be strangers. I
shall work terribly hard, Janek. Sing, think, study –
nothing else. I want to be a – you know – a *grande dame*,
like Miss Marty. Come, sit up here with me, silly, there's
plenty of room. No one's around. So d'you think she
loves anyone?

Janek (*sits on the throne next to her*)   Who?

Kristina   Miss Marty.

Janek   Marty? I expect so.

Kristina   Really? I can't understand why. She's so grand and famous. Why should she love anyone? You don't know what love means for a woman. It's . . . demeaning . . .

Janek   No, it's not!

Kristina   What do you know? I mean it. A woman forgets about herself, stops believing in herself, just follows him around blindly like his servant, like his . . . Oh I could slap myself sometimes!

Janek   But . . .

Kristina   Everyone's in love with Miss Marty, everyone who sees her, and she doesn't give a damn.

Janek   That's not true!

Kristina   She even scares me a bit.

Janek   Kristina! (*Stealing a kiss.*)

Kristina (*letting him*)   Don't Janek, someone might see us!

Prus (*steps forward*)   Don't mind me, I didn't see anything.

Janek (*jumping off the throne*)   Father!

Prus   No need to run away. (*Approaches.*) Miss Kristina, I'm so pleased to meet you. Unfortunately the boy hasn't given me the good news yet!

Kristina (*steps down from the throne and screens* **Janek**)   Excuse me, Mr Prus came here only to . . . to . . .

Prus   Which Mr Prus?

Kristina   This Mr . . .

Prus   This isn't Mr Prus, young woman, this is Janek. How long has he been after you?

Kristina   It's been a year now.

Prus   Fancy! Don't take the little scamp too seriously, miss, I know him. As for you, my boy ... Well, I wouldn't want to interrupt anything, but don't you think this place is a trifle – inappropriate?

Janek   If you think you can embarrass me, Father, you're wrong.

Prus   Excellent. A man should never be embarrassed.

Janek   I never thought you'd snoop on me like this.

Prus   That's good Janek, stand up for yourself!

Janek   I mean it. There are some things which I forbid, which ... about which nobody ...

Prus   Quite right too, my boy. Give me your hand.

Janek (*putting his hands behind him with sudden childish fear*)   No Father, please! Not that!

Prus (*extends his hand*)   Well?

Janek   Father! (*Hesitantly puts out his hand.*)

Prus (*seizes his hand in an iron grip*)   That's better, see? Manly and hearty.

Janek *screws up his face, trying to control himself, finally shouting out in a spasm of pain.*

Prus (*letting go his hand*)   What a hero, he can stand anything!

Kristina (*with tears in her eyes*)   How can you be so cruel!

Prus (*gently takes her hand*)   Ah, but these golden hands will soothe his ...

Vítek (*hurries in*)   Kristy! Kristina! Here you are! (*Stops* *in his tracks.*) Mr Prus?

Prus   Don't let me disturb you. (*Steps aside.*)

Kristina   What is it, Daddy?

Vítek   You're in the papers, Kristy! They're all writing about you! Even in the review on Marty. Fancy, right next to Marty!

Kristina   Show me!

Vítek (*opens the paper*)   Here. 'This little role was sung for the first time by Miss Vítek.' How about that?

Kristina   And the others?

Vítek   Nothing there. You know, just Marty, Marty, Marty. As if there was no one else in the world but Marty.

Kristina (*happily*)   Look Janek, there's my name!

Vítek   Kristy, who is this?

Kristina   This is Mr Prus.

Janek   Janek.

Vítek   How do you know him?

Janek   The young lady was kind enough to . . .

Vítek   Excuse me, my daughter can tell me herself. Come along Kristy

Emilia (*entering, addressing the wings*)   Thank you gentlemen, thank you, now please let me go. (*Notices* **Prus**.) What, another one?

Prus   No, Miss Marty, I wouldn't presume. I'm here on another matter.

Emilia   You weren't at the theatre yesterday?

Prus   Of course I was.

Emilia   I should hope so too! (*Seats herself on the throne.*)

Don't let anyone else in. I've had enough. (*Looks at*
Janek.) This is your son?

Prus Yes. Here, Janek.

Emilia Come Janek, let me look at you. Were you at
the theatre yesterday?

Janek Yes.

Emilia Did you like me?

Janek Yes.

Emilia Can't he say anything but yes?

Janek Yes.

Emilia Your son is an imbecile.

Prus I'm ashamed of him, madame.

Gregor *enters with a bouquet of flowers.*

Emilia Ah, Bertie! Hand them over!

Gregor For yesterday evening. (*Presents the flowers.*)

Emilia Let's see. (*Extracts a jewel-case from the bouquet.*)
Here, take this back. (*Returns the case to him.*) It was good
of you to come. Thanks for the flowers. (*Throwing them
onto the pile of flowers in the corner.*) Did you enjoy my
performance?

Gregor No, I didn't. Your singing is so perfect it
almost hurts. And you . . .

Emilia Yes?

Gregor Well you seemed bored. Your voice is
extraordinary, but not quite human. It's as if you're
bored. You're cold, frozen, numb.

Emilia You felt it? Well maybe there's something in
what you say. I sent that stupid document to your stupid
lawyer. You know, the one about Ellian. So how's the
case going?

Gregor   I don't know. I don't care. I don't think about it any more.

Emilia   So now you're giving me stupid bits of jewellery, you little donkey! Take it back this instant! What possessed you?

Gregor   What do you care?

Emilia   You borrowed money, didn't you? You ran to the money-lenders and borrowed money. (*Rummages through her handbag and flourishes a wad of notes.*) Here, take this!

Gregor (*steps back*)   You're offering me money? What are you thinking of?

Emilia   Take it or I'll box your ears!

Gregor (*flares up*)   I beg your pardon!

Emilia   Don't get on your high horse with me, my boy, or I'll get cross! I'll teach you to run up debts! Take it, you hear me?

Prus (*to* **Gregor**)   For God's sake take the money!

Gregor (*grabs the money; to* **Emilia**)   You have a strange way of talking to me. (*Gives the money to* **Vítek**.) Here, take it to the cashier and deposit it in Miss Marty's account.

Vítek   As you wish, sir.

Emilia   Hey you! It's for him, understand?

Vítek   As you wish, madame.

Emilia   Were you at the theatre last night, Mr Vítek? Did you enjoy my performance?

Vítek   Goodness, I'll say I did! You were like Strada!

Emilia   You heard Strada? Listen, Strada had no voice. She squeaked like a mouse.

Vítek Come now, Strada died a hundred years ago!

Emilia So much the better! You should have heard her. Strada, Strada, Strada! All this fuss about Strada!

Vítek I beg your pardon – of course I didn't hear her, but History tells us . . .

Emilia History tells us lies, you mean! Listen Mr Vítek, Strada squeaked, Corona had dumplings in her throat, Agujari honked like a goose, Faustina wheezed like a walrus. That's History!

Vítek Well if you please . . . In this area . . . in the field of music . . . I don't . . .

Prus (*smiling*) Vítek doesn't give a hang just so long as you don't knock his beloved French Revolution!

Emilia Why is that?

Prus The French Revolution – it's his hobby.

Emilia What's so special about it?

Prus I don't know. Ask him about his Citizen Marat . . .

Vítek Oh no! I'd rather not, if you please!

Emilia Wasn't he the deputy with the sweaty hands?

Vítek No, that isn't true!

Emilia Yes it is, he had hands like a toad! Brr!

Vítek I beg to differ! There's no evidence! It's a mistake!

Emilia I just know, all right? And what about the fat one with the pockmarked face? What's his name?

Vítek Which one, if you please?

Emilia The one who got his head chopped off.

Vítek Danton?

Emilia   That's him. He's even worse.

Prus   Why?

Emilia   His teeth are rotten. *Dégoûtant.*

Vítek (*increasingly aggrieved*)   Please, you really mustn't say such things. History has nothing to say about this ... Danton's teeth weren't rotten. You can't prove it. And even if they were, what would it matter? It's irrelevant.

Emilia   It's not irrelevant, it's disgusting!

Vítek   Please, I cannot permit you to speak like this ... Danton ... I beg your pardon, but you really mustn't. There'd be nothing great left in History.

Emilia   There never was.

Vítek   I beg your pardon?

Emilia   There never was anything great in History. I know.

Vítek   But Danton ...

Emilia   Listen to the man! He's trying to pick a quarrel with me!

Prus   How rude of him.

Emilia   Not rude, just stupid.

Gregor   Shall I bring in some more people for you to be rude to, Vítek?

Emilia   It won't be necessary. They'll come anyway – crawling in on all fours.

Kristina   Janek, let's go.

Emilia (*yawns*)   What a pair, those two! (*To* **Vítek**.) Have they flown to the moon yet?

Vítek   I beg your pardon?

Emilia Come, have they . . . you know . . .
together . . . ?

Vítek For God's sake, no!

Emilia There's nothing to it! Why, would you be
upset if they had?

Vítek Kristy, can it be true . . . ?

Kristina Daddy . . . how can you . . .

Emilia Be quiet, goose. It hasn't happened yet, but it
soon will. It's not worth the bother, you know.

Prus Is anything worth the bother?

Emilia Nothing. Absolutely nothing.

Hauk-Šendorf (*wandering in with a bouquet of
flowers*) Forgive me, I . . .

Emilia Which one is this?

Hauk-Šendorf Forgive me, dear lady . . . (*Kneels before
the throne.*) Madame, if only you knew . . . (*Sobs.*) Forgive
me, forgive me . . .

Emilia What's the matter with him?

Hauk-Šendorf You! You! You're so like her!

Emilia Like who?

Hauk-Šendorf Eugenia! Eugenia Montez!

Emilia (*rises*) Who?

Hauk-Šendorf Eugenia! You see, I knew her . . . God
. . . it was fifty years ago!

Emilia Who's this old boy?

Prus Mr Hauk-Šendorf, madame.

Emilia Maxie? (*Descends from her throne.*) My God, get
up off the floor!

Hauk-Šendorf (*rises*)   May I call you Eugenia?

Emilia   Call me what you like, old man. Am I so like her?

Hauk-Šendorf   Like her? Dear lady, yesterday at the theatre I thought you were her! Eugenia! If only you knew! The voice! The eyes! She was divine! She was beautiful! My God, the forehead . . . (*Suddenly startled.*) But you're taller.

Emilia   Taller?

Hauk-Šendorf   Just a little. May I? See, Eugenia came up to here on me. I could kiss her forehead.

Emilia   I bet you kissed other places too!

Hauk-Šendorf   I beg your pardon? You are – the image of her, dear lady! May I give you these flowers?

Emilia (*takes the flowers*)   Thanks.

Hauk-Šendorf   Let me feast my eyes on you!

Emilia   Come dear, sit down. Quick Bertie, a chair! (*Sits back on her throne.*)

Janek   Just a minute! (*Runs off for a chair.*)

Kristina   Not there! (*Runs off after him.*)

Prus (*to* **Hauk-Šendorf**)   Cher Comte . . .

Hauk-Šendorf   Mr Prus! Forgive me, I didn't see you. What a delightful surprise! How are you?

Prus   Well, and you?

Hauk-Šendorf   How's the case going? Did you send that man packing?

Prus   Far from it! Let me introduce you, Mr Gregor . . .

Hauk-Šendorf   Ah, Mr Gregor! How delightful!

Gregor   Thank you.

Janek *and* **Kristina** *bring in chairs.*

Emilia   Hey lovebirds, have you two been quarrelling?

Janek   Not exactly.

Emilia   Sit down, Maxie.

Hauk-Šendorf   Thank you, how kind. (*Sits down.*)

Emilia   Sit down, you two. Little Bertie can sit on my lap.

Gregor   You're too kind.

Emilia   All right, stand then.

Hauk-Šendorf   Beautiful, divine lady. I beg you on bended knee to forgive me.

Emilia   Forgive you for what?

Hauk-Šendorf   For being an old fool. What do you care about this woman who's been dead all these years?

Emilia   *Is* she dead?

Hauk-Šendorf   Yes.

Emilia   That's bad.

Hauk-Šendorf   Fifty years dead. You see I loved her then, fifty years ago. *Chula negra* they called her down in Andalucia. *Gitana*, the gypsy girl. Yes, she was a gypsy. I was at the embassy in Madrid at the time. Fifty years ago. 1870 it was.

Emilia   Yes.

Hauk-Šendorf   She sang and danced in the market-place. *Alza! Hola!* The world went mad about her! Castanets! *Vaya, gitana!* I was very young then you see, and she was . . .

Emilia   A gypsy.

Hauk-Šendorf *Vaya, querida!* God, she was on fire! She was unforgettable, unforgettable ... Believe me, a man doesn't recover from a thing like that. I lost my mind and didn't ever find it again ...

Emilia Yes.

Hauk-Šendorf You see I'm an idiot, madame. Hauk the idiot. God, what's the word for it?

Gregor Mad?

Hauk-Šendorf That's it. Raving mad. See I left everything with her there, and since then I've been barely alive. *Salero! Mi Dios,* you look so like her! Eugenia! Eugenia! (*Weeps.*)

Prus Steady on, Hauk old chap!

Hauk-Šendorf Perhaps I should go now.

Emilia See you later, Maxie.

Hauk-Šendorf Right ho. So I may ... come again, may I? (*Rises to his feet.*) My deepest respects, madame ... God, when I look at you ...

Emilia (*leaning forward*) Kiss me.

Hauk-Šendorf Forgive me?

Emilia *Besame mucho, bobo!*

Hauk-Šendorf *Jesus mil veces,* Eugenia!

Emilia Animal! *Un besito!*

Hauk-Šendorf Eugenia, *moza negro, nina querida ...* (*Kisses her.*) *Es ella,* it's her! *Gitana endiablada, ven conmigo, pronto!*

Emilia *Yo no lo soy, loco! Hasta mañana!*

Hauk-Šendorf *Vendre, vendre mis amores!*

Emilia *Vaya!*

Hauk-Šendorf (*wandering off*)   *Vendre! Hijo de Dios, ella misma!* (*Exit.*)

Emilia (*clapping her hands*)   Next! Anyone else want something from me?

Vítek   If you please, Miss Marty, if you could kindly autograph this photo for Kristy . . .

Emilia   Silly nonsense! All right, for Kristy then. Pen! (*Signs.*) Run along now.

Vítek (*bows*)   A thousand thanks. (*Exit with* **Kristina**.)

Emilia   Next?

Gregor   When you're alone.

Emilia   Some other time then. Anyone else? Well, I'll be off.

Prus   Please, one moment.

Emilia   You want something?

Prus   Obviously.

Emilia (*yawning*)   Quick, I'm exhausted.

Prus   I wanted to ask you something. You seem to know a lot about Joseph Prus and so on.

Emilia   What if I do?

Prus   Are you perhaps familiar with a certain name?

Emilia   Which name?

Prus   Let's say . . . Makropulos?

Emilia (*stands up abruptly*)   What?

Prus (*also stands*)   Are you familiar with the name Makropulos?

Emilia (*composes herself*)   Absolutely not, never heard of it. Now scram, everyone. Go home, leave me in peace.

Prus (*bowing*)   I apologise.

Emilia   Not you. You stay. Janek can go. What's wrong with him? Has he seen a ghost?

Exit **Janek**.

Emilia (*to* **Gregor**)   And what do you want?

Gregor   I have to talk to you.

Emilia   Not now Bertie, I'm busy.

Gregor   But I must talk to you!

Emilia   Please dear, run along now! You can come back later, all right?

Gregor   I will. (*Leaves, bowing coldly to* **Prus**.)

Emilia   At last!

Pause.

Prus   Forgive me Miss Marty, I'd no idea the name would upset you so much.

Emilia   What does the Makropulos business mean to *you*?

Prus   I'm asking you. Please, madame, sit down. This may take a while. (*Both sit down. Pause.*) First let me ask you a personal question. Perhaps too personal.

Emilia *nods silently.*

Prus   Do you have any special interest in the person of Mr Gregor?

Emilia   No.

Prus   So you've no particular interest in his winning the case?

Emilia   No.

Prus   Thank you. I can't force you to tell me how you

know what was locked in my chest. That's your secret, it seems.

Emilia   Yes.

Prus   Well, you knew there were certain letters in there. You knew Prus's will was in there – still sealed. . . ! Did you happen to know something else was in there too?

Emilia (*rises in great agitation*)   What? You found something else? What is it? Tell me!

Prus   I don't know. I'd like to ask you that.

Emilia   You don't know what it is?

Prus   I thought perhaps Kolenatý . . . or Gregor . . .

Emilia   Not a word.

Prus   Well, lying with the will is a sealed envelope, addressed in Josef Prus's handwriting. 'To be delivered by hand to my son Ferdinand', it says. Nothing more.

Emilia   And you didn't open it?

Prus   Of course not, it's not addressed to me.

Emilia   So give it to me.

Prus (*rising*)   You? Why?

Emilia   Because I want it. Because . . . because . . .

Prus   Well?

Emilia   Because it's mine by right.

Prus   By which right, may I ask?

Emilia   No, you may not. (*Sits.*)

Prus   Ah, another of your secrets.

Emilia   Exactly. Will you give it to me?

Prus   No.

Emilia   In that case, Bertie will give it to me since it belongs to him.

Prus We'll see about that. Tell me what is inside the envelope.

Emilia No. (*Pause.*) So what do you know about this ... Makropulos business?

Prus Sorry, but what do *you* know about this Ellian MacGregor woman?

Emilia You have her letters.

Prus You know anything about her private life? What do you know about the little ... whore?

Emilia (*jumps up*) How dare you?

Prus (*rises*) But dear lady, whatever is the matter? Why should you be interested in some woman of ill-repute who died a hundred years ago?

Emilia I'm not remotely interested in her. (*Sits down.*) So she was a whore, was she?

Prus Look, I've read her letters. A most – ah – passionate little creature.

Emilia You shouldn't have read them ...

Prus There are some extraordinary erotic details there. I'm no longer a young man, madame, but I confess even the most inveterate womaniser wouldn't be up to some of the things this ... good lady got up to in the bedroom.

Emilia You were going to say whore.

Prus The word isn't strong enough, Miss Marty.

Emilia Listen, give me those letters!

Prus What, you want to pick up some of her bedroom tricks?

Emilia Perhaps.

Pause.

Prus You know what I'd like to know?

Emilia What?

Prus What *you're* like in bed.

Emilia So now who's interested in bedroom tricks?

Prus Maybe I am.

Emilia Maybe I remind you of this Ellian.

Prus Heaven forbid!

Emilia All right, she was an adventuress, she slept with men. What's so bad about that?

Prus What was her real name?

Emilia Ellian MacGregor. It's on her letters.

Prus I beg your pardon, there's nothing but 'E.M.' on them.

Emilia It must stand for Ellian MacGregor.

Prus It might stand for any number of names. Emilia Marty, for one. Eugenia Montez. A thousand other names . . .

Emilia But this is Ellian MacGregor, from Scotland!

Prus Or Elina Makropulos, from Crete, in Greece.

Emilia (*suddenly furious*) Damn and blast you! Get out!

Prus I see, so you *do* know something!

Emilia Get out! Leave me alone! (*Pause. Raises her head and stares at him.*) How the devil did you know?

Prus It's quite simple. The will mentions a certain Ferdinand Makropulos, born 20 November 1816, in Loukov.

Emilia *looks away.*

Prus   I read it yesterday evening. This very morning at Loukov, at four a.m., the bailiff was leading me in his nightshirt to see the register of births and deaths. The poor man had to stand there holding a lantern for me while I read it.

Emilia   So what did you find?

Prus   The record of his birth. Here. (*Takes out a notebook and reads.*) '*Nomen infantis*: Ferdinand Makropulos. *Dies nativitatis*: 20 November 1816. Status: illegitimate. Father: blank. Mother: Elina Makropulos, born Crete.' That's all.

Emilia   Anything else?

Prus   Nothing. It's enough.

Emilia   Poor little Bertie! So now Loukov will stay yours, eh Mr Prus?

Prus   As long as we don't hear from Mr Makropulos it will.

Emilia   And the sealed envelope?

Prus   That will be put in safe-keeping for him.

Emilia   And if no Mr Makropulos appears?

Prus   Then no one will get it. It'll just stay there under seal.

Emilia   In that case he'll come, understand? And you'll lose Loukov.

Prus   It's all in the hands of God.

Emilia   How can you be so stupid! (*Pause.*) Listen. Give me the envelope!

Prus   I wish you wouldn't keep talking about that envelope.

Emilia   Makropulos will claim it.

Prus   Who is this Makropulos then? Where are you hiding him? In your luggage?

Emilia   You want to know who Makropulos is? It's Bertie – MacGregor, Gregor, Makropulos – they're all the same!

Prus   Gosh, him again?

Emilia   Yes. Elina Makropulos and Ellian MacGregor were the same person too. MacGregor was just her stage name. Now do you see?

Prus   Perfectly. So Ferdinand Gregor was her son?

Emilia   As I keep trying to tell you.

Prus   Why wasn't he called Makropulos then?

Emilia   Because Ellian wanted the name to vanish from the face of the earth.

Prus   Let's drop the subject, dear lady.

Emilia   You don't believe me?

Prus   I didn't say that. I didn't even ask where you got your information from.

Emilia   Good God, I've nothing to hide! I'll tell you everything, Prus, as long as you keep it to yourself. This Ellian – Elina Makropulos – was my aunt.

Prus   Your aunt?

Emilia   Yes, my mother's sister. There, now you know everything.

Prus   Of course. What a terribly simple explanation.

Emilia   You see?

Prus   (*rises*)   What a pity none of it's true, Miss Marty.

Emilia   You're calling me a liar?

Prus   I'm afraid I am, yes. It would have made more

sense to say she was your aunt's great-grandmother.

Emilia   Of course, you're right. (*Pauses, gives* **Prus** *her hand.*) Goodbye.

Prus (*kisses her hand*)   Perhaps I may express my admiration for you some other time.

Emilia   Thank you.

Prus *moves to leave.*

Emilia   Wait! Give me the envelope!

Prus (*turns around*)   Say that again?

Emilia   I'll buy it! I'll buy the letters. How much do you want? Name your price!

Prus (*walks back to her*)   I'm sorry, miss. I can't discuss this with you here. You'd better send someone to me to negotiate for you.

Emilia   Why?

Prus   So I can throw them out of the door. (*Leaves with a slight bow.*)

Pause. **Emilia** *sits without moving, her eyes closed.* **Gregor** *enters the room and stands there silently.*

Emilia (*after a pause*)   Is that you, Bertie?

Gregor   Why are your eyes closed? Has someone hurt you? Are you in pain?

Emilia   I'm tired, Bertie. Keep your voice down.

Gregor (*approaches her*)   Really? I warn you. If I do, I won't be responsible for what I say. I'll just keep saying foolish things to you, do you hear me, Emilia? I implore you, forbid me to be quiet! I love you! I adore you! I'm possessed by you! You're not laughing? I thought you'd jump up and slap me in the face, and I'd have loved you even more for it! I love you. What, are you asleep?

Emilia I'm cold, Bertie, I'm icy cold. Don't let me make you cold, Bertie.

Gregor I love you, Emilia! Be warned, you treat me badly but it makes me happy! I could strangle you when you humiliate me. You drive me wild, Emilia, you make me want to kill you. There's something horrible about you. But even that is beautiful. You're evil, Emilia, you're wicked and terrible. An animal, without human feelings . . .

Emilia Come Bertie, that's not true!

Gregor Yes it is! Nothing matters to you. You're cold, like a knife, like a corpse risen from the grave. It's perverse to love you, but I do. I'm yours, Emilia. I love you so much I could tear the flesh from my own body. . . !

Emilia Tell me, do you like the name Makropulos?

Gregor Stop! Don't torment me! I'd give my life to possess you. Do whatever you like with me. Anything. Perverse, unheard-of things. I love you, Emilia, I'm a lost man!

Emilia So listen, go to that lawyer of yours and make him give me back the document I sent him.

Gregor Is it forged?

Emilia No, Albert, on my honour. But we need another one, with the name Makropulos on it. Wait, let me explain. Ellian . . .

Gregor Don't bother. I've heard enough of your stories.

Emilia No, wait. You must be rich, Bertie. I want you to be very, very rich.

Gregor Will you love me then?

Emilia Stop it, Bertie. You promised to get me the

Greek papers. Prus has them, do you hear? First you get the inheritance, then you give me the papers.

Gregor   Will you love me then?

Emilia   Never, do you understand? Never!

Gregor (*sits down*)   I'll kill you, Emilia, I swear I will!

Emilia   Nonsense. Three little words and it's all over, finished. So he wants to kill me. See this scar here on my neck? That was another man who wanted to kill me. Shall I take my clothes off and show you all my other little love mementoes? You think I'm here to give you the pleasure of killing me?

Gregor   I love you!

Emilia   Love, love, love. So kill yourself, silly boy. How ridiculous you all are. If only you knew how tired I am, and how little I care! If you only knew!

Gregor   What's wrong? Tell me what's wrong!

Emilia (*wringing her hands*)   Wretched Elina!

Gregor (*softly*)   Come Emilia, we'll go away together. Nobody has ever loved you as I do. I know ... there's something dreadful about you. But I'm young, Emilia, I'm strong. I'll flood you, melt you with love, you'll forget everything. Then you can cast me aside like an empty shell. How about it, Emilia?

Loud, regular snores are audible from **Emilia**.

Gregor (*jumps up angrily*)   What? Asleep? She's made a fool of me. She's sleeping like a drunk! (*Reaches out to her.*) Emilia it's me, me, nobody else is here. (*Bends closer to her.*)

The **Cleaner**, *standing behind them, coughs to warn him of her presence.*

Gregor (*stands up*)   Oh it's you. The young lady has fallen asleep. Don't wake her. (*Kisses* **Emilia**'s *hand and* *hurries off.*)

Cleaner (*approaches* **Emilia** *and silently watches her*)   Poor thing. I can't help feeling sorry for her. (*Exit.*)

Pause. **Janek** *enters from the wings, stops ten paces from* **Emilia** *and turns to her.*

Emilia (*stirs*)   Is that you, Bertie?

Janek (*retreats*)   No it's just me, Janek.

Emilia   Janek, come here. Will you do me a favour?

Janek   Yes Miss Marty, anything.

Emilia   Anything I want?

Janek   Yes, Miss Marty.

Emilia   Something great, Janek? Something heroic?

Janek   Yes, Miss Marty.

Emilia   And what will you want from me in return?

Janek   Nothing, Miss Marty.

Emilia   Come closer. That's better. You know, you can do something really nice for me. Your father has a sealed envelope at home. 'To be delivered by hand to my son Ferdinand', it says. I'm not sure where it is – in his desk or his safe perhaps. *Compris?*

Janek   Yes, Miss Marty.

Emilia   Bring it to me.

Janek   Will Father give it to me?

Emilia   No he won't. You'll have to take it from him.

Janek   I couldn't do that, Miss Marty!

Emilia   Is my little boy scared of his Daddy?

Janek   I'm not scared, it's just . . .

Emilia   Just what? Janek, it's of sentimental value only,

I swear. But I want it, desperately.

Janek   Well, I'll try.

Emilia   Really?

Prus (*entering from the shadows*)   Don't bother looking, Janek, it's in the safe.

Janek   Father! You again!

Prus   Go! (*To* **Emilia**.) Well well, Miss Marty, what a surprise! I thought he was hanging around the theatre because of his Kristina, when in fact he . . .

Emilia   And you? Why are you hanging about the theatre?

Prus   I was hoping to see you.

Emilia (*comes very close to him*)   So give me the envelope.

Prus   It's not mine.

Emilia   Then get it for me.

Prus   When?

Emilia   Tonight.

Prus   It's a deal.

Curtain.

Act Three

*A hotel suite. On the left a window, on the right a door into the corridor. In the middle is the entrance to **Emilia**'s bedroom, separated from the rest of the suite by heavy drapes. **Emilia** enters from the bedroom in her peignoir, followed by **Prus** in dinner jacket but no collar. **Prus** sits silently on the right. **Emilia** goes to the window and pulls up the blinds, flooding the room with early morning light.*

Emilia (*turns from the window*)   Well? (*Pause, goes to **Prus**.*) Give it to me.

Pause.

You hear? Give me the envelope!

Prus *silently takes a leather wallet from his pocket and removes a sealed envelope which he places on the table. **Emilia** takes the envelope, goes to her dressing-table, switches on the lamp and examines the seal. Hesitating briefly, she rips open the envelope with her hairpin and pulls out a yellowing folded manuscript. She reads with a gasp of joy, then quickly folds it and tucks it into the décolletage of her nightgown. Gets up.*

Emilia   Excellent!

Pause.

Prus (*quietly*)   You cheated me.

Emilia   You got what you wanted.

Prus   You cheated me. You were cold as ice. I felt I was holding a corpse. (*Shivers.*) To think I stole someone's papers for that! Thank you very much!

Emilia   What do you care about one little sealed envelope?

Prus   I'm sorry I ever met you. I should never have given it to you. I feel like a thief. Disgusting! Disgusting! Disgusting!

Emilia   You want breakfast?

Prus   I want nothing from you. Nothing! (*Stands, goes to her and peers at her.*) Look at me, show me your face! I don't know what I gave you . . . Maybe it has some value . . . Maybe its only value was the seal on it – and my ignorance . . . (*Waves his hand in despair.*)

Emilia (*rises*)   You want to spit in my face?

Prus   No, in my own face.

Emilia   Go ahead. (*A knock at the door. She goes to it.*) Who is it?

Maid   It's me, madam.

Emilia   Come in. (*Unlocks the door.*) Bring us some breakfast.

Maid (*enters in her nightdress and dressing-gown, out of breath*)   Excuse me madam, is Mr Prus here?

Prus (*turns round*)   Why? What is it?

Maid   Mr Prus's manservant is downstairs. Says he has something to tell him.

Prus   How the devil did he . . . ? Tell him to wait. No stay here. (*He goes to the bedroom.*)

Emilia (*to* **Maid**)   Do my hair. (*Sits at her dressing-table.*)

Maid (*letting down* **Emilia**'s *hair*)   I had such a fright, madam. The janitor called me and said Mr Prus's manservant was here and wanted to see you. Lord, he was in such a state, he couldn't speak. I was shocked, madam. Something terrible must have happened.

Emilia   Careful, you're pulling my hair!

Maid   White as a sheet he was, madam. I got such a fright.

Prus (*appears from the bedroom wearing his collar and tie*)   Will you excuse me a moment? (*Exit stage-right.*)

Maid (*brushing* **Emilia**'s *hair*)   Some bigwig isn't he? I wish I knew what happened. Lord, you should have seen his servant, shivering and shaking.

Emilia   I should like some scrambled eggs please.

Maid   He was holding some papers in his hand. Should I go down and listen?

Emilia (*yawning*)   What time is it?

Maid   Just after seven.

Emilia   Switch the lights off and stop jabbering.

Pause.

Maid   That servant, his lips were all blue . . .

Emilia   You're pulling my hair, stupid. Show me the comb. Look at those hairs!

Maid   Sorry madam, I can't help it, my hands are shaking. Something awful must have happened.

Emilia   So I'm supposed to let you tear my hair out? Pull yourself together!

Prus *returns from the corridor mechanically smoothing an unopened letter in his hand.*

Emilia   That didn't take long.

Prus *reaches for a chair and collapses into it.*

Emilia   What will you have for breakfast?

Prus (*hoarsely*)   Send the girl away.

Emilia (*to* **Maid**)   You may leave. I'll ring when I need you.

Exit **Maid**.

Emilia   Well?

Prus   Janek. He shot himself.

Emilia   Oh no!

Prus   His head . . . shattered . . . unrecognisable. He's dead.

Emilia   Poor thing. Who's the letter from?

Prus   My servant told me . . . This letter . . . Janek wrote it. They found it on his . . . Look, blood . . .

Emilia   So what does he say?

Prus   I can't open it . . . I'm afraid . . . How did he know I was here with you? Why did he send it to me here? Do you think he . . . ?

Emilia   What, saw you?

Prus   Why did he do it? Why did he kill himself?

Emilia   Read it and find out.

Prus   Could you . . . read it first?

Emilia   No I couldn't.

Prus   I think it concerns you too. Won't you please open it?

Emilia   Certainly not.

Prus   I should go to him . . . I should . . . shall I open it?

Emilia   By all means.

Prus   So be it. (*Tears the envelope and removes the letter.*)

Emilia *attends to her nails.*

Prus *reads silently, then drops the letter with a gasp.*

Emilia   How old was he?

Prus   So that was the reason!

Emilia   Poor Janek.

Prus   He was in love with you.

Emilia Really?

Prus (*sobbing*) My child, my only son . . . (*Covers his face with his hands.*) Just eighteen years old! My boy! My Janek! Christ, I was so hard on him, I never kissed him, never praised him! He wanted me to, but I thought, no, life is hard, he must be tough like me. I never knew him! God, that boy worshipped me!

Emilia And you didn't know?

Prus Christ, if only he was alive! To fall in love so pointlessly. He saw me coming to see you, he waited two hours by the gate. Then he went home and . . .

Emilia (*takes the comb and combs her hair*) Poor thing.

Prus Eighteen years old! My Janek, my child, look at his childish handwriting, 'Daddy, now I know what life is about, I want you to be happy. But I . . .' (*Gets up.*) What on earth are you doing?

Emilia (*with hair-pins in her mouth*) Combing my hair, stupid, what do you think?

Prus Perhaps you don't understand. Janek was in love with you. He killed himself for you!

Emilia Ah well, so many of them killed themselves.

Prus And you go on playing with your hair?

Emilia Am I supposed to run around with my hair a mess because of him? Do you want me to tear it out? My maid pulls it enough as it is.

Prus (*backs away from her*) Be quiet, or I'll . . . !

A knock at the door.

Emilia Come in!

Maid (*enters now dressed*) A Mr Hauk-Šendorf wishes to see you, madam.

Emilia Send him in.

Exit **Maid**.

Prus   You're going to see him now, in front of me?

Emilia   Go to the bedroom, then.

Prus (*lifts the drapes and goes to the bedroom*)   *Canaille!*

Enter **Hauk-Šendorf**.

Emilia   *Buenos Dios*, Maxie. Why so early?

Hauk-Šendorf Hush! (*Tiptoes towards her and kisses the nape of her neck.*) Get dressed Eugenia, we're leaving!

Emilia   Where?

Hauk-Šendorf   Home, to Spain. Tee-hee, my wife doesn't know! I can't go back to her now, you see! *Por Dios*, Eugenia, hurry up!

Emilia   Are you mad?

Hauk-Šendorf   Yes I am! God forgive me, I'm a certified lunatic! They can send me back whenever they want, like a parcel! See, I have to get away from them. And you're going to take care of me!

Emilia   In Spain? What would I do there?

Hauk-Šendorf   *Hola*, you'll dance, of course! *Mi Dios hija*, I used to be so jealous! You'll dance, *sabe*? And I'll clap my hands. (*Produces a pair of castanets from his pocket.*) *Ay salero, vaya querida!* (*Pauses.*) Stop, who's that crying?

Emilia   Oh, nobody.

Hauk-Šendorf   Hush! It's a man's voice.

Emilia   Oh yes. It's someone in the other room. Apparently his son died or something.

Hauk-Šendorf   Died? That's sad. *Vamos, gitana!* See what I'm taking with me? Jewels, Mathilda's jewels! Mathilda's my wife, you see. But she's old. It's ugly to be old. It's horrible, horrible to be old. I was old myself, but then you came back, and . . . *Chiquirita!* Now I'm twenty again! Do you believe me?

Emilia   *Si, si, señor.*

Hauk-Šendorf   You haven't grown old either. Listen my dear, you must never grow old. Lunatics live long lives, you see? And I'm going to live for a long, long time. Live and love! (*Clicks his castanets.*) Love and live, la, la, la! My gypsy, will you come?

Emilia   Yes, I'll come.

Hauk-Šendorf   A new life! We'll start again at twenty, what? God, what bliss. Remember? (*Laughs.*) You remember? Nothing else matters. *Nada!* Shall we go?

Emilia   *Si, ven aqui, chucho.*

A knock at the door.

Come in.

Maid   Mr Gregor wants to see you, madam.

Emilia   Let him in.

Hauk-Šendorf   What does he want? *Mi Dios.* Let's hurry.

Emilia   Wait.

Enter **Gregor**, **Kolenatý**, **Kristina** *and* **Vítek**.

Emilia   Hello, Bertie. For goodness' sake who else have you brought here with you?

Gregor   You're not alone?

Hauk-Šendorf   Ah Mr Gregor, how delightful. How are you?

Gregor (*pushes* **Kristina** *before* **Emilia**)   Look at this child's eyes. You heard what happened?

Emilia   Janek?

Gregor   And you know why?

Emilia   Pah!

Gregor   You have that boy on your conscience, understand?

Emilia   Is that the reason you've brought all these people to see me, including a lawyer?

Gregor   Not the only reason, no. And you can drop that tone with me.

Emilia (*flares up*)   How dare you! What do you want with me?

Gregor   You'll find out. (*Sits down without ceremony.*) Kindly tell me what your real name is.

Emilia   You want to interrogate me?

Kolenatý   Nothing of the sort, Miss Marty. Just a friendly chat.

Gregor   Mr Vítek, the picture please. (*Takes the photo of* **Emilia** *from* **Vítek**.) Did you sign this for Miss Kristina? Is this your signature?

Emilia   Of course it is.

Kolenatý   I see. May I ask if you sent me this document yesterday? It's a handwritten statement by one Ellian MacGregor, dated 1836, stating that she is the mother of Ferdinand MacGregor. Is it genuine?

Emilia   It is, yes.

Gregor   The ink on it is fresh. You know what that means? It means it's a forgery, your ladyship!

Emilia   How does that concern me?

Gregor   The ink is fresh. Watch please, gentlemen. (*Wets his finger and rubs it on the paper.*) It's still smudging. Any comment, Miss Marty?

Emilia   No.

Gregor   It was written yesterday, understand? By the same hand that signed this photograph. And with a most distinctive signature.

Kolenatý   Like Greek. The 'a', for instance . . .

Gregor   Did you or did you not sign this document?

Emilia   I will not be interrogated by you!

Hauk-Šendorf   Forgive me gentlemen, really, but . . .

Kolenatý   Keep out of this, sir. It's a serious matter. Can you tell us, Miss Marty, how you came by this document?

Emilia   It was written by Ellian MacGregor, I swear.

Kolenatý   When? Yesterday morning?

Emilia   What does it matter?

Kolenatý   It matters very much, dear lady. Very much indeed. When did Ellian MacGregor die?

Emilia   Stop it! I'm not saying another word!

Prus (*enters quickly from the bedroom*)   Please, let me see the document.

Kolenatý (*rises*)   God, you! Emilia, what is the meaning of this?

Hauk-Šendorf   Mr Prus, what a delightful surprise! How are you?

Gregor   Your son . . .

Prus   I know. The document, please.

Kolenatý *hands it over.*

Prus   Thank you. (*Raises his monocle and reads.*)

Gregor (*crosses over to* **Emilia**, *quietly*)   What is he doing here? I have a right to know.

Emilia (*eyes him*)   What right would that be?

Gregor   The right of a man who is going out of his mind.

Prus (*puts down the document*)   The handwriting is genuine.

Kolenatý   So it was written by Ellian MacGregor, dammit!

Prus   No. It was written by the Greek woman, Elina Makropulos. The same handwriting as on my letters, there's no doubt about it.

Kolenatý   But those were written by . . .

Prus   Elina Makropulos. There never was an Ellian MacGregor, gentlemen. It was a mistake.

Kolenatý   You could have fooled me. And the signature on the photograph?

Prus (*looks at it*)   Undoubtedly the handwriting of Elina Makropulos.

Kolenatý   Well I never! And the writing's identical to the signature on your photograph, Kristina!

Kristina   Leave Miss Marty alone!

Prus (*returning the photograph*)   Thank you. Forgive me for interfering. (*Sits to one side with his head in his hands.*)

Kolenatý   For God's sake, how are we to clear up this mess?

Vítek   If you please sir, maybe Miss Marty's signature just happens to be similar.

Kolenatý   But of course. And Miss Marty just happens to come to our office. And this just happens to be a forgery. You know what you can do with that sort of talk, Vítek!

Emilia   May I remind you, gentlemen, that I'm

planning to leave the country this morning?

Kolenatý   For God's sake Miss Marty, you can't do that! Please stay on your own surety, so we won't have to call . . .

Emilia   You want to put me behind bars!

Gregor   Not yet. You have the chance . . .

A knock at the door.

Kolenatý   Come in!

Maid (*puts her head round the door*)   Two men are downstairs. They're looking for Mr Hauk-Šendorf.

Hauk-Šendorf   What? I'm not going . . . ! For God's sake, I implore you, not that . . . !

Vítek   I'll ask them what they want. (*Exit.*)

Kolenatý (*goes to* **Kristina**)   Kristina, stop crying! I'm so dreadfully sorry . . .

Hauk-Šendorf   Dear me, isn't she lovely. Now then young lady, don't cry.

Gregor (*stands by* **Emilia**, *quietly*)   My car is downstairs. Come with me, we'll cross the border. Or . . .

Emilia   Hah, don't count on it!

Gregor   It's either me or the police. Are you coming?

Emilia   No.

Vítek (*returns*)   Mr Hauk is wanted by his . . . ah . . . doctor, and another man. They want to escort him home.

Hauk-Šendorf   Forgive me. (*Giggles.*) They've caught up with me! Ask them to wait, will you?

Vítek   I did, sir.

Gregor   Gentlemen, since Miss Marty isn't prepared to

explain herself, we have no option but to search her luggage.

Kolenatý   Oh we've no right to do that, Gregor! Privacy, harassment laws and so on.

Gregor   Shall I call the police then?

Kolenatý   I wash my hands of it.

Hauk-Šendorf   Excuse me Mr Gregor, but as a gentleman . . .

Gregor   Sir, your doctor and a detective are outside. Shall I ask them to come in?

Hauk-Šendorf   Please, not that. But Mr Prus, surely . . .

Prus   Go on, do what you like with the woman . . .

Gregor   Very well then, let's start. (*Goes to* **Emilia**'s *writing desk.*)

Emilia   Keep away from there! (*Jumps up and reaches in the drawer of her dressing-table.*) Don't you dare!

Kolenatý (*lunges at her*)   No you don't, miss. (*Grabs something from her hand.*)

Gregor (*opens the drawer without turning round*)   What, was she going to shoot me?

Kolenatý   It's loaded too. We'd better leave it. Shall I call someone in?

Gregor   No, we'll sort this out ourselves. (*Goes through* **Emilia**'s *drawers.*) Talk among yourselves. Don't bother me.

Emilia (*to* **Hauk-Šendorf**)   You're a gentleman, Max. *Y usted quiere pasar por caballero?*

Hauk-Šendorf   *Cielo de mi*, what can I do?

Emilia (*to* **Kolenatý**)   Doctor, you're an honourable man.

Kolenatý I'm sorry miss, you're wrong. I am a well-known villain and a scoundrel, and my real name is the Thief of Baghdad.

Emilia (*to* **Prus**) Prus then, you're a gentleman, you can't . . .

Prus Please, don't talk to me.

Kristina (*sobbing*) You're all horrible! I can't bear you doing this to Miss Marty. Leave her alone!

Kolenatý My thoughts exactly, child. It's horrible what we're doing, horrible and unpleasant.

Gregor (*throws a bunch of papers onto the table*) Here Miss Marty, I see you carry an entire archive around with you. (*Goes to the bedroom.*)

Kolenatý Lots of material here for you to look at, Mr Vítek. Excellent stuff, a real treat. Do you want to sort it out?

Emilia Don't you dare!

Kolenatý Dear lady, I'm asking you politely not to move. Otherwise I might cause you grievous bodily harm, according to paragraph 91 of the Criminal Code.

Emilia You call yourself a lawyer?

Kolenatý I think I'm beginning to acquire a taste for crime. I've always had a talent for it, but sometimes a man only realises his true vocation in his middle years.

Vítek Tell me Miss Marty, when is your next singing engagement?

Emilia *says nothing.*

Hauk-Šendorf *Mon dieu, je suis désolé, désolé.*

Vítek Did you read your reviews today?

Emilia   No.

Vítek (*takes some newspaper clippings from his pocket*)   They're excellent, Miss Marty. Listen: 'A voice of breathtaking beauty and power . . . Extraordinary fullness in the upper register . . . Supreme confidence . . .' And here: 'Her spellbinding beauty and dramatic power . . . A performance unique in the history of our opera, possibly in the history of music itself . . .' The entire history of music, Miss Marty, pretty good eh?

Kristina   But it's true!

Gregor (*returns from bedroom with an armful of documents*)   Here Doctor, this is all so far. (*Throws more documents onto the table.*) Get busy.

Kolenatý   With pleasure. (*Sniffs the documents.*) They've got the dust of history on them, Miss Marty. This is historic dust, Vítek.

Gregor   We also found a seal bearing the initials E.M., the same seal as we found on the documents of Ellian MacGregor.

Prus (*rising*)   Show me.

Kolenatý (*looking through the documents*)   My God Vítek, the date on this is 1603!

Prus (*handing him back the seal*)   This is the seal of Elina Makropulos. (*Sits down.*)

Kolenatý (*looks at the documents*)   There's no knowing what we may find.

Hauk-Šendorf   Good God . . .

Gregor   Mr Hauk, do you recognise this medallion? Isn't that your coat-of-arms?

Hauk-Šendorf (*examines the medallion*)   Yes, it is. I gave it to her myself!

Gregor   When?

Hauk-Šendorf Then! Fifty years ago, in Spain!

Gregor Who did you give it to?

Hauk-Šendorf To her, Eugenia! Eugenia Montez! Don't you understand?

Kolenatý (*looking up from the documents*) There's something in Spanish here. Do you speak Spanish?

Hauk-Šendorf Yes, yes, of course. Let me see. (*Giggles.*) Eugenia, this is from Madrid!

Kolenatý What?

Hauk-Šendorf From the police. Deportation order for immoral conduct. Ramera the Gypsy, also known as Eugenia Montez. Forgive me Eugenia, it was because of that quarrel we had, wasn't it?

Kolenatý My apologies. (*Looks through more papers.*) Passport, Elsa Miller, 79 . . . Death certificate Ellian MacGregor 1836 . . . Everything jumbled up together. Wait Miss Marty, let's arrange it by name. Ekaterina Myshkina, who's that?

Vítek Ekaterina Myshkina was a Russian singer in the forties, if you please sir.

Kolenatý You know everything, old chap!

Gregor It's amazing. They all have the same initials, E.M.

Kolenatý Miss Marty seems to be collecting these initials. I wonder if it's her hobby. Aha, '*Dein Peppy*', that would be your great-great-uncle, am I right Prus? Shall I read it to you? '*Meine liebste, liebste Ellian.*'

Prus Don't you mean Elina?

Kolenatý No it says Ellian, and on the envelope too, 'Ellian MacGregor, Hofoper, Wien.' Just wait, Gregor, we may win this case thanks to our *liebste, liebste* Ellian!

Emilia (*rises to her feet*)   Stop. Don't read any more.
These papers are mine!

Kolenatý   But we find them so incredibly fascinating!

Emilia   Don't read any more. I'll tell you everything.
Everything you want to know.

Kolenatý   Really?

Emilia   I swear it.

Kolenatý (*folds the documents and put them down*)   We
entreat your forgiveness, Miss Marty, for forcing you
to . . .

Emilia   Will you pass judgement on me?

Kolenatý   Heaven forbid, Miss Marty. Just a friendly
chat!

Emilia   No, I want a proper trial.

Kolenatý   I see. We'll do our best then, within our
competence. Shall we begin?

Emilia   No, it must look like a real court of law. With
a crucifix and all the rest of it.

Kolenatý   You're right. What else?

Emilia   First let me eat something and put on a dress.
I refuse to appear in court in my nightgown.

Kolenatý   Quite right too. It's important for the
defendant to be decently attired.

Gregor   What a farce.

Kolenatý   Quiet please, show respect for the court!
The accused is allowed ten minutes – will that be
enough for your toilette?

Emilia   Are you serious? I need at least an hour.

Kolenatý   Half an hour then, to prepare yourself and
consider your plea. We shall send for you. Now go.

Emilia   Thank you. (*Goes to the bedroom.*)

Prus   I must go . . . to Janek.

Kolenatý   Be back in half an hour.

Gregor   Doctor, can't you please be a bit serious?

Kolenatý   Quiet, Gregor. I'm being terribly serious. I know how to deal with her. She's a hysteric. Mr Vítek?

Vítek   Yes sir?

Kolenatý   Hurry to the undertakers and get us some crucifixes and crosses – candles, black crêpe, a Bible, all the usual paraphernalia. Run along now!

Vítek   Certainly, sir.

Kolenatý   And a skull!

Vítek   A human one?

Kolenatý   Human, cow, doesn't matter, so long as it represents death.

Curtain.

Act Four

Transformation

The same room, rearranged as a court. Dressing-table and writing-table, sofa and chairs are covered in black crêpe. On the larger table is a crucifix, a Bible, burning candles and a skull.
Kolenatý *presides behind the table as judge.* **Vítek** *is clerk.*
Gregor *sits at the smaller table as prosecutor.* **Prus, Hauk-Šendorf** *and* **Kristina** *sit on the sofa as jurors. To the right is an empty chair.*

Kolenatý She should be here by now.

Vítek Lord, I hope she didn't take poison!

Gregor Nonsense, she loves herself too much for that.

Kolenatý Bring in the accused.

Vítek *coughs and enters the bedroom.*

Prus Couldn't you have left me out of it?

Kolenatý No, we need your vote on the jury.

Kristina (*weeping*) It's . . . it's like a funeral!

Kolenatý Don't cry, Kristy dear, let the dead rest in peace.

Vítek *leads in* **Emilia**, *dressed in a magnificent outfit, holding a whisky bottle and a glass in her hand.*

Kolenatý Lead the accused to her place.

Vítek May I just say, sir, that the accused has been drinking whisky?

Kolenatý Is she drunk?

Vítek Yes sir. Very.

Emilia (*slumping against the wall*) Leave me alone! It was to give me courage. I'm thirsty!

Kolenatý Take the bottle from her!

Emilia (*clutches the bottle to her bosom*) No! I won't let you! Otherwise I can't speak! (*Laughs.*) You look like undertakers! How funny! Hah, look at little Bertie! Cut it out, Theotokos, I'll split my sides!

Kolenatý (*severely to* **Emilia**) Order in court!

Emilia (*startled*) Trying to scare me? Bertie, tell me this is just a joke?

Kolenatý Kindly speak only when asked to by the court. This is your place. Please be seated. The prosecutor will now present the case against you.

Emilia (*uncertainly*) Should I take the oath?

Kolenatý The accused never takes the oath.

Gregor The accused, Emilia Marty, a singer, is accused before God and this court of committing perjury and of forging documents for pecuniary gain, thus violating all laws of trust, decency and life itself, and thereby putting herself beyond human jurisdiction, which means that she must now answer before a higher court.

Kolenatý Does anyone have anything to add to the accusation? No? Then let us proceed to the cross-examination. The accused will rise. What is your name?

Emilia (*rising*) Me?

Kolenatý Yes, you, you, you! Speak up! What is your name?

Emilia Elina Makropulos.

Kolenatý (*whistles*) What did you say?

Emilia Elina Makropulos.

Kolenatý Place of birth?

Emilia Crete.

Kolenatý   Date of birth?

Emilia   You mean which year?

Kolenatý   How old are you?

Emilia   Guess!

Kolenatý   Around thirty?

Vítek   I'd say over thirty, sir.

Kristina   Over forty.

Emilia (*sticks her tongue out at her*)   Idiot!

Kolenatý   Don't trifle with this court please, madame!

Emilia   Do I look that old?

Kolenatý   For heaven's sake, just tell us when you were born!

Emilia   In 1585.

Kolenatý (*jumps up*)   When?

Emilia   The year fifteen hundred and eighty-five.

Kolenatý (*sits down*)   '85. So I suppose that makes you thirty-seven?

Emilia   Three hundred and thirty-seven. Yes.

Kolenatý   I must insist that you answer me seriously. How old are you?

Emilia   I am three hundred and thirty-seven years old.

Kolenatý   I'm warning you, Miss Marty! So who was your father?

Emilia   Hieronymus Makropulos, personal physician to Emperor Rudolf II.

Kolenatý   By Christ, I'm not asking her any more questions!

Prus   What is your real name?

Emilia   Elina Makropulos.

Prus   The same family as the Elina Makropulos who was the mistress of Josef Prus?

Emilia   The same.

Prus   How can that be?

Emilia   I was the mistress of Peppy Prus, you see. That Ferdy Gregor was our son.

Gregor   And Ellian MacGregor?

Emilia   I was her too.

Gregor   Are you mad?

Emilia   I'm your . . . great-great-grandmother, or something. Ferdy Gregor was my son, all right?

Gregor   Which Ferdy?

Emilia   Ferdinand Gregor of course, but he was registered as Ferdinand Makropulos, because I had to give my real name. Sometimes you have to.

Kolenatý   Naturally. And your date of birth?

Emilia   1585. *Christos Soter*, how many times do I have to tell you!

Hauk-Šendorf   Aha . . . forgive me . . . So you *are* Eugenia Montez!

Emilia   I was, Maxie, I was. But then I was only two hundred and ninety. I was Ekaterina Myshkina and Elsa Müller too, and God knows who else. One can't live with you people for three hundred years with the same name.

Kolenatý   Especially if you're a singer.

Emilia   I should think not.

Pause.

Vítek   So you lived in the eighteenth century too?

Emilia   Obviously.

Vítek   And you . . . you knew Danton – personally?

Emilia   I'll say I did. Disgusting creature.

Prus   So how is it you knew the contents of a sealed will?

Emilia   Because Peppy showed it to me before he put it there, so I'd tell that stupid Ferdy Gregor about it.

Gregor   Why didn't you?

Emilia   I never cared much about my offspring.

Hauk-Šendorf   Dear me, what a way for a lady to talk!

Emilia   It's years since I've been a lady, dear!

Vítek   Did you have other children?

Emilia   Twenty or so. One can't keep track of everything. A drink, anyone? Mother of God, I'm parched! My mouth is on fire! (*Collapses on a chair.*)

Prus   These letters signed 'Emilia' – were they all written by you?

Emilia   Yes, me. Listen, why don't you give them back to me? Sometimes I like to read them. Dirty, aren't they?

Prus   Did you write them as Elina Makropulos or as Ellian MacGregor?

Emilia   What does it matter? Peppy knew who I was. I told Peppy everything. I loved Peppy.

Hauk-Šendorf (*rises in a fury*)   Eugenia!

Emilia   Be quiet Maxie. Life was sweet with you too, old soldier! But Peppy was . . . (*Bursts into tears.*) I loved him more than any of the others! That's why I lent it to him. He begged and begged me . . .

Prus   What did you lend him?

Emilia   The secret. The document you gave back to me today. The sealed envelope. He said he wanted to try it. He promised he'd return it. But he hid it with his will! Maybe to make sure I came and collected it. But I didn't come till now. How did he die?

Prus   In a fever, in terrible pain.

Emilia   It was because of the formula! I knew it! Santa Maria, I told him so!

Gregor   So you came here just for this Greek thing?

Emilia   Haha, you're not having it now, Bertie! It's mine! I don't care about your stupid lawsuit! I don't care if you're one of my brats. I don't care how many thousands of them are running around the world. I just want the secret. I had to get my hands on it or I'd . . . I'd . . .

Gregor   You'd what?

Emilia   I'm growing old, Bertie. I'm at the end. I need to take it again. Touch me, Bertie, I'm like ice. (*Rises.*) Touch me, feel my hands! God, my hands!

Hauk-Šendorf   Tell us, what is this Makropulos secret?

Emilia   It shows you how to do it.

Hauk-Šendorf   To do what?

Emilia   How to keep a person alive for three hundred years. Keep them young for three hundred years. My father invented the formula for the Emperor Rudolf. You wouldn't know him, would you?

Vítek   Only from history, if you please.

Emilia   History teaches you nothing. History's rubbish.

God, what was I saying? (*Takes a sniff from a box.*) Anyone want some?

Gregor   What is it?

Emilia   Nothing. Cocaine or something. What was I saying?

Vítek   About Emperor Rudolf.

Emilia   Oh, him, he was bad! Alchemy, science – God, the things I could tell you about the man! Who was that astronomer who burst his bladder because he wasn't allowed to stand before him?

Kolenatý   Kindly keep to the subject.

Emilia   Anyway, so when he started getting old he began looking around for some miracle to make him young again – the elixir of life, you know. So then my father came to him and invented this secret remedy so he could stay young for three hundred years. Rudolf was afraid it might poison him, so he ordered him to try it out on his daughter. That was me. I was sixteen at the time. So Father tried it on me. They said it was a kind of miracle. But it wasn't, it was something else.

Hauk-Šendorf   What was it?

Emilia (*shivering*)   I can't tell you. No one can! For over a week I lay there delirious, in a high fever. But then I got better.

Vítek   And the Emperor?

Emilia   Nothing. He was livid. How could he be sure I'd live three hundred years? He locked my father in a tower, and I ran off with everything he'd written and ended up in Hungary or Turkey, I can't remember where now.

Kolenatý   Did you ever show the Makropulos secret to anyone?

Emilia   A few people over the years. A priest from the Tyrol in 1660, or something. Maybe he's still alive, I don't know. He was a pope once. Alexander, he called himself, or Pius. Something like that. Then there was an Italian officer. He was called Hugo. But he got killed. He was a handsome man. Wait, there was Nageli, and Ondrey, and that bastard Bombita, then Peppy Prus, who died of it. Peppy was the last, and it stayed with him. I don't know any more. Ask Bombita. Bombita's still alive, but I don't know what he calls himself now. You know he's one of those – what d'you call them – they marry rich widows for their money?

Kolenatý   So according to you, you are now two hundred and forty-seven years old?

Emilia   No, three hundred and thirty-seven!

Kolenatý   You're drunk! From 1585 to today makes two hundred and forty-seven!

Emilia   God, don't confuse me! It's three hundred and thirty-seven!

Kolenatý   What did you forge Ellian MacGregor's signature on those documents for?

Emilia   But I *am* Ellian MacGregor!

Kolenatý   Don't lie to us. You are Emilia Marty!

Emilia   Yes, but only for the last twelve years.

Kolenatý   Then you admit stealing that medallion from Eugenia Montez?

Emilia   Mother of God, it isn't true. Eugenia Montez . . .

Kolenatý   It's recorded in the minutes. You've already admitted it.

Emilia   It's not true!

Kolenatý   What are the names of your accomplices?

Emilia I have no accomplices!

Kolenatý Don't lie to us! We know everything. When were you born?

Emilia (*trembles*) 1585.

Kolenatý (*fills a glass*) Here! Drink this! All of it!

Emilia No, I won't! Leave me alone!

Kolenatý Drink. To the bottom. Quick!

Emilia (*in anguish*) What are you doing to me? Bertie? (*Drinks.*) My head – it's spinning . . . it's . . .

Kolenatý (*rises and goes to her*) What is your name?

Emilia I feel dizzy. (*Falls off the chair.*)

Kolenatý (*grabs her and lowers her to the floor*) What is your name?

Emilia Elina Makro . . .

Kolenatý Don't lie to me! You know who I am? I'm a priest! You're confessing to me!

Emilia *Pater – hemon – hos – eis – en – uranois –*

Kolenatý What is your name?

Emilia Elina – pulos.

Kolenatý The skull! Lord, take the soul of Thine unworthy servant Emilia Marty . . . mumble, mumble . . . *In saecolum* Amen . . . mumble, mumble . . . That's it. (*Drapes the skull with the black cloth and holds it before* **Emilia**.) Get up! Who are you?

Emilia Elina. (*Loses consciousness.*)

Kolenatý (*drops her on the floor with a thud*) Damn you! (*Stands and puts down the skull.*)

Gregor What happened?

Kolenatý She wasn't lying. Take all this stuff away.

Quick. (*Rings his buzzer.*) Gregor, get a doctor.

Kristina Did you give her poison?

Kolenatý Just a little.

Gregor (*standing by the door into the corridor*) Is the doctor still here?

Doctor (*enters*) Come along now Mr Hauk, we've been waiting for you over an hour. Let's get you home.

Kolenatý Wait. First this one please, Doctor.

Doctor (*standing over* **Emilia**) Passed out?

Kolenatý Poison.

Doctor Which one? (*Kneels by* **Emilia** *and sniffs her breath.*) Aha. (*Stands up.*) Make her comfortable.

Kolenatý You're her next of kin Gregor, take her to the bedroom.

Doctor Is there some hot water?

Prus Yes.

Doctor Lovely woman, eh? (*Writes a prescription.*) There, black coffee. And take this to the chemist. (*Goes to the bedroom.*)

Maid (*enters*) Madam rang?

Kolenatý Yes, she did. She needs black coffee, make it strong. And collect this from the chemist. Run along now.

Exit **Maid**.

Kolenatý (*sits in the middle of the room*) Dammit, there was something in what the woman said.

Prus Did you have to make her drunk to find that out?

Hauk-Šendorf I . . . forgive me, please don't laugh,

but I believe her.

Kolenatý You too, Prus?

Prus Oh yes.

Kolenatý Me too. You know what it means?

Prus That Gregor will get Loukov.

Kolenatý Do you mind?

Prus No. I've no heirs.

Gregor *returns with his hand wrapped in a cloth.*

Hauk-Šendorf How is she?

Gregor A bit better. But you know what? She bit me! Like an animal! And you know what? I believe her!

Kolenatý So do we, I'm afraid.

Pause.

Hauk-Šendorf My God, three hundred years old! Three – hundred – years!

Kolenatý Gentlemen, I must request utter discretion!

Kristina (*shudders*) Three hundred years! How horrible!

Maid *enters with the coffee.*

Kolenatý Kristy, you take it to Miss Marty like a sister of mercy!

Kristina *goes to the bedroom with the coffee. Exit* **Maid**.

Kolenatý (*after checking that both doors are closed*) Well now gentlemen, let's get our wits together. What are we going to do with it?

Gregor With what?

Kolenatý The Makropulos secret. This recipe for three hundred years of life. It's ours if we want it.

Prus It's in the cleavage of her dress.

Kolenatý We can get it out of there, gentlemen. This

matter can have unimaginable consequence. Now we must decide what to do with it.

Gregor You're not doing anything with it. That formula belongs to me. I am her heir.

Kolenatý Use your brain, man. As long as she's alive there'll be no heir. And she may stay alive for another three hundred years if she feels like it. But we can get it, understand?

Gregor Steal it, you mean?

Kolenatý If need be. Put aside your qualms, this is too important, for us and for humanity, to, ah . . . You follow me, gentlemen? Why should we let her keep it? Why should she and that scoundrel Bombita be the only ones to benefit from it?

Gregor Her descendants should come first.

Kolenatý Good grief, there could be any number of them! You'll hardly be the only one. Say you had such a thing in your hands, Prus, would you lend it to me? You know, so I could live for three hundred years?

Prus Certainly not!

Kolenatý You see, gentlemen? We must agree among ourselves what we should do with the secret.

Vítek (*rises*) I think we should make it public property.

Kolenatý No, no, Vítek, I don't think so.

Vítek We'll give it to everyone, to all humanity. Everyone has the same right to life! God, our lives are so short! Such a little time to be a man!

Kolenatý That can't be helped, Vítek.

Vítek It makes you weep, sir! Imagine, this human soul, this thirst for knowledge, a man's brain, his work, his love and creativity – all this, my God, and what does he achieve in his sixty years of life? What does he

learn? What can he enjoy? He never picks the fruit from
the tree he planted. He never even knows what men
knew before him. We leave our work unfinished without
being able to set an example. We die without having
lived! Jesus, we live so little!

Kolenatý Good God, man . . .

Vítek No time for joy, no time for thought. No time
for anything but endlessly scurrying around for our daily
crust! We see nothing, we learn nothing, we finish
nothing, not even ourselves – we're just particles. Why
did we live? Was it worth it?

Kolenatý Stop that Vítek, you want to make me
weep?

Vítek We die like beasts. God, what comes after life,
what is the immortality of the soul but a desperate cry
against the shortness of our lives? Man has never
accepted this animal span of life. We can't endure it, it's
too unjust. Man is more than a tortoise or a raven. Man
needs more time to live. Sixty years is slavery, an animal
existence, ignorance . . . !

Hauk-Šendorf Oh dear, oh dear, and I'm already
seventy-six!

Vítek Let's give everyone three hundred years of life!
It'll be the greatest thing since the creation! A liberation,
a completely new creation of man! God, what might we
achieve in three hundred years! A child and a pupil for
fifty years! Discover the world and everything in it for
fifty. A hundred years of useful labour. Then when
we've learnt everything, another hundred years of
wisdom – to rule, teach, set an example. Just think how
valuable a human life could be if it lasted three hundred
years. There'd be no wars. No rush, no fear, no
selfishness. Each person would have knowledge and
dignity. (*Clasps his hands.*) Sovereign, perfect, all-knowing,
the son of God, not a freak of nature. Let's give people

life! A full and human life!

Kolenatý That's all very nice, Vítek, but . . .

Gregor Three hundred years filing invoices. Three hundred years darning socks. Thanks a lot!

Vítek But . . .

Gregor Sovereign, all-knowing rubbish! You know perfectly well that most human jobs are bearable only because of ignorance.

Kolenatý From the legal and economic position alone it's untenable, man. Our social economic system is based on short lives. Contracts, pension schemes, securities, inheritance laws and so forth. And what about marriage? Who in their right mind would enter into an agreement with someone for three hundred years! You're an anarchist, Vítek! You want to destabilise the social order!

Hauk-Šendorf Forgive me – but after three hundred, everyone would get young all over again!

Kolenatý And live for ever! No, it wouldn't work.

Vítek One could forbid that. After three hundred years people would have to die.

Kolenatý You see! Now these human feelings of yours would order people to die?

Hauk-Šendorf With all due respect, I . . . perhaps we could divide the formula into smaller doses.

Kolenatý How would that work?

Hauk-Šendorf We could divide it into years, you see. One dose for each ten years of life. Three hundred is too many. No one would buy it. Ten years now, everyone would buy ten years.

Kolenatý So we set ourselves up in trade, selling years? It's an attractive idea! I can already see the orders: 'Rush us one thousand two hundred years of your formula.' 'Send two million years under plain cover to our Vienna branch.' Doesn't sound bad, Hauk!

Hauk-Šendorf   Well I'm not a businessman, but when one starts getting on in life one wants to buy a bit more. Three hundred years is too much though.

Vítek   Not for knowledge, it isn't.

Hauk-Šendorf   No one will buy knowledge. But ten years of happiness – gladly, yes.

Maid (*enters*)   This is from the chemist, sir.

Kolenatý   Thanks Louisa. How long would you like to live?

Maid (*giggles*)   Thirty years, maybe!

Kolenatý   No more?

Maid   No, what would I do with it? (*Exit.*)

Kolenatý   See, Vítek? (*Goes towards the bedroom.*)

Doctor (*comes out of the bedroom and takes the medicine*)   Thanks.

Hauk-Šendorf   How is she?

Doctor   Sick. (*Goes back into the bedroom.*)

Hauk-Šendorf   Oh dear, poor thing.

Prus (*rises*)   Gentlemen, a strange chain of coincidences has placed in our hands a certain secret which concerns the prolongation of life – assuming that it works, and that no one intends to misuse it for his own personal gain.

Vítek   My feelings exactly. We have to use it to prolong the life of everyone!

Prus   I think not. Only the strongest. The most capable. For the masses even the life of a mayfly is too long.

Vítek   With respect, sir . . . !

Prus   I'm not going to bandy words with you Vítek, I'll merely say that a normal stupid man never dies, a normal stupid man lives for ever without your help. Smallness reproduces itself without respite, like flies or mice. Only greatness dies. Only strength and talent die, because they're irreplaceable. It may be in our power to preserve them, to establish an aristocracy of long life.

Vítek   An aristocracy? You hear that, gentlemen? The privilege of life?

Prus   That's just it. Only the best deserve to live and breed. Capable men, leaders. No need to mention women here. But there are some ten, twenty thousand men who are irreplaceable. We can preserve them, give them supernatural power, develop their brains to superhuman levels of intelligence. Ten, twenty, a thousand superhuman rulers and creators.

Vítek   You mean a breed of bosses?

Prus   Exactly. Select those who have the right to unlimited life.

Kolenatý   And may I ask who would nominate such individuals? Governments? Plebiscite? The Swedish Academy?

Prus   No stupid voting! From hand to hand the strongest would pass life on. The masters of matter to the masters of spirit. Inventors to soldiers. Businessmen to dictators. The masters of life. A dynasty independent of the uncivilised herd.

Vítek   Until that herd claims *their* right to life!

Prus   No, the masters will claim it from *them*! From time to time a few of the strong ones will be killed, but what of it? Revolution is the privilege of slaves. Progress means replacing small, weak despots with stronger, bigger ones. The rule of the chosen few, who'll live long and privileged lives. The rule of reason over the masses. A superhuman authority of knowledge and power. These rulers will become unchallenged rulers of humanity. We have it in our power, gentlemen. We can abuse that power. I have no more to say. (*Sits down.*)

Kolenatý   Hm. Am I or Gregor to be among this chosen few?

Prus   No.

Gregor   But you are?

Prus   No longer, I fear.

Gregor   Gentlemen, stop this senseless talk. The formula is the possession of the Makropulos family. Let them do with it as they wish.

Vítek   What would that be?

Gregor   Only the heir of Elina Makropulos can decide that, whoever he may be.

Kolenatý   And he'll live for ever just because he was hatched from a union with some crazy hysterical female and a disreputable baron? A priceless inheritance, to be sure!

Gregor   Never mind that.

Kolenatý   I have the honour to know one gentleman from this family who is, if you'll forgive me, dear man ... To hell with it, he's a degenerate criminal. Nice clean family, eh?

Gregor   If you say so. They can be idiots, apes, cripples or fools for all it matters. They can be evil incarnate, it's not important. It's theirs. End of story.

Doctor (*enters from the bedroom*)   She'll be all right. Just keep her in bed.

Hauk-Šendorf   Yes, yes, in bed. That's good.

Doctor Come home now, Mr Hauk. I'll take you.

Hauk-Šendorf Oh dear, we were having such an important discussion. Please let me stay a little longer. You see . . .

Doctor They're waiting outside the door for you, Mr Hauk. Now be a good chap and come quietly.

Hauk-Šendorf Yes, yes . . . I . . . I'm coming.

Doctor Glad to be of assistance, gentlemen. (*Exit.*)

Kolenatý Keep your voices down. She needs to sleep.

Kolenatý (*to* **Kristina**) Come here, child. Would you like to live for three hundred years?

Kristina No I wouldn't.

Kolenatý And if you had the formula for it, what would you do with it?

Kristina I don't know.

Vítek Would you share it with everyone?

Kristina D'you think they'd be happier if they lived that long?

Kolenatý I think life's a bloody marvellous thing, don't you?

Kristina I . . . Don't ask me.

Hauk-Šendorf I'm sure we just all want to be happy, Miss Kristina!

Kristina (*covering her eyes*) Sometimes . . . sometimes we don't.

Pause.

Prus (*comes up close to her*) Thank you for that.

Kristina For what?

Prus For thinking of him.

Kristina   Thinking of him? I think of nothing else!

Kolenatý   And here we are, quarrelling about life eternal!

Emilia *enters like a shadow, a towel on her head. All rise.*

Emilia   I'm sorry I had to leave you for a while.

Gregor   How are you feeling?

Emilia   Empty. Horrible. My head is aching.

Hauk-Šendorf   There, there, it'll pass.

Emilia   No it won't. It'll never pass. I've had it for two hundred years.

Kolenatý   What exactly?

Emilia   Boredom. Melancholy. Emptiness. It's . . . oh you humans . . . you have no word for it. No language has a word for it. Bombita talked about it. It's horrible.

Gregor   What is?

Emilia   I don't know. Everything's so stupid. Empty, pointless. Do you really exist? Pehaps you're not real, perhaps you're objects, or shadows. What am I supposed to do with you?

Kolenatý   Would you like us to leave you?

Emilia   It makes no difference. To die or disappear behind doors, it's all the same. It's all the same if something exists or not – and you're getting all worked up about this stupid death of yours! You're strange – bah!

Vítek   What's wrong with you?

Emilia   It's not right to live so long!

Vítek   Why not?

Emilia   We weren't meant to. A hundred, a hundred and thirty years maybe. Then . . . then you realise, and your soul dies inside you.

Vítek   What do you realise?

Emilia   God, there are no words for it. You find you
don't believe in anything. Nothing. Just this emptiness.
Remember, Bertie, you said when I sang I was
frozen. See, art still keeps its meaning long after life has
lost it. It's just that once you've got the hang of it you
realise it's useless. As useless, Kristy, as snoring. Singing's
the same as silence. Everything's the same. There's no
difference.

Vítek   That's not true! When you sing . . . it changes
people, they become greater, better.

Emilia   People never get better. Nothing changes,
nothing. Nothing matters, nothing happens. Shootings,
earthquakes, the end of the world – nothing! You're
here, and I'm somewhere far, far away, three hundred
years away. If you only knew how easy your lives are!

Kolenatý   Why do you say that?

Emilia   You're close to things. Everything means
something! Everything has value in your few short years
of life, so of course you live it to the full. Oh my God,
if only I could get . . . (*Wrings her hands.*) Fools,
you're so happy! It's disgusting to see you so happy!
And all because of the stupid accident that you'll soon
be dead! You're interested in everything, like monkeys.
You believe in everything. Love, yourselves, honour,
progress, humanity, everything! Maxie, you believe in
pleasure. Kristina, you believe in love and faithfulness.
Prus, you believe in power. Vítek believes in all his
rubbish. Everyone, everyone believes in something. What
a life, you fools! What a wonderful life!

Vítek (*agitated*)   With respect madame, there are higher
things, values, ideals . . . aspirations . . .

Emilia   There are, but only for you. How can I put

it? Perhaps there's love, but it's only in your minds.
Grasp it and it's gone, nowhere, nowhere in the
universe. No one can love for three hundred years. Or
hope, or write, or sing. You can't keep your eyes open
for three hundred years. It's unbearable. Everything
grows cold, numb. Numb to good, numb to evil. Numb
to heaven, numb to earth. Then you see nothing exists.
Nothing. No sin, no pain, not even the earth, nothing.
The only thing that exists is something which has
meaning. And for you everything has meaning. Oh God,
I was once like you! I was a girl, I was a woman, I was
happy, I . . . I was a human being! God in heaven!

Hauk-Šendorf   So what happened, for God's sake?
What happened?

Emilia   If you only knew what Bombita told me. He
said we – we old ones know too much. But you know
much more, you fools. Much, much more! You know
love, greatness, purpose. You have everything. You
couldn't ask for more. You still have your lives! While
we go on and on, numb, frozen. Jesus Christ, I can't go
on. God, the solitude!

Prus   Why did you come for the formula, then? Why
did you want to live all over again?

Emilia   Because I dread death.

Prus   God, so not even the immortals are spared that?

Emilia   No.

Pause.

Prus   Miss Makropulos, we have been very unkind to
you.

Emilia   I don't feel it. But you were right. It's
degrading to live so long, to be so old. You know that
children run away from me? Kristina, do you hate me
very much?

Kristina   No, I just pity you terribly.

Emilia   Pity? You don't even envy me? (*Pause. Shivers and takes from her cleavage a folded document.*) It's written here: 'Ego Hieronymous Makropulos iatros kiasaros Rodolfu'. And so on, words and words of it, what you have to do. (*Stands.*) Take it Bertie. I don't want it any more.

Gregor   Thanks. I don't want it.

Emilia   No? Then you, Maxie. You want so much to live. You'll be able to make lots of love. Take it!

Hauk-Šendorf   Forgive me, but can one die of it? Does it hurt?

Emilia   Yes, it can hurt. Are you afraid?

Hauk-Šendorf   Yes.

Emilia   But you'll live for three hundred years.

Hauk-Šendorf   If . . . if it didn't hurt . . . (*Giggles.*) No, I don't want it.

Emilia (*to* **Kolenatý**)   Doctor, you're a clever man. Think what it could do for you. You want it?

Kolenatý   You're very kind, madame, but I want nothing to do with it.

Emilia   Vítek, you're a funny man, I'll give it to you. Who knows, perhaps you'll make humanity happy with it!

Vítek (*backs off*)   No, no thank you, if you please. I think I'd – rather not.

Emilia   Prus, you're strong, are you afraid of three hundred years?

Prus   Yes.

Emilia   God, nobody wants it then? No one's interested? (*To* **Kristina**.) You child, you haven't made a sound. Poor girl, I took your boyfriend – you have it.

You're beautiful. You'll live three hundred years. You'll sing like Emilia Marty. You'll be famous. Imagine, in a few years you'll start growing old, then you'll be sorry. Take it, child.

Kristina (*takes the paper*) Thank you.

Vítek What will you do with it, Kristy?

Kristina (*opens the paper*) I don't know.

Gregor You'll try it?

Kolenatý For God's sake, she's not afraid. Give it back to her!

Vítek Yes, give it back!

Emilia Leave her!

Pause.

Kristina *silently puts the formula over the flame of a burning candle.*

Vítek Don't burn it! It's a part of History!

Kolenatý   Look out!

Hauk-Šendorf } (*together*) For God's sake!

Gregor Take it from her!

Prus (*holds them back*) Let her!

A stunned silence.

Hauk-Šendorf Oh dear, oh dear! It doesn't want to burn!

Gregor It's parchment.

Kolenatý How slowly it's turning to ashes. Don't burn yourself, Kristy!

Hauk-Šendorf Leave just a little piece for me!

Silence.

Vítek   Eternal life! Now people will be looking for it for ever. Perhaps we had it here.

Kolenatý   And we might have lived for ever! Thanks a lot!

Prus   For ever? You have children?

Kolenatý   I have.

Prus   See, eternal life! If we thought of birth instead of death, life wouldn't be short! We can be creators of life . . .

Gregor   It's burning down. What a wild idea to live for ever. God, I can't help longing for it, yet I feel better for knowing it's impossible now.

Kolenatý   We're no longer young. Only Kristina could burn our fear of death so beautifully. Thank you Kristy, you did it well.

Hauk-Šendorf   Forgive me . . . may I . . . there's a strange smell in here of . . .

Vítek   (*opens the window*)   . . . burnt ashes.

Emilia   Haha, the end of immortality!

Curtain.

The White Plague

Characters

Court Counsellor Professor Sigelius
Doctor Galen
Father
Mother
Son
Daughter
First Clinic Assistant
Second Assistant
Marshal
Baron Krug
Baron Krug's son
Four Professors
Commissar
General
Marshal's daughter, *Annette*
Marshal's entourage
Minister of Health
Minister of Information
Adjutant
Nurse
First journalist
Second journalist
Doctors
Nurses
Three Lepers
Crowd

Act One

Three bandaged **Lepers.**

First Leper It's the Plague, that's what it is! There's one in every house! Hey neighbour, there's a white spot on your chin! That's all right, I can't feel a thing. Next he's falling to bits like me. It's the Plague!

Second Leper Nah, it's leprosy, the White Death. God's punishment. There must be a reason. A disease like this doesn't come from nowhere.

Third Leper Sweet Jesus – God in heaven – sweet Jesus!

First Leper Punishment, punishment! What for, tell me that! I've not lived, I've only known poverty. What sort of god punishes those who are punished already?

Second Leper It's God's curse, there must be a reason. It's skin now – you wait till it starts eating you up inside like him. (*Pointing to* **Third Leper.**)

Third Leper Sweet Jesus – God in heaven – sweet Jesus!

First Leper 'Course there's a reason. There's too many of us – half of us must snuff it to make room. You're a baker, you make room for another baker. I'm a poor man, I make room for another poor man so someone else can go cold and hungry. That's the reason for the Plague.

Second Leper It's not the Plague, it's leprosy! You go black with the Plague. With leprosy you're white as chalk, like us.

First Leper White or black, we've all had it. If only I didn't smell so bad.

Third Leper Sweet Jesus – merciful Christ!

Second Leper It's all right for you, you're on your own. Imagine when your poor wife and children can't stand you any more! What they have to suffer! Now my wife's found a spot on her breast. There's an upholsterer next door, screaming day and night, day and night . . .

Third Leper Sweet Jesus – merciful Christ – sweet Jesus!

First Leper Shut up, stupid leper! Nobody asked you!

Office of Court Counsellor Professor **Sigelius** *in the Lilienthal State Clinic.* **Sigelius** *sits at his desk. Enter* **Journalist**.

Sigelius Ah, Editor, do sit down. I can only spare you a few minutes. My patients, you know.

Journalist Sir, my paper needs information from the highest source . . .

Sigelius Ah, the so-called Peking Leprosy. I'm afraid you media chaps have sensationalised the whole thing – naively in my view. The moment journalists get hold of it, people start searching their bodies for symptoms! Let's leave medical matters to medical men!

Journalist Yes, but our paper wishes to reassure . . .

Sigelius Reassure? How will you do that? This is an appalling disease, and it's spreading. It's only three years since the virus first appeared. Clinics throughout the world are working flat out to find a cure. (*Shrugs.*) Science is still powerless . . . You just tell people if they're worried to pop in to their G.P. for a chat.

Journalist And he can . . . ?

Sigelius . . . prescribe ointments. Manganese for the poor ones. Peruvian balsam for those who can afford it.

Journalist Does that help?

Sigelius Yes, counteracts the stench when the wounds open. That's the second stage.

Journalist   And the third stage?

Sigelius   Straight morphine, young man. You don't
want to know about that. It's a nasty business.

Journalist   Is it very contagious?

Sigelius (*in pontificating professorial tone*)   That depends.
The layman will be unfamiliar with the microbe which
transmits our disease. We know only that it is spreading
at unusual speed. Furthermore it is not transmitted
through animals, and cannot be injected artificially into
humans – not young humans at any rate. That
remarkable experiment was performed on himself by
Doctor Hirota of Tokyo. We're fighting an unknown
enemy, my friend! Write that in our clinic we've been
working on the virus for three years. We've published a
good number of articles on the subject and have been
cited in all the respectable journals . . . (*Presses his buzzer.*)
In the process we have discovered beyond all shadow of
doubt . . . I'm afraid I have only three minutes left . . .

Nurse (*enters*)   Professor?

Sigelius   Please prepare a selection of our scientific
publications for my young friend.

Exit **Nurse**.

Sigelius   Quote from them, old chap. It will reassure
people that we're fighting the Peking Leprosy. Of course
we don't call it that. Leprosy, or *leprosis maculosa,* is a
skin disease. This is purely internal. My colleagues from
dermatology have assumed the right to lecture on it . . .
Politics, my dear chap! Our disease knocks the spots off
leprosy, you can assure the public of that! We are much,
much bigger than mere pus and scabs!

Journalist   It's . . . is it more dangerous than leprosy
then?

Sigelius   Infinitely! And much, much more interesting!
All the initial symptoms are reminiscent of leprosy. A

little patch of white on the body's surface. Cold as
marble. Quite numb. The so-called *macula marmorea*, or
marble spot. That's why the disease is sometimes called
the White Virus. However its aetiology is entirely
distinctive from the common *leprosis maculosa*. We doctors
simply call it *morbus chengi* – the Cheng virus to you –
after Doctor Cheng, a disciple of Charcot and a
specialist in internal medicine, who as you know first
described the disease, illustrating his article with several
cases from his Peking hospital. Fascinating stuff. I
reviewed it recently, before anyone dreamt the disease
would become a pandemic . . .

Journalist   A what?

Sigelius   A pandemic. An illness which spreads
uncontrollably and eventually affects the entire
population of the world. Some fascinating new disease
emerges almost every year in China. It's the poverty,
you see. But none has hitherto been as interesting as the
Cheng virus. It's the disease of the moment! Five million
deaths! Twenty million registered! At least three times
that number running around not knowing that a tiny
spot no bigger than a lentil is lurking somewhere on
their bodies. And the first case in Europe was diagnosed
right here in my clinic! That's something we're
extremely proud of, my friend. One particularly fine
symptom of the virus has been named the Sigelius
symptom . . .

Journalist (*writing*)   'Court Counsellor – Professor –
Doctor – Sigelius symptom – '

Sigelius   In my view, and that of my school, which is
proud to bear the name of the great Lilienthal, my late
father-in-law (you can write that), according to the
classic Lilienthal school, *morbus chengi* is highly infectious,
and affects only persons of forty-five to fifty years and
upward. It seems the normal organic changes of ageing

provide the appropriate environment for the microbe to flourish.

Journalist That's enormously interesting.

Sigelius You think so? How old are you?

Journalist I'm thirty, sir.

Sigelius I see. If you were any older you wouldn't find it so interesting. We know beyond all doubt that preconditions for infection are the first signs of physical ageing, and that the moment the first symptoms appear the prognosis is hopeless. I think we may omit the symptoms and aetiology, they're not terribly pleasant. Death usually follows in three to five months, usually from total sepsis. As for treatment – *sedativa tantum praescribere opportet.*

Journalist I beg your pardon?

Sigelius Never mind, young man, that's for us doctors. A classic prescription from the great Lilienthal. A great physician, my friend. If only he was still with us! Any more questions? I've a couple of minutes.

Journalist If you don't mind, Professor, our readers are chiefly interested in how to avoid the disease.

Sigelius Avoid it? It's unavoidable! It'll get us all, my friend! Everyone over fifty! What do you care – you're only thirty! While we, in our prime . . . Ten times a day I examine myself in the mirror, and your readers want to know how to avoid disintegrating alive! I bet they would – so would I! Here, see anything? Anything on my face yet? No? (*Sinks back, head in hands.*) God, how powerless is human science!

Journalist Maybe you could conclude with a few encouraging words?

Sigelius Yes – write in your newspaper that we must resign ourselves to the inevitable. (*The telephone rings.* **Sigelius** *lifts the receiver.*) Yes. . . ? I'm not available . . .

Doctor . . . ? Ah, Doctor Galen . . . Any references . . . ?
What does he want . . . ? 'In the interests of science' if
you please! I've no time for science, let him bother my
Second Assistant with that . . . I see, five times already
. . . Just a couple of minutes, then . . . (*Puts down the
receiver.*) See, my friend, how hard it is to concentrate on
scientific work?

Journalist   It's been a great honour, sir. You must
forgive me for intruding on your valuable time.

Sigelius   Don't worry, dear fellow. Science and the
people must serve each other. If you need anything, just
ask. (*Shakes his hand.*)

Journalist *bows himself out. A knock at the door.*

Sigelius (*sits at his desk, grabs a pen and starts
writing*)   Enter!

Galen *enters and remains standing by the door.*

Sigelius (*continues writing busily, then finally raises his
head*)   You wish to see me, colleague?

Galen   Excuse me for disturbing you, Professor. My
name is Doctor Galen.

Sigelius   I know that. How may I help you, Doctor
Galen?

Galen   As you know, Professor, this disease is rioting
through the slums of our city. I run a medical-aid clinic
in the suburbs, sir. I have the chance to see hundreds of
cases . . .

Sigelius   Rioting, you said?

Galen   That's right. Through the poor suburbs.

Sigelius   I see. We doctors must avoid wild language,
dear colleague.

Galen   I agree. The uncontrollable spread of the White
Virus . . .

Sigelius   *Morbus chengi*, dear friend, *morbus chengi*. A scientist must learn to express himself concisely and accurately.

Galen   When you see the horror of it, people rotting alive in front of their families, the poverty, the stench . . .

Sigelius   Then you must prescribe remedies to alleviate the smell, dear colleague.

Galen   Yes, but I want to save their lives, not stand there in despair . . .

Sigelius   There you are wrong. A doctor must never despair.

Galen   It's monstrous, Professor. I must do something. I've read all the literature on the subject, and with respect, it says nothing. About a cure, I mean.

Sigelius   (*starts writing again*)   And you think you've found a cure?

Galen   Yes, I think I have, sir.

Sigelius   (*lays down his pen*)   So you've your own theories about the virus?

Galen   I think I do, sir.

Sigelius   Come, Doctor. Where there's no cure, a theory can always be found. In my view the general practitioner should stick to the tried and tested methods. Not very fair on your clients is it, using them as guinea-pigs for your experiments? We have special clinics for that sort of thing . . .

Galen   Yes. That's why . . .

Sigelius   Let me finish, Doctor. We only have a couple of minutes left. As regards *morbus chengi*, I recommend the well-established anti-odorants. From then on it's morphine, dear colleague. Ultimately our aim is to relieve pain, at least for our fee-paying clients. I have no more to say on the subject. Delighted to have met you. (*Picks up his pen again.*)

Galen   But Professor, I have ...

Sigelius   You have something more to say?

Galen   Yes, you see I have found a cure for the White Virus.

Sigelius   You're at least the twelfth person who's come to tell me that, young man! Including several top specialists!

Galen   But I've already used my vaccine clinically on several hundred cases. With definite results.

Sigelius   What percentage cured?

Galen   About sixty. A further twenty not yet established.

Sigelius   (*lays down his pen*)   If you'd said a hundred per cent I'd have thrown you out as a madman or a fraud. What am I going to do with you, dear colleague! Look, I understand, it must be sorely tempting to dream up a cure. Wonderful clientele, university chair, Nobel Prize, name in lights – bigger than Pasteur, Koch, Lilienthal! But we've suffered so many set-backs ...

Galen   I'm asking you to let me try out my vaccine in your clinic, Professor.

Sigelius   My clinic? That's terribly naive of you, dear chap. Where are you from again?

Galen   From Pergamon. I'm Greek.

Sigelius   I'm afraid I couldn't possibly allow a foreigner into our Lilienthal State Medical Institute.

Galen   I'm a citizen of this country, sir. I was born here.

Sigelius   Origins are origins, dear sir!

Galen   What about Lilienthal's origins?

Sigelius   I might remind you, young man, that Court Counsellor Professor Lilienthal was my father-in-law. Anyway things change, you know that. And I've my doubts whether even the great Lilienthal would agree to some medical-aid doctor working in his institute.

Galen   He would agree, Professor. I was his assistant.

Sigelius (*jumps up*)   His...? My dear sir, why didn't you say so! Please be seated! Strange, I don't recall him mentioning your name.

Galen (*on the edge of his seat*)   'Babyface', he called me.

Sigelius   My God, so you're Babyface! 'My best pupil', he used to say. He was terribly sorry to lose you. Why on earth did you leave?

Galen   Things got difficult, Professor. You can't feed a family as an assistant.

Sigelius   You slipped up there! I'm always telling my students, if you want to dedicate yourself to science don't marry! If you do, marry money. Cigarette?

Galen   No thanks. I suffer from angina.

Sigelius   Nonsense! Want me to examine your chest?

Galen   No thanks, I've no time. I'd like you to let me run tests here on some cases you consider hopeless.

Sigelius   They're all hopeless, old chap! Tricky business, wouldn't be at all popular ... Look, since it's you, my father-in-law's favourite pupil, I'll tell you what. You give us the formula for your vaccine, and we'll consider it, then conduct clinical trials if appropriate. Hang on, I'll see we're not disturbed. (*Reaches for the buzzer.*)

Galen   Sorry Professor, but I can't disclose my formula until it's been clinically tested.

Sigelius   Not even to me?

Galen   Not even to you, Professor.

Sigelius   In that case forget it. Sorry Galen, it would contravene clinical propriety, as well as – how shall we say? – your scientific responsibilities.

Galen   Perhaps. I have my reasons.

Sigelius   Please yourself. We'll say no more about it. Despite everything, I'm honoured to have met you, Doctor Babyface!

Galen   Listen sir, please – you . . . must . . . let me work in your clinic!

Sigelius   Why?

Galen   No one ever writes about the slum patients, but I can vouch for my cure! We've had not a single relapse! See this letter from my colleagues. They're sending me patients from all over the city! Please, look at the letters.

Sigelius   They're of no interest to me. (*Stands up.*) There's nothing more to talk about.

Galen   That's a great pity. (*Hovers by the door.*) Such a dreadful disease . . . You yourself one day . . .

Sigelius   You had no call to say that, Galen. (*Paces the floor.*) I don't much fancy falling apart alive . . .

Galen   In that case the Professor can treat himself with anti-odorants . . .

Sigelius   Show me the letters. (**Galen** *hands them over.* **Sigelius** *clears his throat and reads.*) Doctor Stradela, my pupil – tall chap?

Galen   Yes, very tall.

Sigelius (*reads on*)   My goodness! (*Shakes his head.*) This is astounding! They're just GPs, but dammit Galen, you

have some extraordinary results! Look old boy, I'm
going to meet you half-way – I'll take your vaccine, run
a few tests. Couldn't ask for more, eh?

Galen   No. I know it would be a tremendous honour,
but . . .

Sigelius   But you want to do it yourself?

Galen   Yes Professor, I want to test it myself at your
clinic.

Sigelius   Then publish the results?

Galen   Yes – under certain conditions.

Sigelius   Namely?

Galen   We'll discuss that later, Professor.

Sigelius (*sits behind the desk*)   I see, you want our clinic
to test your cure, and give you the monopoly on its
application. That your plan, eh?

Galen   Yes, but . . .

Sigelius   That's extraordinarily impertinent of you,
Doctor Galen, approaching the Lilienthal Clinic with
such a demand. I've a good mind to kick you
downstairs. Of course every physician must profit from
his speciality, but to turn a medical procedure into an
industrial secret is conduct more becoming to a faith-
healer than to a physician! Primarily, dear colleague, it
is inhuman to suffering humanity. Secondly . . .

Galen   Professor, I . . .

Sigelius   Secondly, it violates medical ethics. We all of
us want to cure our clients, it's our livelihood. For you,
it is merely a source of private gain. I unfortunately
must approach things as a scientist and a physician,
conscious of his duties to humanity. Our attitudes, dear
Doctor Galen, appear diametrically opposed. One

minute. (*Presses the buzzer.*) Send in my First Assistant. Yes, this instant! The depths to which medicine has sunk! Endless miracle-workers trying to squeeze cash from secret cures! And he wants to use our clinic for publicity purposes! Damn profiteers!

A knock at the door.

Come in!

First Assistant (*enters*) You called, sir.

Sigelius Which wards are occupied by *morbus chengi*?

First Assistant Almost all, sir. Two, Four, Five . . .

Sigelius And the slum patients?

First Assistant Our non-fee-paying patients are in Ward Thirteen, sir.

Sigelius Who's in charge there?

First Assistant Our Second Assistant, sir.

Sigelius Kindly inform him that from now on my colleague Doctor Galen here will be in charge of all medical procedures on that ward.

First Assistant Very good sir, but . . .

Sigelius Excellent. I feared you might have objections. Tell our Second Assistant not to concern himself with Doctor Galen's methods of treatment. Those are my specific instructions.

First Assistant Very well, Professor. (*Exit.*)

Galen My dear Counsellor, I don't know how to thank you!

Sigelius No need, sir. I am acting exclusively in the interests of medical science. All else must take second place. Even my strongest antipathy. If you wish, you may inspect Ward Thirteen straight away. (*Rings the buzzer.*) Staff Nurse, be kind enough to take Doctor

Galen to Ward Thirteen. How long will you need, Doctor?

Galen   Six weeks will be enough.

Sigelius   Six weeks? You really are planning miracles, Doctor!

Galen (*goes to the door*)   I am deeply grateful to you, sir. (*Exit.*)

Sigelius   Good luck. (*Takes his pen, then flings it down. Rises, goes to the mirror and inspects his face.*) Nothing so far . . .

A comfortable family sitting-room.

Father (*reading the newspaper under the evening lamp*)   This damn disease! Give us a break, we've enough problems of our own!

Mother   That woman on the third floor is in a terrible way. No one's allowed up there any more . . . Have you noticed the smell on the stairs?

Father   No, I have not. Hah, interview here with Court Counsellor Sigelius. I've a lot of time for that chap. He's a top specialist, he'll prove me right.

Mother   How, dear?

Father   It's been blown out of all proportion. One sneeze, and it's the White Plague. One or two cases and the papers go mad!

Mother   My sister says there's a lot of it around in the country too.

Father   Nonsense, Mother, it's just scare stories! See, Sigelius here says it comes from China. Why should we pay to support these backward countries? Hunger and poverty, plagues and viruses – they're breeding-grounds for disease! Make them a colony of Europe, I say – get them organised, show them some discipline, that'll sort them out! Sigelius says here it's infectious. Pack them off to camps so they don't contaminate us! Simple as that! Soon as someone gets the white spot, off he goes. It's a disgrace, letting that witch stay up there to die. You dread coming home to the stench . . .

Mother   The poor woman's all on her own up there. I should take her some soup . . .

Father   No way! You and your soft heart – you'll bring it down here! They should disinfect the corridor.

Mother   What with?

Father (*reading*)   Hang on. Stupid man!

Mother   Who?

Father   Journalist. He says here . . . Idiot! They shouldn't be allowed to write this rubbish!

Mother   What does he say?

Father   He says we can't escape, we'll all cop it by the time we're fifty . . .

Mother   Show me.

Father (*hurling the paper at the table, runs around the room screaming*)   Cretin! It's ridiculous! Fifty's nothing! I'll never buy his paper again! They'll hear from me!

Mother (*reads*)   But Father, Court Counsellor Sigelius said it . . . !

Father   Nonsense! At our stage of scientific knowledge? This isn't the Dark Ages. Chap at our office got it – he was only forty-five! Where's the justice in striking people down at fifty?

Daughter (*who has been lying on the sofa all this time reading a magazine*)   It's obvious why, Dad – to make room for the young ones, get them started . . .

Father   Hear that, Mother? Your parents feed you and sweat blood for you, and now they're in the way. Very nice! Let them pass on to make room!

Mother   She didn't mean it that way, Daddy!

Father   No, but she said it. All right for you if Mum and Dad snuff it when they're fifty?

Daughter   Don't take it personally, Dad! It's just hard for us to get started. There's no jobs. Something has to give, so we can live our lives, have families . . .

Mother   She has a point, Father.

Father   So you're on her side – according to you we should all kick the bucket in our prime?

Enter **Son**.

Son   What's he in a state about?

Mother   Nothing, dear. He just read an article about this illness . . .

Daughter   I said something had to give, to make room for more people.

Son   That's what everyone's saying, Dad! I don't know what we'd do without the plague! Sister couldn't get married, I'd be slogging my guts out for endless exams . . .

Father   High time too, my lad!

Son   Degrees are no use now anyway. Maybe things will change when the old people have gone. Only joking!

Hospital corridor outside Wards Twelve and Thirteen.

Sigelius (*at the head of a group of visiting foreign professors*)   Here we are dear colleagues. *Par ici chers confrères. Ich bitte, meine verehrten Herren Kollegen* . . . (*Leads them into Ward Thirteen.*)

First Assistant Listen to the old man prattling on. It's Galen this, Galen that. Now he's dragging around our top world specialists to witness his miracles. You can bet your life the spots will return!

Second Assistant Why?

First Assistant I wasn't born yesterday, medicine has its limits. The governor's going soft if he thinks he's found a cure. This is my eighth year here. I'll soon have my own little private practice treating the Cheng virus!

Second Assistant Using Galen's method?

First Assistant Lilienthal's. This is a fantastic window for me!

Second Assistant Galen's so secretive . . .

First Assistant Galen can take a hike. We don't speak. The nurse on Ward Thirteen told me he's stuffing his patients with this vaccine that looks like mustard. So I mixed up the usual minerals and vitamins, added some yellow dye and tried it out on myself. No side effects! Patients will even improve for a bit. So I'll start with that. Not bad eh? (*Listening at the door.*) The old boy's still at it. 'We must delay publication of our method . . .' Smart guy! He knows as much as I do! Now he's preaching to the pundits in English. Always had an ear for languages, the old charmer! Clever move, marrying into his career. God, I hope Galen doesn't publish before I open my practice!

Second Assistant Otherwise everyone will rush to see him instead.

First Assistant I'm not bothered. He gave his word of honour not to treat our fee-paying patients until clinical tests were finished. That'll give me time to get going.

Second Assistant And Galen is keeping his word as a . . .

First Assistant (*shrugging*)   As an idiot! I hear he even closed his other practice – some shack in the back of beyond, apparently. Nurse on Ward Thirteen says he can't even afford to eat! Just carries a couple of bread-rolls in his pocket. She was going to take him some lunch, but the catering manager wouldn't hear of it. Said Galen wasn't on his list. Quite right too.

Second Assistant   My mother found a white spot on the back of her neck. I asked Galen to take a look. 'Sorry my friend,' he said. 'I gave Sigelius my word.'

First Assistant   Bloody nerve! Just like him. Totally unprofessional.

Second Assistant   So I asked the governor to have a word with him to make an exception, seeing as it's my mother.

First Assistant   And what did he say?

Second Assistant   He said 'Dear Second Assistant, I make no exceptions in my clinic!'

First Assistant   Heart of stone. Of course he could do it. What's a promise amongst colleagues? He's a nasty bit of work!

Second Assistant   It's my mother! She saved every penny so I could finish medical school. I'm sure he could cure her.

First Assistant   Galen? I wouldn't bet on it!

Second Assistant   But his results are a miracle!

Sigelius *and the other professors emerge from Ward Thirteen.*

First Professor   *Wirklich überraschend! Ja, es ist erstaunlicht!*

Second Professor   *Mes félicitations, mon ami! C'est un miracle!*

Third Professor   I congratulate you, Professor!

Splendid, splendid!

The guests move down the corridor talking.

Fourth Professor (*to* **Sigelius**)   One minute, colleague. Congratulations, a remarkable success!

Sigelius   Not my success, Professor, the success of the Lilienthal Clinic!

Fourth Professor   Tell me, who was that little fellow?

Sigelius   On Ward Thirteen? That was Doctor Galen, I believe.

Fourth Professor   Your assistant?

Sigelius   No, heaven forbid. He just drops in occasionally. One of Lilienthal's disciples. He's not interested in the Cheng virus.

Fourth Professor   Phenomenal success. (*Confidentially.*) Look, I've a patient with the white spot, a real big shot. He's . . . (*Whispers in his ear.*)

Sigelius (*whistles*)   Poor fellow.

Fourth Professor   Might I . . . ?

Sigelius   Only too happy, Professor. Tell him to report to me in person. We don't apply our method yet to patients outside the clinic . . .

Fourth Professor   Quite right too.

Sigelius   Glad to be of assistance . . .

Fourth Professor   And since we're talking of such a patient . . . Yes?

Sigelius   No charge, of course dear colleague. My pleasure. (*Leaving with the rest of the group.*)

First Assistant   See? We're talking megabucks here.

Second Assistant   And with my mother it was 'we make no exceptions'.

First Assistant   Hell, this is different – money, connections. I wish to God I had his patients!

Galen (*sticking his head out of the door of Ward Thirteen*)   Are they gone?

Second Assistant   Can we help you, Doctor?

Galen   No, thank you.

First Assistant   We'd better scoot. Doctor Galen wants to be alone.

Exeunt. **Galen** *looks around. When they have gone he takes a roll from his pocket and starts to eat.*

Sigelius (*returns*)   Hah, glad to have caught you! Congratulations, Babyface, on our phenemonal success!

Galen (*gulping down his roll*)   We must still wait, Professor.

Sigelius   Of course, Babyface! Oh, and before I forget, there'll be one private client.

Galen   But I don't treat private patients.

Sigelius   I know that. Most commendable, dear Galen. Dedicating yourself to science and all that. But I've personally selected this case. He's a very special client.

Galen   But I gave you my word that I would test my method only on Ward Thirteen . . .

Sigelius   Very true. But on this occasion I shall release you from your word.

Galen   I would prefer to keep it, sir.

Sigelius   I repeat, Galen, I have already made a personal commitment. I might remind you that this is my clinic. I am in charge here, and I make the rules.

Galen   Sir, if you put your patient in Ward Thirteen, then of course . . .

Sigelius   What are you saying?

Galen   Ward Thirteen. On the floor. We have no spare beds on Ward Thirteen.

Sigelius   My good man, it's completely out of the question! He'd rather die! We can't just dump a man like this in a public ward with those. . . ! He's an extremely important client, he's . . . Come, Doctor Babyface, don't trifle with me!

Galen   I will treat patients only in Ward Thirteen. I gave you my word. Now if you will excuse me, sir. I was delayed by the professors' visit. I must go to my patients.

Sigelius   You can go to hell, you, you . . . !

Galen   Thank you. (*Slips back into the ward.*)

Sigelius   Bloody idiot, leading me this dance!

First Assistant (*enters, clearing his throat*)   If the Professor would permit . . . I couldn't help overhearing . . . I confess I find Galen's behaviour quite outrageous! I might add that I have made a serum similar in appearance to Galen's – almost identical in fact.

Sigelius   What's it good for?

First Assistant   It can be used in place of Galen's preparation. It's perfectly harmless.

Sigelius   And its medical effects?

First Assistant   It contains some tonic ingredients which you yourself prescribe. It will alleviate pain for a while.

Sigelius   But the illness will progress?

First Assistant   Galen's injections also have no effect in certain cases, Professor . . .

Sigelius   You're right, young man. But Professor

Sigelius doesn't do things like that.

First Assistant   I know . . . but the Professor won't refuse a valued client.

Sigelius   Point taken. (*Taking out his prescription pad and writing. With cold contempt.*) You're wasted on scientific research. Wouldn't you be better off in private practice?

First Assistant   Yes, and that's exactly where I intend to be!

Sigelius (*tears off the prescription*)   Come and speak to my colleague. He'll introduce you to our patient. I wish you well! (*Exit quickly.*)

First Assistant (*bowing*)   Thank you kindly, Court Counsellor. (*Shakes his own hand.*) Congratulations, Doctor, I think we've cracked it!

A line of orderlies in white medical gowns stand to attention in the corridor. The **Commissar** *glances at his watch.*

Second Assistant (*runs in breathlessly holding a walkie-talkie to his ear*)   The Marshal has just stepped into his car!

Commissar   Let's run through it one more time. All rooms with patients . . .

Second Assistant   To be closed from 0900 hours. All staff to assemble downstairs in the hall . . . The Minister of Health has arrived, must fly . . . ! (*Exit.*)

Commissar   Attention!

Orderlies stand to attention.

Commissar   For the last time, nobody is to pass here except his Excellency's entourage. At ease!

Sound of motor sirens.

He's here! Atten – shun! (*Retreats backstage.*)

Silence. From the floor below we hear speeches of welcome. Two men in civilian dress hurry down the corridor and the orderlies salute as the **Marshal** *enters in battledress, with* **Sigelius** *on one side and the* **Minister of Health** *on the other, and followed by* **Marshal***'s entourage of generals and doctors.*

Sigelius   Here in Ward Twelve we have our control group of patients. We're not using our new treatment on them, so we can compare the results achieved.

Marshal   I see. Let me inspect them.

Sigelius   Your Excellency, a word of caution. The disease is highly contagious and the sight is horrendous, and despite our best efforts, the stench is nauseating.

Marshal   We soldiers can take anything! Forward!

Turns into Ward Twelve with his entourage. A moment of silence. We hear **Sigelius***'s voice from inside the ward. Then the* **General** *staggers out gagging, supported by* **Second Assistant***.*

General (*shrieks*)   Horrible! Horrible! Horrible!

Other members of the party push their way out.

Minister   It's a bloody nightmare! Open the window!

Adjutant (*holding his handkerchief to his nose*)   It's a scandal, bringing guests here!

Member of entourage   Jesus!

General   How can the Marshal stand it?

Minister   Gentlemen, I almost fainted!

Adjutant   How dare they bring the Marshal here? They'll regret it!

Member of entourage   You saw . . . You saw . . . You saw . . .

General   The things I saw in there . . . B-r-r, don't talk about it, sir. I'll remember it as long as I live. And as a soldier I've seen a bit.

Second Assistant   I'll fetch some eau-de-cologne, gentlemen.

Minister   You should have brought some with you.

Second Assistant *runs off.*

Adjutant   Attention!

All move from the door as the **Marshal** *emerges, followed by* **Sigelius** *and doctors.*

Marshal (*stops*)   I see you gentlemen haven't the stomach for it. Lead on, Sigelius!

Sigelius   Now in Ward Thirteen you'll find a totally different picture. Here we are applying our new method. Your Excellency will see for himself.

Marshal *enters Ward Thirteen followed by* **Sigelius** *and doctors. Entourage peeps hesitantly around the door and silently enters. Silence, except for* **Sigelius**'s *muffled words.*

Voice (*backstage*)   Stop!

Another voice   Take your hands off me! Let me pass!

Commissar (*runs on as* **Galen** *enters, struggling to free himself from the clutches of two men in white coats*)   Who's this? Who let him in? What do you want, young man?

Galen   I must go to my patients!

Second Assistant *returns with the eau-de-cologne.*

Commissar (*to* **Second Assistant**)   Do you know this man?

Second Assistant   It's Doctor Galen. Sir.

Commissar   Does he work here?

Second Assistant   Well, yes. He works on Ward Thirteen.

Commissar   In that case I apologise, Doctor. Let him

go! Why weren't you here by nine, like the other doctors?

Galen (*rubbing his arms*)   I didn't have time. I was busy preparing my patients' medication.

Second Assistant (*quietly*)   He wasn't invited.

Commissar   I see. You'll have to wait here with me, you can't go in before the Marshal leaves.

Galen   But I . . .

Commissar   Kindly follow me. (*Escorts* **Galen** *backstage.*)

Marshal, **Sigelius** *etc. leave Ward Thirteen.*

Marshal   I congratulate you, Sigelius. It's nothing short of a miracle!

Minister (*reads from a piece of paper*)   'Dear Excellency, our revered Marshal, allow me in the name of our Department . . .'

Marshal   Thank you Minister, that will do. (*Turns to* **Sigelius**.)

Sigelius   Your Excellency, I am lost for words. Such an honour for our scientific work. We at the Lilienthal Clinic are only too aware how small is our merit in comparison with the incalculably more dangerous plague of perversion, the gangrene of degeneracy, the leprosy of licentiousness . . .

The crowd murmurs its approval.

Let me take this opportunity as a simple doctor to pay tribute to the great healer who with surgical precision has saved us all from a national epidemic of anarchy which threatens racial death to our national organism . . . (*Bows to the* **Marshal**, *amid cries of 'Bravo!' 'Bravo!'*)

Marshal (*stretching out his hand*)   Sterling work, Sigelius, it's nothing short of a miracle!

Sigelius   I am profoundly grateful to you, Excellency.

Exit **Marshal**, *followed by* **Sigelius**, *entourage, doctors etc.*

Commissar (*emerges from the wings*)   Ready! Attention!
Pair off! Forward march! (*Men in white coats follow the
entourage.*)

Galen   May I go into the ward now?

Commissar   One moment, Doctor, the Marshal
hasn't left yet. (*Approaches Ward Twelve, puts his nose around
the door and hastily shuts it.*) My God, you doctors actually
go in there?

Galen   What? Certainly.

Commissar   He's a great man our Marshal, a hero.
He stood it for (*Checks his watch.*) exactly two minutes.
(*The sirens of the departing motorcade.*) You can go in now,
Doctor. Sorry we had to detain you . . .

Galen   Don't worry. My pleasure. (*Slips into Ward
Thirteen.*)

Second Assistant (*runs in*)   Quick, where's the press?
(*Runs off.*)

Commissar (*looks at his watch*)   Didn't go on too long,
thank God.

Voice of Second Assistant   Follow me, gentlemen.
The Court Counsellor will be here shortly.

Enter group of **Journalists** *with* **Second Assistant**.

Second Assistant   This way please, gentlemen. On
Ward Twelve here you can see what the so-called White
Plague looks like when it's not treated by our method.
However, I would strongly recommend you not to . . .

Journalists (*enter Ward Twelve but immediately rush out
again*)   Back! Nightmare! Don't go in! Revolting!

Journalist (*to* **Second Assistant**)   They're gonners,
aren't they?

Second Assistant   For sure. Here on Ward Thirteen, however, you can see for yourself the results of a few weeks' application of our treatment. No need for concern, follow me.

A few of the **Journalists** *hesitantly enter Ward Thirteen, followed by the others. Enter* **Sigelius**, *glowing with pride.*

Second Assistant   Sir, I beg to inform you that the gentlemen of the press are inspecting Ward Thirteen.

Sigelius   I wish they'd leave me alone, my heart is so full. All right, let's meet them.

Second Assistant (*at the door of Ward Thirteen*) Notepads ready, gentlemen! The Court Counsellor will give us a quick briefing.

Journalists (*milling around the corridor*)   It's a miracle! Marvellous! Wonderful! Splendid!

Sigelius   You gentlemen must excuse me if my emotions occasionally get the better of me. If you had seen the compassion and fortitude of our Marshal as he bent over the sick and dying. Gentlemen, it was an inspiration!

Journalist   What did he say?

Sigelius   Afterwards, he was full of praise for . . .

Second Assistant   If the Court Counsellor might allow me to remind him, he said 'Sterling work, Sigelius, it's nothing short of a miracle!'

Sigelius   The Marshal overestimates my contribution, of course. Now we have a cure for the so-called White Virus, gentlemen, you may write that it was the most dreadful disease in the history of the world. No point mincing words here – it was a greater danger than the Black Death. I am proud, dear sirs, that our nation bears the glory for this success, and that it was achieved here in the clinic of my great predecessor and mentor, Professor Lilienthal!

Dr **Galen** *leans wearily against the door of Ward Thirteen.*

Sigelius   Come, Galen. Gentlemen, let me introduce you to one of my co-fighters in merit. We medical scientists don't push personal success, we work for all humanity. Don't be shy, little Babyface! All of us, even down to the humblest nurse, have fulfilled our duty. I am delighted that on this great day I can express my humble gratitude to my dedicated colleagues.

Journalist   Could you explain to us the precise nature of your cure, sir?

Sigelius   Not mine, sir, not mine. The Lilienthal Clinic's. Its precise nature will be announced to the medical world. Medical methods should be handled only by specialists. Simply tell the public what you saw. Write: 'The remedy for the most dreadful disease in the world has now been found.' That's all. And if you want to celebrate further this joyous day, write about our glorious Leader, who went among the lepers braving fear, disease and infection. It was superhuman, gentlemen. Words fail me. Now if you will excuse me, my patients are waiting. My pleasure, at your service. (*Leaves quickly.*)

Journalist   That's it then?

Galen (*steps forward*)   One minute please, gentlemen. Please tell them that I, Doctor Galen, the doctor of the poor . . .

Journalist   Tell who?

Galen   Tell all the governments of the world, the kings and rulers. Tell them that I went to the war as a doctor, and as a doctor I don't want another one. Please, write that.

Journalist   What makes you think they'll listen to you?

Galen   They will. They must, or they'll all be wiped out by the White Plague. Tell them the cure is mine, and I won't reveal it until they promise to stop the killing. Nobody else knows my remedy. Ask anyone here. Tell the rulers of the world they'll disintegrate alive, like the patients in this clinic. Tell them it'll happen to everybody . . .

Second Journalist   You'd let them die like that?

Galen   You'd let them be slaughtered by land-mines and nerve-gas, and expect us doctors to save them? If you knew how much it took to save one child from leukaemia . . . Each day we're fighting heart-disease, cataracts, osteomyelitis, cancer . . . Now they want us to fight another war! I'm not a soldier, I'm a doctor, fighting for human life . . .

Journalist   How do you intend to do that?

Galen   Simple. When they agree to pull back from war, they can have my vaccine.

Second Assistant *runs off.*

Journalist   How do you imagine the rulers of the world . . . ?

Galen   Yes, how? That's the hard bit, isn't it? I know they won't talk to me, but if you write that no nation will get the vaccine until it pledges not to fight . . .

Second Journalist   Idealism! No state will buy it!

Galen   No? They'd let millions die a horrible death for nothing? You think people will buy that? What happens when the rulers start falling apart? They'll be terrified, man!

Journalist   He has a point. But what if no government will agree?

Galen That would be terribly sad. I simply couldn't release my vaccine.

Journalist What would you do with it?

Galen Take it back to the slums, man. No lack of patients there! I can prove a million times over that the White Plague is curable!

Journalist And you won't treat the rich?

Galen I'm afraid not. The rich have the power. If they want peace they can just snap their fingers for it.

Journalist That's a bit tough on the rich.

Galen It's tough to be poor. The poor die younger. Everyone has the right to live. It doesn't have to be like that.

Sigelius *and* **Second Assistant** *hurry in.*

Sigelius Gentlemen of the press, kindly leave the clinic. Doctor Galen appears to be having a nervous breakdown!

Journalist But we would be interested still to hear . . .

Sigelius Gentlemen, behind these doors a lethal epidemic is raging. I advise you to leave. My assistant will see you to the door.

Journalists *are ushered out by* **Second Assistant**.

Sigelius Have you taken leave of your senses, Galen? I will not permit the expression of such views within the walls of my clinic! And on this of all days! I should have you arrested on the spot! All right, I can see you're overworked. Come here now Babyface.

Galen What for?

Sigelius Come here and tell me the precise chemical formula and application of your remedy, then you can take a nice rest – you clearly need one.

Galen   Dear Court Counsellor I have stated my terms. Otherwise . . .

Sigelius   Otherwise what?

Galen   I beg your pardon, sir, but otherwise I can't reveal my formula.

Sigelius   Then you're either a madman or a foul traitor. I order you to remember your duties as a doctor. Nothing else concerns you.

Galen   As a doctor it's my duty to stop people killing each other.

Sigelius   I forbid the expression of such views in my clinic! We do not serve some abstract humanity, we serve the state! This is a state institute!

Galen   So why should that stop our state making peace?

Sigelius   Because it cannot and must not, Doctor Galen! As one of foreign extraction you can have no conception of our state's mission and destiny. But enough of this! I am asking you for the last time, Galen, as the head of this clinic – tell me your formula!

Galen   I'm sorry, Counsellor. I can't.

Sigelius   Get out! Never set foot in my clinic again!

Galen   As you wish, Counsellor. I'm sorry.

Sigelius   Me too, sonny boy! You think I'm not sorry for all the patients who'll die? How does this make me look, solemnly announcing a cure for the leprosy, and suddenly it's not there any more? It'll be curtains for my career, Doctor Babyarse! Imagine the disgrace! I'd rather the whole world croaked than suffer your pacifist plague!

Galen   How can you say that as a doctor!

Sigelius   I'm not merely a doctor, sir. I also serve my state, thank God. Kindly leave my clinic.

Curtain.

Act Two

Family sitting-room.

Father (*reading the newspaper under the evening lamp*) Look Mother, it says here they've found a cure for the plague!

Mother God be praised!

Father What did I tell you? They wouldn't let people die in this day and age. Fifty's too young! B-r-r, it gave me the creeps! Glad to be alive! Over thirty chaps in our office have passed away – all in their fifties.

Mother Poor devils.

Father So, you'll never guess – I was going to surprise you, but since today's such a happy day . . . This morning Baron Krug calls me in. 'Look here colleague,' he says, 'our Head of Accounts has just died so I'm putting you in charge. In a fortnight's time, you'll be our new Head of Accounts!' There! What do you think?

Mother That's nice for you.

Father And not for you, Mother? Just think, an extra twelve thousand a year! Where's that bottle I gave you for your birthday?

Mother Shouldn't we wait for the children?

Father What for? She's out with her boyfriend, he's got his exams. Crack it open!

Mother If you want. (*Exit.*)

Father (*reading paper*) Hm. 'A greater danger than the Black Death.' People these days won't stand for dying such a stupid death – it's not the Middle Ages any more. (*Reads on.*) Our Marshal, what a hero, visiting the lepers! Wild horses wouldn't drag me there. (*Rubs his hands.*) Head of Accounts! 'Good morning sir!' 'Let me take your coat, sir.' 'Did you pass a reasonable night, sir?' The responsibility . . . !

Mother *returns with a bottle and one glass.*

Father   Only one glass? Not drinking with me?

Mother   No, I won't drink.

Father   Your good health. (*Drinks.*) Give us a little kiss, Mother.

Mother   No, leave me alone, please.

Father (*pours another glass*)   My God, Krug's Head of Accounts! Millions pouring through my hands every day! It's no job for a weakling! Then they go making chaps of fifty redundant! I'll show you redundant! Who'd have thought when I started at Krug thirty years ago that I'd end up Head of Accounts! What a career, Mother! Toiled away for thirty years, and now the Baron calls me colleague. Not sir, like the young ones. Colleague. 'Look here colleague, I'm putting you in charge.' That's what he said. Five others had their eye on the job. All of them dead now . . . You could almost say . . .

Mother   What?

Father   Think about it – our daughter can marry, her bloke has a job, our boy can work in our office when he passes his exams. You could almost say thank your lucky stars for the plague!

Mother   Lord, how can you say that?

Father   It's true! It's helped people like us to get on. Without it we'd be nowhere. And now they've found the cure, we're laughing all the way to the bank! (*Picks up the paper again.*) I always said Sigelius was smart – they discovered it at his clinic. Our Marshal was there. Superhuman, he was. I can well believe it. I saw him driving past once. A great man and a great soldier.

Mother   Will there definitely be a war?

Father   With a leader like that it would be a sin not
to! We're working three shifts a day, turning out
munitions. I'll tell you a secret – we've started making
this new gas. They say it's special. The Baron's building
six new factories. Imagine, Head of Accounts now!
Shows he trusts me! I'm doing my patriotic duty.

Mother   I hope they won't call up our boy.

Father   He must do his duty too, Mother. (*Drinks.*)
Don't worry, they probably won't want him. It'll all be
over in a week. We'll smash 'em before they know what
day it is. That's the way with wars now, Mother. (*Pause
as he reads on, then slams down the paper.*) Hell and
damnation! How dare he! Put him against a wall and
shoot him! Bloody traitor!

Mother   Who, Father?

Father   The cheek! It says here this doctor who
discovered the vaccine won't let any government have it
unless they promise not to make war!

Mother   What's wrong with that?

Father   Don't be daft, Mother! What do we spend
millions on arms for – peace? Shut down Krug's
factories and throw two hundred thousand out of work?
It's criminal to talk peace now. Throw him in jail!

Mother   But if he has the cure . . .

Father   That's open to question. If you ask me the
chap's not a doctor, he's in the pay of a foreign power.
Arrest him! Put a gun to his neck and make him talk!
That's what they should do!

Mother   But if he really has discovered . . . (*Takes the
newspaper.*)

Father   Put his fingers in a thumb-screw, and screw it
tighter, tighter, tighter . . . till he squeaks! We've the
technology to make him talk. Imagine that bastard

letting us all perish just for some stupid peace! To hell with peace!

Mother (*reads the newspaper*)   But he only says...

Father   Traitor! What about our national glory? Our living space? Think they'll hand it to us on a plate? Preaching against war is against our sacred interests, understand? If I had to choose between the plague and peace, I'd pick the plague!

Mother   If you say so, Father.

Father   What's up with you today? What's that scarf around your neck? Have you a cold?

Mother   No.

Father   Take it off then, let me see! (*Pulls off the scarf.*)

Mother *stands before him in silence.*

Father   Merciful Jesus! The white spot!

A queue of patients outside **Doctor Galen**'s *surgery. The last in line are* **Father** *and* **Mother**.

First Patient   Look at your neck!

Second Patient   Healing nicely! He told me last time I was almost better!

First Patient   We're almost back to normal!

Second Patient   At first he didn't want to take me. 'If you're a baker you're not really poor,' he says. 'I only treat the poor.' But I say to him, 'Doctor, when the baker gets sick no one will buy a bread-roll from him – I'm worse than a beggar!' So in the end he took me ... (*Entering the surgery.*)

Father   See Mother, he took him in the end.

Mother   God, I'm frightened!

Father   I'll fall on my knees and say, 'Doctor take pity on me, my children aren't provided for!' Is it a crime to work your way to the top? All our lives we've scrimped and saved. He can't be that cruel.

Mother   But he treats only the poor.

Father   I'll see he treats you. I'll tell him what I think . . .

Mother   Please, Father, don't lose your temper.

Father   I'll tell him it's his human duty. I'll say, 'Never mind the cost, Doctor. This is my wife.'

Galen (*enters*)   Yes my friend, what can I do for you?

Father   Doctor, if you would be good enough – my wife here . . .

Galen   What is your job?

Father   Head of Accounts, Krug Corporation.

Galen   Krug? I'm terribly sorry, sir, I can't.

Father   Doctor, take pity on us, we'll be eternally grateful to you . . .

Galen   Stop, please. It's terribly hard for me to refuse you but I only treat the poor. They need me, the rest can . . .

Father   I don't care what it costs . . .

Galen   Then you can tell your Baron Krug to shut down his production-line . . .

Father   With all my heart, Doctor, but there's nothing I personally can do . . .

Galen   That's what they all say. Krug can stop the war. He has the power. Persuade him to use it.

Father   Impossible, out of the question, I wouldn't presume . . . !

Galen   See? What can I do? Terribly sorry, but . . .

Father   Doctor, in the name of humanity . . .

Galen   Believe me, I do this in the name of humanity.
If you stopped working for Baron Krug, refused to take
his money . . .

Father   What would I do then? I'd never get a job as
Head of Accounts in another firm. Thirty years I've
worked for this. You can't expect me to throw it away!

Galen   I expect nothing. Goodbye sir.

Mother   You see, you see!

Father   Let's go. Heartless swine, expecting me to
throw it all away!

The office of **Professor Sigelius**.

Sigelius (*at the door*)   Do come in, dear Baron.

Krug   Thank you, sir. I thought I'd never get here.

Sigelius   I can believe it. We live in dangerous times.
Please take a seat. Yes, challenging times, my dear sir!

Krug   Indeed.

Sigelius   But stirring times!

Krug   Politically, you mean? Yes, great and difficult
times, sir.

Sigelius   Especially difficult for you I imagine, dear
Baron, as you prepare us for this war, which thank God
appears inevitable. To be managing the Krug
Corporation at such a moment must be no joke . . .

Krug   True. Listen Counsellor, I thought of making a
donation to your leprosy fund.

Sigelius   That is typical of you, Baron, thinking about
scientific research at such a great and difficult period of

our nation's history! Always the same – grand, magnanimous yet modest! We humbly accept, sir, and will do our best to use it for further research.

Krug Thank you. (*Places a fat envelope on the table.*)

Sigelius Do you want a receipt?

Krug No need. So, how are you getting on?

Sigelius *Morbus chengi*, you mean? Roaring ahead nicely, thanks. Luckily people have their heads too full of the war to worry about it. Morale is excellent. Wonderful fighting spirit.

Krug Fighting the disease, you mean?

Sigelius No, fighting the war! Our nation puts its trust in the Marshal, our heroic army and you, dear Baron! Things have never looked so propitious . . .

Krug Still no cure?

Sigelius Nothing so far. We're still working on it.

Krug What about your former Assistant? Apparently he has a private practice and no end of patients. They say he's using the Lilienthal method . . .

Sigelius There's nothing in it, dear Baron. Between you and me, it's a simple case of fraud. I was glad to be shot of him.

Krug Well, well. What happened to that hare-brained doctor of yours, by the way?

Sigelius Galen? He's almost forgotten. Disappeared among his poor. Complete crackpot, though he certainly gets results.

Krug Reliable?

Sigelius Unfortunately almost a hundred per cent. Good thing the public have their wits about them . . . The lunatic thought he could use his miracle cure to blackmail us into his idiotic peace utopia, but fortunately no one paid any attention to him. No one who counts, anyway. Between you and me, the police are keeping a discreet eye on him. Remarkable how patriotic our people are.

Krug   So he still refuses to cure the rich?

Sigelius   Pure fanaticism, I fear. Wretched man still dreams of eternal peace. Dreaming about peace at such a time – there are places for people like him! Good job we have my former Assistant here. All the top people are flocking to see him. There's a rumour he took Galen's secret formula. No results yet, but his practice is flourishing.

Krug   So you've still found no way to stop the virus?

Sigelius   I have, Baron, thank God I have! It will be triumphant in stopping its spread!

Krug   I'm delighted to hear it, Sigelius! Tell me about it.

Sigelius   Still very hush-hush. But in the next few days we'll be issuing legislation imposing compulsory quarantine orders on all plague victims. This is my work, Baron. The Marshal pulled a few strings of course. We have to defend ourselves. It'll be our greatest success to date in the fight against the virus!

Krug   I'm sure it will be a huge success. What sort of quarantine have you in mind?

Sigelius   Camps, Baron. Each new sufferer helps spread the disease. So all those with the white spot will be sent to camps.

Krug   I see, and left to die there?

Sigelius   Humanely. Under proper medical supervision. Anyone attempting to escape will be shot. All citizens over forty will be required to undergo a monthly medical test. The epidemic must be suppressed by force, Baron. It's them or us! Sentimentality would be a crime!

Krug I'm sure you're right, Sigelius. It's a pity you didn't think of it sooner.

Sigelius A great pity. We wasted weeks on that stupid Galen business. But it won't be long before we have every leper in the country behind barbed wire. And no exceptions!

Krug (*rises from his chair, then sinks back*) No exceptions Counsellor, that's the main thing. Thank you.

Sigelius (*gets up*) My dear Baron, are you unwell?

Krug (*suddenly tears open his shirt*) Here, Professor, would you just look . . . ?

Sigelius Show me, man, for God's sake. (*Turns* **Krug** *to face the light and taps his chest with a paper knife.*) Feel anything? (*After a pause.*) You can do up your shirt now, Baron.

Krug Is it . . . ?

Sigelius We can't be sure yet. Just a little white spot. Could be mere *dermatosa nervosa* . . .

Krug What do you recommend?

Sigelius (*with helpless gesture*) If we could persuade Galen to take a look at you . . .

Krug Thank you, Professor. I suppose I can't shake your hand?

Sigelius No more shaking hands now, Baron.

Krug (*goes to the door*) You say the quarantine order will come into force in a few days? I must order them to increase our production of barbed-wire.

The surgery of **Doctor Galen**.

Galen   You can get dressed now, my friend, you're doing fine.

First Leper   When's my next appointment, Doctor?

Galen   Come back in a fortnight. After that you probably won't need another appointment. (*Opens the door.*) Next!

Enter **Baron Krug**, *dirty and unshaven, in beggar's clothes.*

Galen   What can I do for you, my friend?

Krug   I have this white spot, Doctor.

Galen   Take off your shirt, man. (*To* **First Leper**.) Off you go.

First Leper   How much do I owe you, Doctor?

Galen   You owe me nothing.

First Leper *slips out of the door.*

Galen (*to* **Krug**)   Let me examine you. (*Examines him.*) Not too bad yet. It's the White Virus of course, but . . . So what do you do?

Krug   Unemployed, Doctor. Used to be a steel-worker.

Galen   And now?

Krug   Whatever I can find. I heard the doctor helped the poor, so . . .

Galen   Listen, it'll take a fortnight, after that you could be well again. Six injections. Could you pay for them?

Krug   Of course . . . That's to say, it depends how much, of course.

Galen   It would be very, very expensive, Baron Krug.

Krug   That's not my name, Doctor!

Galen   Don't waste my time, please. We have nothing further to discuss.

Krug You're right, Doctor, let's not waste time. Look, if you agree to treat me I'll give you – what, a million? – for your own personal use.

Galen (*aghast*) One million?

Krug All right, five. That's a handsome sum. Make it ten. You could do a lot with ten million. Think of the publicity that would buy if you have propaganda in mind.

Galen Wait, ten million you say?

Krug Twenty.

Galen For peace?

Krug Whatever you want. You can buy the press! Even I don't spend that much a year on propaganda.

Galen (*nonplussed*) It would cost that much to get the press to support peace?

Krug Yes – or war.

Galen You see, it never occurred to me. (*Disinfecting his syringe in alcohol.*) We're so cut off here. How does one go about it?

Krug You need connections.

Galen My God, it's hard to make connections. Terribly time-consuming, isn't it?

Krug You could spend your whole life on it.

Galen In that case I . . . (*Soaking cotton-wool in alcohol.*) Why don't you take care of it?

Krug You mean run your peace campaign for you?

Galen Precisely. (*Rubs the cotton-wool on **Krug**'s arm.*) You have the connections. In return I shall cure you.

Krug Sorry Doctor, I'm afraid I can't.

Galen You can't? (*Throws away the cotton-wool.*) That's very interesting. In your own way you're an honest man.

Krug   Maybe Doctor, but you are a naive one if you think you can impose world peace all on your own.

Galen   Not on my own sir, I have a mighty ally.

Krug   Yes, the White Plague, and fear. Jesus, I know that fear. If you could rule people through fear, you wouldn't need war. Don't you think most people are afraid? Yet despite it there'll be war – there'll always be war.

Galen (*picks up the syringe*)   So what *will* make people listen?

Krug   I tried money. Usually works, Doctor. It's all I have. A generous offer, you might say. Twenty . . . thirty million for a single life.

Galen   You're so afraid of the White Virus? (*Slowly fills the syringe.*)

Krug   Yes.

Galen (*approaches* **Krug**, *syringe in hand*)   I'm asking you to close down your factories. Can't you do that?

Krug   No, I can't.

Galen   What can you offer me then?

Krug   Only money.

Galen   I don't want money. Money is pointless. (*Lays syringe on table.*) Money is no use to me.

Krug   You won't take me as your patient?

Galen   I'm sorry. You must get dressed now, Baron.

Krug   That's it? Merciful Christ!

Galen   You'll be back.

Krug (*dressing behind the screen*)   Will I?

Galen   Yes, and you can read behind the screen how much your consultation cost.

Krug (*leaves, buttoning his jacket*)   Seems to me you're not as naive as I thought, Doctor.

Galen (*opens the door for* **Krug**)   Next please!

Marshal's *office.*

Adjutant (*enters*)   Baron Krug, your Excellency!

Marshal (*writing at his desk*)   Show him in.

Adjutant *leads in* **Baron Krug**.

Marshal   Take a seat Baron, I'll be with you in a minute. (*Lays down his pen.*) So what have you to report, Krug? Do sit down, I called you in to hear it from the horse's mouth. What are our present capabilities?

Krug   We're working at full capacity, sir. With due regard to the current situation.

Marshal   And the results?

Krug   I'm still not satisfied. Sixty-five heavy tanks a day . . .

Marshal   Instead of the eighty requested.

Krug   Seven hundred jets. A hundred and twenty bombers. We must increase output. We're not turning them out for fun.

Marshal   Naturally. And?

Krug   Everything fine on the munitions front. Thirty per cent more than ordered by HQ.

Marshal   And Gas C?

Krug   Unlimited supplies. Bit of a catastrophe yesterday. Bloody cylinder exploded.

Marshal Fatalities?

Krug Total. Forty girls and three men up in smoke. Death was instantaneous.

Marshal Most unfortunate. But otherwise a pleasing result. Congratulations, Krug.

Krug Thank you, Excellency.

Marshal I knew I could count on you. By the way, how is your nephew doing?

Krug Thank you Excellency, he's doing splendidly.

Marshal I hear about him from my daughter. Seems there's a bit of a family connection building up between us, old chap!

Krug (*rises from his chair*) That would indeed be an honour, Excellency.

Marshal (*also rises*) The honour would be mutual, Baron. I wouldn't be where I am today without you. One doesn't forget these things, my friend.

Krug I did my duty, sir. I acted in the interests of my shareholders and my country.

Marshal (*approaching him*) Do you remember when we shook hands before I led my men against the government?

Krug Dear Marshal, one doesn't forget things like that!

Marshal Well let's shake hands before an even greater and more glorious enterprise. (*Stretches out both his hands.*)

Krug I'm afraid I can't shake hands with you, Excellency.

Marshal Why ever not?

Krug Excellency, I am stricken . . .

Marshal (*backs away from him*)   God sir, have you been to Sigelius?

Krug   Yes.

Marshal   And?

Krug   He sent me to Galen.

Marshal   And?

Krug   Galen said he could cure me in a fortnight . . .

Marshal   Thank God! You don't know how happy I am for you!

Krug   Provided I agree to one condition.

Marshal   Do it Krug, I order you! We can't lose you, there's too much at stake. What's the condition?

Krug   That my factories stop production of war materials.

Marshal   I see. So Galen really is mad.

Krug   In your eyes certainly, Excellency.

Marshal   And not yours?

Krug   With respect, Marshal, I view the matter from a slightly different perspective.

Marshal   It's out of the question! Impossible!

Krug   Technically it's not impossible, Excellency.

Marshal   Politically it is. You must force Galen to change his terms.

Krug   His only terms are peace.

Marshal   We won't be blackmailed by this nonsense. You say he can cure you in a fortnight. So stop production of war materials for a fortnight. It will be unpleasant, but what can we do? We can announce it as a last-minute attempt to resolve the conflict through negotiation. Dammit, I'll do it for you, Krug. And when you're well . . .

Krug   Thank you, Excellency, but it wouldn't be fair play.

Marshal   There's no fair play in war.

Krug   I know that, Excellency. But Galen is no fool. He could prolong the treatment . . .

Marshal   Yes, he has you by the short hairs. What do you think, Krug?

Krug   Excellency, last night I was all set to accept his condition.

Marshal   Have you gone mad, Krug!

Krug   Yes, fear is maddening, Excellency.

Marshal   Are you so afraid?

Krug (*shrugs helplessly*)   Marshal, if you knew the ghastly feeling when fear penetrates your body to your fingertips. It's disgusting. I see myself jabbering behind the barbed-wire – 'Jesus Christ, somebody help me! Merciful God, take pity on me!'

Marshal   I like you, Krug, you're like a brother to me. What are we going to do with you?

Krug   Make peace, Excellency, make peace! (*Drops to his knees.*) Save me Marshal, save us all . . . !

Marshal (*stands up*)   Get up, Krug.

Krug (*rises from his knees*)   Yes, your Excellency . . .

Marshal   I'm not satisfied with those figures. You are to increase your output of gas, understand?

Krug   Yes, Excellency.

Marshal   I expect you to fulfil your patriotic duty to the last.

Krug   Yes, Excellency.

Marshal (*approaches him*)   Give me your hand.

Krug   I cannot Marshal, I am a leper.

Marshal   The moment I feel fear is the moment I cease to be your commander. I order you to give me your hand, Baron Krug!

Krug (*tentatively stretches out his hand*)   As you command, Marshal.

Marshal   Thank you, Baron.

Krug *staggers out.* **Marshal** *presses the buzzer.*

Adjutant   Yes, Excellency?

Marshal   Find Doctor Galen.

Adjutant (*reappears in the doorway*)   Doctor Galen is here, sir.

Marshal (*writing*)   Show him in.

Adjutant *leads in* **Doctor Galen**. *Both stop by the door.*

Marshal (*continues writing. After a pause*)   Galen?

Galen (*absent-mindedly*)   Yes, Professor.

Marshal (*still writing*)   Excellency, Galen, not Professor.

Galen   Sorry Prof . . . Excellency.

Marshal (*puts down his pen and observes* **Galen** *for a while*)   Congratulations, Galen! My departments are bombarding me with reports on your work. (*Picks up a sheaf of documents.*) The results have been verified. Remarkable, quite remarkable!

Galen (*embarrassed*)   Thank you humbly -- your Excellency.

Marshal   I am embarking on a project to convert the hospital of the Holy Spirit into the State Institute for the fight against the White Plague. I plan to put you in charge, Galen.

Galen   I'm afraid I can't, Excellency. I have my patients.

Marshal   Take that as an order, Doctor Galen.

Galen   In normal circumstances I would, Excellency. But I . . .

Marshal   Put it another way. (*Glances at his* **Adjutant**, *who leaves the room.*) You have refused to treat Baron Krug?

Galen   Not exactly. It depended on certain conditions.

Marshal   I know. But you will now treat Baron Krug without conditions. Understood?

Galen   I'm sorry, Excellency, but I must insist on my conditions.

Marshal   Doctor, we have ways of forcing people to obey commands.

Galen   Look here, obviously you can arrest me, but . . .

Marshal   As you wish. (*Reaches for the buzzer.*)

Galen   Don't do it, sir. I have so many patients. If you arrest me you'll kill them.

Marshal (*releases the buzzer*)   They wouldn't be my first. Just think it over. (*Rises and approaches him.*) What are you, Galen, madman or hero?

Galen (*backs away*)   Definitely not a hero. I was a field doctor in the war. And when I saw so many people dying, so many healthy men . . .

Marshal   I was in the war too. The men I saw were fighting for their Fatherland. I led them back as conquerors.

Galen   That's the difference, Excellency. I saw the

ones you didn't lead back.

Marshal What was your rank?

Galen (*clicks his heels*) Assistant Field Doctor of the 36th Infantry Regiment, Marshal sir!

Marshal Excellent regiment. Any decorations?

Galen Golden Cross for exceptional bravery, sir!

Marshal (*offers his hand*) Well done!

Galen Thank you, Marshal.

Marshal Now go and report to Baron Krug.

Galen You'd better arrest me, Excellency, for disobeying an order.

Marshal *shrugs and presses the buzzer. His* **Adjutant** *appears in the doorway.*

Marshal Place Doctor Galen under arrest.

Adjutant Very well, Excellency.

Galen Don't! You mustn't do it!

Marshal Why not?

Galen Because perhaps you'll need me one day.

Marshal Not me. (*To the* **Adjutant**.) That's all, you may go.

Exit **Adjutant**.

Marshal Sit down, Galen. (*Sits beside him.*) How shall I put it to you, stubborn man? I am personally concerned for Baron Krug, he is an exceptionally important figure and my only friend. You don't know how lonely it is to be a dictator. Save Krug, Doctor. It's a long time since I asked anyone a favour.

Galen First I have a favour to ask you. You are a statesman, you have power. The whole world is afraid of

you, that's why they're arming themselves to the teeth.
If you offered them peace, how happy they would
be . . . !

Marshal (*pause*)   We were discussing Baron Krug,
Doctor.

Galen   Quite so. You can save him, and all the others.

Marshal   The Baron cannot accept your conditions.

Galen   But you can, sir. You can do anything you
want.

Marshal   I cannot. Must I explain it to you like a
baby? Do you really think war and peace depend on
me? I must obey the interests of my nation. If my
people go to war, it's my duty to lead them to their
destiny.

Galen   If it wasn't for you, they wouldn't fight in the
first place.

Marshal   No they wouldn't. Now, thank God, they
can fulfil their historic mission. I'm just the agent of
their will . . .

Galen   Which you've whipped up.

Marshal   I've awakened their will to live. You believe
peace is better than war? I believe a victorious war is
better than a shameful peace. I can't deprive my nation
of victory.

Galen   And their dead?

Marshal   And their dead. Only the blood of the fallen
heroes turns a piece of earth into the Fatherland. Only
war makes a nation out of people, and turns men into
heroes.

Galen   And corpses. In the war I saw more of the
corpses, sir.

Marshal   That's your business, Doctor. In my line of

business I see more heroes.

Galen   Yes, they were usually in the rear. We didn't have many in the trenches.

Marshal   What were you decorated for?

Galen   Just bandaging a few wounded.

Marshal   Wasn't that heroism? You and your peace. By whose authority? Who gave you this mission?

Galen   Mission?

Marshal (*whispering*)   The Divine Will, old chap. We all have our mission. I do, otherwise I couldn't lead my men . . .

Galen   Whose children will be slaughtered in the struggle . . .

Marshal   And be victorious in its name . . .

Galen   Whose fathers and mothers will perish of the plague . . .

Marshal   I'm not interested in them when they get old, Doctor. They're no use to me as soldiers. I don't know why I haven't arrested you yet. (*Rises.*) You will cure Baron Krug. Our Fatherland needs him.

Galen (*also rises*)   Let the Baron visit me, Marshal.

Marshal   And accept your ridiculous conditions?

Galen   Yes Excellency, and accept my ridiculous conditions.

Marshal   In that case . . . (*Approaches the table. The telephone rings. The* **Marshal** *lifts the receiver.*) Yes. Speaking. He's . . . ? When did this happen? Thank you. (*Replaces the receiver. In a hoarse voice.*) You may go. Fortunately for you, five minutes ago Baron Krug shot himself.

Curtain.

Act Three

Marshal's *office.*

Minister of Information Peace demonstrations are spreading. Especially in Britain. The British have always had a horror of disease. According to the British press their government received a petition with several million signatures . . .

Marshal Good. That'll weaken them internally. Go on!

Minister of Information I'm afraid this time it's reached the highest circles. Apparently a member of the royal household is involved.

Marshal I know.

Minister of Information It seems Her Royal Highness has a pathological dread of the White Plague. It got her aunt. The King is preparing a proclamation to all governments, to be presented at an international peace conference . . .

Marshal That would be most awkward. Can't we stop him?

Minister of Information It's gone too far, Excellency. World opinion is fiercely opposed to war. It comes down to their terror of the plague – they're not interested in politics, they want to live. I'm getting reports that even our people are losing faith. Becoming almost anti-war. Health, not medals, they say.

Marshal Cowards! Only once in every century does such a moment occur! I rely on you to suppress these sentiments!

Minister of Information Won't last long, Excellency. The young are full of enthusiasm and will follow you through fire. The older ones are different.

Fear and anxiety is spreading . . .

Marshal   I'm more concerned with the young.

Minister of Information   Certainly. But the older ones have the economic power and hold the key positions. In wartime they might give us problems. It's imperative to soothe public opinion.

Marshal   How?

Minister of Information   Force this Galen chap to reveal his formula.

Marshal   Won't work, old boy, even if you put him on the rack. I know Galen.

Minister of Information   We have our methŏds.

Marshal   Yes, and they're usually fatal, thanks. It would make a bad impression.

Minister of Information   Then we'll have to give in to his demands – temporarily.

Marshal   And lose our military advantage? Forget it.

Minister of Information   The only option, then, is to make a lightning strike before the peace movement gets going. Attack the weakest link. The *causa belli* is in the bag – intrigues against the state, continual acts of provocation and sabotage . . . All we need is a minor political assassination, a word to the press, mass round-ups, organised war rallies, and hey presto! Go for it! I can vouch for people's patriotic fervour!

Marshal   My dear Minister, I knew I could rely on you. I shall finally lead my people to greatness!

The **Marshal***'s office a few days later. A door opens onto the balcony, where the* **Marshal** *stands addressing the crowd. The sounds of military marches, drums and bugles are drowned by a swelling chorus of cheers. Inside, the* **Marshal's daughter** *and* **Krug Junior** *in military uniform.*

Marshal (*to the crowd*) At this historic moment, when our silver-winged bombers sow death over the land of our enemy . . . (*Wild cheers.*) I want to share with my people the reason for this difficult step. (*Cries of 'Long live the Marshal!', 'Hurrah!!'*) Yes, I started this war. Yes, I made a pre-emptive strike. I did it to save the lives of thousands of our children, who at this moment are winning their first battles before the enemy has time to recover from the shock. I am asking you now for your support. (*Wild cries of 'We support you!', 'Long live our Marshal!'*) I initiated hostilities without humiliating negotiations with a wretched little enemy which thought it could insult our mighty nation unpunished (*Angry jeers.*), infiltrating their hired agents to destabilise our national order and security! (*Roars of 'Traitors!', 'Lynch them!', 'Hang them!'*) Quiet, shouting won't rid us of this evil! Only one thing will do that – send in punitive detachments! Let the other powers show their cards, we fear nobody! Exterminate them! (*Shouts of 'We're not afraid!', 'Long live the Marshal!', 'Hurrah for the war!'*) I knew you'd be behind me. It's for your honour I'm sending our magnificent army into battle! I swear before the world we didn't want this war, but we shall be victorious. By God's will we shall win! (*Thumps his chest.*) Our cause is just! (*His voice fading.*) Justice . . . (*Shouts of 'Our cause is just!', 'Long live war!'* **Marshal** *staggers from the balcony into the room, clutching his chest.*) Our cause is just! God's will be done . . .

Krug Junior (*approaching*) What's up, Excellency?

Marshal's daughter What is it, Daddy?

Marshal Go, leave me. (*Beats his chest.*) Our cause is just! (*Pulls open his jacket and unbuttons his shirt.*) Justice! (*Tears his shirt open.*) Look!

Krug Junior Show us!

Krug Junior *and the* **Marshal's daughter** *lean over* **Marshal**.

Marshal (*pummelling his chest*)   I can't feel anything. It's like marble . . . !

Marshal's daughter (*with an effort*)   It's nothing, Daddy. You mustn't look.

Marshal   Leave me alone! (*Pummels his heart.*) No feeling, totally numb . . .

Marshal's daughter   It's nothing Daddy, you'll see!

Outside, swelling roars of 'Marshal! Marshal! Marshal!'

Marshal   I know what it is. Go, leave me child, leave me.

From the street, more roars of 'Marshal! Marshal! We want our Marshal!'

Marshal   Coming!

Marshal *buttons his jacket and goes to the balcony, his hand out to greet the crowd. Wild cries of 'We love our Marshal!', 'Long live the Marshal!'* **Marshal's daughter** *weeps.*

Krug Junior (*to* **Marshal's daughter**)   Don't cry dear, don't cry . . . (*Goes to the telephone, feverishly scans the directory then dials a number.*) Counsellor Sigelius? Krug speaking. Report at once to the Marshal's palace . . . Yes, the Marshal. Yes, The white spot. (*Hangs up.*)

Shouts from outside of 'Long live our Marshal!', 'Long live the Army!', 'Glory to the Marshal!'

Marshal (*returning from the balcony*)   At least they like me. This is a great day, my darling. You mustn't cry.

Krug Junior   Sir, I've taken the liberty of calling Court Counsellor Sigelius . . .

Marshal   So I can be ill according to all the scientific regulations? (*Waves him away.*) No communiqués from our airforce yet?

Sounds of singing and military bands playing on the street.

Listen to them. At last I've made a nation of them. (*Feels his chest under his uniform.*) Strange. Stone cold, as if it wasn't me any more.

Cries from the street of 'Marshal!', 'Marshal!', 'Marshal!'

Coming, coming! (*Lurches out to the balcony.*)

Krug Junior   Allow me, your Excellency. (*Runs to the balcony and motions to the crowd.*) His Excellency the Marshal wishes to express his thanks. He has just returned to work.

Cries of 'Long live our Marshal!', 'Long live victory!'

Marshal (*to his* **Daughter**)   He's a nice young man. I was fond of old Krug. (*Sits down.*) Poor Baron, wretched man . . .

Krug Junior (*returns from balcony, to* **Marshal's daughter**)   I beg you, Annette. (*Points to the windows.*)

They draw the heavy curtains and switch on the table-lamp. Semi-darkness. Silence. Muffled echoes of singing and marching from the street.

Marshal   Yes. Now it looks like an invalid's room.

Marshal's daughter (*sits at his feet*)   You won't be ill, Daddy. The best doctors from all over the world will come and make you better. Lie down now, Daddy.

Marshal   Now is no time to be ill, little one, I must fight. I'll just rest here with you for a bit. It was all that shouting . . . Just crawl into the darkness and hold someone's hand . . . It'll pass, you'll see. I'm leading a war. I must wait for the news. Listen, they're singing in the street. Sounds as if it's coming from another world . . .

Krug Junior   If they disturb you, Excellency . . .

Marshal   No, leave it, the flags are flying. You should drive through the town. Be seen. Tell everyone justice is at hand ... Tell them we ... we ... (*Squeezes his chest.*)

Marshal's daughter   Stop thinking about it, Daddy.

Marshal   You're right. I'll lead our soldiers as a conqueror! You were too little to see me in the last war, leading them home. But now you'll be so proud of me. War is a glorious thing for a man, Pavel! The greatest thing there is! Advance the right flank! Encircle! Throw in ten divisions ... !

Adjutant (*at the door*)   Court Counsellor Sigelius is here, Excellency.

Marshal's daughter   Show him in to Daddy's room.

Exit **Adjutant.**

Marshal   The best doctors in the world, eh? (*Gets up.*) Pity. I felt better alone with you. (*Exit.*)

The silence is broken by the sounds of **Marshal's daughter** *weeping and military marches outside.*

Krug Junior   It's horrible, it's so far advanced. He's all eaten away. How is it he didn't notice?

Marshal's daughter   He never thinks about himself. He ignores his own health ... (*Leans against the fireplace sobbing.*)

Krug Junior   This evening I shall report to the regiment, Annette.

Marshal's daughter   You don't have to.

Krug Junior   In our family we don't evade our duties. Silly tradition, eh?

Marshal's daughter   This war won't last long. Just a few days, Daddy said.

Krug Junior   Maybe. But you'll be alone a bit. You

must be brave now.

Adjutant (*enters*) Urgent cable for his Excellency. (*Leaves it on the* **Marshal**'s *table and exits.*)

Krug Junior (*goes to the table and reads*) I know I shouldn't, but ... It's unbelievable...! Digging in like moles! They've pushed us back from the capital. Eighty planes shot down! Our tanks meeting stiff resistance at the border...

Marshal's daughter Is it very bad?

Krug Junior We're losing time, they're calling in reinforcements. The Marshal gambled on a *Blitzkrieg* ... We've had ultimatums from two superpowers ... Christ, they're already mobilising...! Three, four, five ultimatums...!

Marshal's daughter Should we tell him?

Krug Junior I think we must. Don't worry Annette, he's strong. Illness won't break him. We'll see him poring over his maps again. He's a soldier.

Marshal (*reels into the office sobbing, his nightgown flowing behind him*) Sweet Jesus! God in heaven! Jesus crucified!

Marshal's daughter Daddy!

Krug Junior (*runs to him*) Courage, sir! (*Leads him to the sofa.*)

Marshal Leave me, it will pass! God in heaven, six weeks the doctor said! Six weeks, then the end! You can't imagine it till it happens to you! Merciful God! Sweet Jesus!

Krug Junior (*gestures to* **Marshal's daughter** *to let him handle it*) Excellency, we have a communiqué here from the front.

Marshal What is it? I can't ... Leave me alone ... Can't you see ...?

Krug Junior   Bad news I fear, sir.

Marshal   What? Hand it over. (*Takes the cable and reads it silently.*) Yes, this changes everything. (*Rises.*) Summon – no better not, I'll issue my commands here. (*Sits at his desk and writes.*)

Krug Junior *stands behind him.* **Marshal's daughter** *stands motionless. Singing is heard from the street.*

Marshal (*scribbling frantically*)   Mobilise our youth reserves!

Krug Junior (*takes the paper*)   Very well, sir.

Marshal (*presses the pen so hard that it breaks.* **Krug Junior** *hands him another*)   Directives to the airforce.

Krug Junior (*takes the paper*)   Very well, sir.

Marshal   Here . . . (*Feverishly crosses something out.*) No, no. (*Tears paper from the desk, rips it up and hurls it in the bin.*) We must try another way. (*Starts writing again.*) No, that won't work. (*Lays his head on the table.* **Krug Junior** *looks hopelessly at his daughter.*) Sweet Jesus! Merciful God!

Krug Junior   I await your commands, sir.

Marshal (*lifts his head*)   Yes . . . (*Staggers centre-stage.*) I am in command. From tomorrow, Annette, I shall assume supreme power over my army and direct all offensive operations. This is my sacred mission! Mounted on my white horse, I shall lead my men in the victory parade through the ruins of the enemy capital. (*Sounds of military marching from the street.*) The flesh will have fallen off me, only my eyes will be left. I shall ride in front of my soldiers, a skeleton on a white horse, and the people will cheer, 'Long live our Marshal! Long live his Excellency Death!'

Marshal's daughter *covers her face and weeps.*

Krug Junior   You mustn't talk like that, sir!

Marshal You're right, Pavel! Don't worry, it won't come to that. Tomorrow I shall stand before my soldiers, not at HQ, my High Command mightn't care for the smell ... I'll stand there, sabre in hand, leading the attack. Forward boys, follow me! And if I fall, Pavel, they can avenge their fallen Marshal. Forward boys, fix bayonets! Fight like devils! We won, we, we. . .! (*Clutches his chest.*) Annette, I'm afraid!

Marshal's daughter (*talking to him quietly, as though he were a child*) Don't say that, Daddy. Sit here, stop worrying about it. (*Helps him to the armchair.*)

Marshal At the clinic this old chap stood up to salute me, and a huge lump of flesh fell off him. Christ Jesus, is there no mercy?

Krug Junior *exchanges looks with the* **Marshal's daughter**, *goes to the telephone and searches the directory.*

Marshal I have to win this war first. My God, just six months I need – a year at most ...

Krug Junior (*dials*) Galen? Krug here. Come to the Marshal, Doctor ... Yes, very sick ... Only you ... Yes, any conditions ... Peace treaty. Yes, I'll tell him ... (*Covers the receiver with his hand.*)

Marshal (*jumps up*) No, no! I don't want peace! Have you gone mad, Pavel? I've a war to win! I can't call it off now! The humiliation! Justice is on our side!

Krug Junior No it isn't, Marshal.

Marshal I know that, young man, but we shall be victorious. I don't matter, our nation does. Put the phone down, Pavel. I want to die for my nation.

Krug Junior (*hands the receiver to Annette*) You can do that sir, but then what?

Marshal After my death? I'm only mortal you know.

Krug Junior You refused to accept that, sir. No one

can replace you now. If you go, God save us from the consequences!

Marshal   You're right, Pavel. I have to win before I go.

Krug Junior   It won't be over in six weeks, Marshal, sir!

Marshal   Six weeks! Sweet Jesus, why did you do this to me?

Marshal's daughter (*into the receiver*)   Doctor ...? No, his daughter ... Yes, he accepts your terms ... No, but he has no choice ... You'll save him ...? I'll tell him ... (*Puts her hand over the mouthpiece.*) Father, he wants a word with you ...

Marshal   Hang up, Annette. I ... can't. The matter is closed.

Krug Junior (*calmly*)   I beg your pardon, Your Excellency, you have no choice.

Marshal   What, declare peace? Recall our troops? Is that what you want?

Krug Junior   Yes, sir.

Marshal   Apologise? Accept punishment?

Krug Junior   Yes, sir.

Marshal   Horribly and senselessly to humiliate my nation?

Krug Junior   Yes, sir.

Marshal   Resign my post in disgrace?

Krug Junior   Yes sir. Leave when we are at peace, sir.

Marshal   No, do you hear! No! Let somebody else do it! There are plenty who are against me – let them make a shameful peace!

Krug Junior That would mean civil war. Only you can order your troops to retreat.

Marshal This nation must govern itself or leave the stage of history. Let me go – manage by yourselves.

Krug Junior You didn't teach us how, sir.

Marshal There's only one thing left for me – the officer's way. (*Heads for the door.*)

Krug Junior (*bars his way*) You won't do that, sir.

Marshal He's a nice boy, Annette, but he thinks too much. He'll never achieve anything . . .

Marshal's daughter Here, Daddy. (*Hands him the receiver.*) I'm begging you. For all the sick people. I implore you.

Marshal For all the sick people! You're right, Annette. Maybe my place is with them now! With the millions of lepers and plague victims all over the world! Out of the way! Here stands the Marshal of Lepers, heading his army of sick, stinking flesh. Justice is ours! We demand mercy! Let me, Annette. (*Grabs the receiver.*) Doctor? Yes, I agree, thank you. (*Hangs up.*) Well that's that. He'll be with us in a few minutes.

Marshal's daughter God be praised! (*Weeps for joy.*) I'm so happy, Daddy . . . So happy, Pavel!

Marshal (*strokes her hair*) We'll go away somewhere – then there'll be peace. When the doctor arrives I'll stop the offensive. It won't be easy, Pavel . . . (*Sweeps his commands off the desk onto the floor.*) Yes, stop the offensive. Inform all governments . . . Pity. Could have been a great war. It was a beautiful army, my darling! Twenty years of my life . . . If I live . . . God's will . . . My sacred mission . . . Where's that doctor, Annette? Where is he?

The street. Crowds with flags singing and shouting, 'Long live our Marshal!', 'War! War! War! War!', 'Glory to our Marshal!'

Son (*from Act One*) All together now, 'Hurrah for war!'

Crowd Hurrah for war!

Son Our Marshal is leading us!

Crowd Our Marshal is leading us!

Son Long live our Leader!

Crowd Long live our Leader!

Sounds of a car hooting backstage, unable to get through.

Galen (*leaps out clutching his medical bag*) I'll go on foot . . . Please let me through . . . I'm in a hurry, someone's waiting for me . . .

Son Come on citizens, shout with me, 'Long live our Marshal! Hurrah for war!'

Galen No, no! There must be no war!

Howls of 'What did he say?', 'Traitor!', 'String him up!', 'We'll fix him!'

There must be peace! Let me through . . . I must get to the Marshal!

*Shouts of 'He's slandering our Marshal!', 'Hang him from the lamp-post!', 'Shoot him!' The crowd closes in on **Galen** in a violent and noisy turmoil. Crowd disperses to reveal **Galen** lying on the ground with his bag.*

Son (*kicks **Galen***) Get up, you bastard! Clear off, or . . .

One of the crowd (*bending over the motionless **Galen***) Wait, I think he's dead!

Son Who cares. One traitor less! Glory to our Marshal!

Crowd Marshal! Marshal! Long live our Marshal!

Son (*opens* **Galen**'s *bag*)   Look, he was a doctor! (*Smashing ampoules on the ground.*) So-o! Hurrah for the war! Long live our Marshal!

Crowd (*rolling forward*)   Marshal! Marshal! Long live the Marshal!

Curtain.